AACR2R with MARC21

Cataloging Practice for 21st Century

AACR2R with MARC21
Cataloging Practice for 21st Century

R.S. Aswal

Ess Ess Publications

4837/24, Ansari Road, Darya Ganj,
New Delhi-110002
✆ : 23260807, 51563444
Fax : 011-51563334
E-mail: info@essessreference.com
url:http://www.essessreference.com

First Published 2005

ISBN: 81-7000-440-3

Ess Ess
Rs.1000/-

Published by:
Ess Ess Publications
4837/24, Ansari Road, Darya Ganj,
New Delhi-110 002.
Phone: 51563444
Fax: 51563334
E-mail: info@essessreference.com
url: http://www.essessreference.com

Printed in India at:
Printline, New Delhi

TABLE OF CONTENTS

PREFACE

Due to explosion of information technology, the proliferation of computer systems in libraries and rapidly growth of centralized cooperative bibliographic services and resource sharing, it becomes apparent that a standard system is needed. AACR2R and MARC 21 is such standard system, where in AACR2R use in the construction of catalogues and the MARC 21 facilitate the exchange of bibliographic and related information. MACR 21 support the revised rules of AACR2R for integrating resources both in print (loose-leaves) and electronic format (updating databases and web sites).

This new manual aims to maintain the tradition established by AACR2 and MARC 21 and seeks to fulfill the same aims that is to provide a clear and comprehensively overview of modern cataloging theory, policy and practice and to provide a depth description of various fields of AACR2R into MARC 21.

To facilitate reading and understanding the book is presented in 2 parts (Part-I Description and Part-II Choice of Access points). This volume is intended as a blueprint of good cataloging practice. Thus this book is a must for librarians and students of library science.

The cataloging rules (AACR2R) and MARC coding standards (MARC21) mean to create edit or retrieve records effectively. It has been tried to provides the guideline to user between AACR2 and MARC21 through this book. This book is very useful create simple records and identify specific current rules of AACR2R and MARC 21 coding.

The AACR2R Rules cover the description of, and the provision of access points for, all library materials commonly collected at the present time with MARC 21 standard. All changes approved by the Joint Steering Committee for Revision of AACR2R have been incorporated in this book.

AACR2 2002 [*Anglo-American Cataloging Rules, 2nd ed., 2002 revision*] and the related MACR 21 Standard format introduce new terms or revise certain rules.The bibliographic resources are classified by their type of issuance: continuing/finite, discrete/non-discrete. Type of issuance determines whether a bibliographic resource is cataloged as a monograph, a serial, or an integrating resource. Multipart monographs are handled differently from serials, but because multiparts are issued in "parts," they may be confused with serials. Conversely, special issues of serials are sometimes confused with monographs and sometimes get into the monograph cataloging workflow by mistake.

MARC [Machine-Readable Cataloging] fields or certain types of notes as denoting a "serial." As a result of the recent revision to AACR2, staff will begin to see these "serial" MARC fields in records for monographs and integrating resources. For that reason, determining whether a bibliographic resource is a monograph, a serial, or an integrating resource will sometimes depend on the more abstract and complex categories of type of issuance: discrete/not discrete; finite/continuing. In addition, the information on the item in hand may not be that explicit.

The I part "Description" brings together the cataloging rules and the MACR 21 coding standards for the Books, Cartographic Materials, Sound Recordings, Motion Pictures and Video-recordings, Electronic Resources, Microforms, and Continuing Resources [Serials]. In the chapter of "special cataloging rules" provides theses and dissertations, multi-volumes and analytics and technical reports. The opening chapter "New Amendment Rules in AACR2" introduces a general changes in 2002 edition of AACR 2.

The rules in part II deal with the choice of access points for main and added entries, with the form of name headings and uniform titles with references.

The presentation of the examples in standard format is only intended to help in the use of the rules. Finally, the text is close with appendix of initial with glossary of technical terms.

Acknowledgements

My primary gratitude goes to Dr. Shankar Singh, Sr. Manager (Lib & Inf. Services) Central Public Sector, PFC, New Delhi who has provides the right spirit, necessary information, consistent support and continuous persistence. I am thankful to my colleagues of VTLS Pvt. Ltd., who supported and encouraged me. I would like to personally thank to my wife who motivated and cooperated me. My special thanks to my publishers M/s Ess Ess Publication for their friendly cooperation and untiring efforts in bringing out this book in excellent form in short time.

I request the readers to convey the feedback along with any suggestions, comments and criticism for further improvement of this book.

RS ASWAL

Assistant Manager (Lib & Inf. Services)

VTLS PVT LTD, NOIDA

E-mail: *rajendra_vtls@yahoo.com*

Introduction
New Amended Rules In AACR2 2002

The 2002 revision of the Anglo American Cataloging Rules, 2nd edition, included a major overhaul of the rules dealing with serial.

AACR2 rule 1.1B1 has to do with titles proper and introductory words at the start of the title. It says: Do not transcribe the words that serve as an introduction that are not intended to be part of the title. It's appearing most often with videos and popular journals.

When creating a preliminary record, create an additional title access field 246 that includes the title phrase as part of the title for the benefit of other searchers.

EXAMPLES:

245	0	0	$a Rainy day.
246	1	--	$i Title appear on item as: $a Disney presents Rainy day.

245	0	0	$a Today's world.
246	1	--	$i Title appear on item as: $a Welcome to today's world.

Rule 0.24. It is important to bring out all aspects of the item being described, including its content, its carrier, its type of publication, its bibliographic

relationships, and whether it is published or unpublished.

Rule 1.4D4. Elimination of rule 1.4D4

Rule 1.4D6. Renumbered – Name of publisher, distributor, etc. from 1.4D7. Rule expanded to cover dates for serials, integrating resources, and multipart items; with an option to supply beginning and/or ending date(s) if first and/or last issue/part not available.

RULE 1.4F8 (Dates in 260 $c and first part is not in hand). This rule applies to transcription of publication dates in 260 $c. It addresses the question of what to do when the first/last issue is not in hand at the time of cataloging.

1.4F8. Serials.

RULES:

* If the first/last issue is not in hand, dates are NOT recorded in 260 $c
* If information about the first/last issue is available from another source, it may be recorded in field 362 1, e.g. 362 1# $a Began in 2000.

If the first/last issue is not in hand, record must have a 500 "Description based on" note

1.4F8. Integrating resources (updating loose-leafs)

* If the first iteration isn't in hand, there may or may not be a date.
* If information about the first/last iteration is available from another source, it may be recorded in field 362 1
* If the first/last iteration is not in hand, record must have a 500 "Description based on" note

1.4F8 Multipart monographs. As with integrating resources, the rules listed have been simplified:

* If the first part isn't in hand, there may or may not be a date in 260 $c. If there is a date, the date will be in square brackets [date of first vol.] or angle brackets <date of earliest/latest available volumes>
* If the first part isn't in hand, a 362 1 field will be used only if there is no square bracket date. Even in that case the 362 1 field is only entered if information is readily available, so in reality you won't see it very often on multipart records.
* 500 "Description based on" note is always used

EXAMPLE:

260	_	_	$a ______ : $b ______ , $c <2003>
362	1	_	$a Began publication in 1999?
500	_	_	$a Description based on v. 3, published 2003.

Cartographic Materials: Change in GMD to [cartographic material](no longer [globe] or [map])

Electronic Resources. Change in name from 'Computer file' to 'Electronic resources' data, games, graphics, images, music, programs, statistics etc.

Local and remote resources: Local: you insert... Remote: you access...

9.0B1. Chief Source of Information for electronic resources is the resource itself. "If the information ... varies in degree of fullness, prefer the source that provides the most complete information."

9.0B2: Prescribed Sources of Information. "The item itself, information issued by publisher, creator, etc., or any source, depending on area of description."

9.1C: General Material Designation. Optional, but "[electronic resource]" if used.

9.3: Type and Extent of Resource Area. "Type of resource" part of Area 3 (9.3B1) is required for resources available by remote access electronic data and program(s). "Extent of resource" part of Area 3 (9.3B2) is not required for resources available by remote access.

9.4B1: "Record information about the place, name, and date of all types of publishing, distributing, etc., activities as instructed in 1.4B."

9.4B2:"Consider all remote access electronic resources to be published."

9.5: Physical Description Area. As per footnote 2, under 9.5, "Do not give a physical description for an electronic resource that is available only by remote access. See 9.7B1c and 9.7B10."

9.7B1c: "Mode of access. If a resource is available only be remote access, always specify the mode of access. Begin the note with Mode of access:"

9.7B10: "Physical description... If the resource is available only by remote access, give the physical details [in a note] (e.g., color, sound) if they are readily available and considered important."

9.5B1: Optionally, use conventional terminology to record specific format of the physical carrier 1 CD-ROM (rather than 1 Computer optical disk)

9.7B1a: "Nature and scope. Make notes on the nature and scope of the resource unless it is apparent from the rest of the description."

9.7B1b: "System requirements. Make a note on the systems requirements of the resource if the information is readily available."

9.7B1c: "Mode of access. If a resource is available only be remote access, always specify the mode of access. Begin the note with Mode of access."

9.7B3: Source of the Title Proper Note

"Always give the source of the title proper."

9.7B8: Type and Extent of Resource Note

"Give information relating to the type and extent of the resource if it is considered to be important and not found elsewhere in the description."

Electronic journal. Resource size varies.

TYPOGRAPHIC ERROR IN SERIAL 245 $a (AACR2 12.1B1). Although the correction of typographic errors in serial titles is a new AACR2 rule, it has been standard serial cataloging practice for some time because of Library of Congress practice. Access to the incorrect form is provided through the 246 field. Note that 246 access is generally provided only if the typo was on the issue used as the basis for the description (i.e. issue #1). Typos on later issues are generally ignored.

EXAMPLE:

245	0	0	$a Ohio adventures.
246	1	_	$i Title on no. 1: $a Ohioo adventures.

12.0B1: Basis of the description

Serials: Base the description of a serial on the first issue or part or, lacking this, on the earliest available issue or part.

Integrating resources: Base the description of an integrating resource, except the beginning date of publication, on the current iteration of that resource.

12.1B8: Change in title proper

Serials: If a major change in the title proper occurs, make a new description. If a minor change occurs in the title proper on a subsequent issue or part, in general, give the later title in a note.

Integrating resources: If any change in the title proper occurs on a subsequent iteration, change the title and statement of responsibility area to reflect the current iteration and, in general, give the earlier title in a note.

12.1F3: Serials Editors: Do not record as statements of responsibility relating to persons who are editors.

Integrating resources: Record statements relating to persons who are editors as statements of responsibility if considered to be important

12.3: Numbering area.

Serials: Give this area for serials if cataloging from the first and/or last issue or part.

Integrating resources: This area is not generally applicable.

12.4: Publication Information.

Serials: If the place of publication or name of publisher changes on a subsequent issue or part, give the later place or name in a note if considered to be important.

Integrating resources: If the place of publication or the name of the publisher changes on a subsequent iteration, change the place of publication or name of publisher to reflect the current iteration and give the earlier place or name in a note if considered to be important.

12.5B1 - Extent of item (including specific material designation)

For printed serials, use only the specific material designation "v." does not use "no." or "pt." Also do not use "v. in," etc.

12.5B2 - Extent of item (including specific material designation)

Designation on last issue: Volume 1, number 3

Extent of item recorded as: 3 v.

12.7B1 - Frequency

Always make a note on the known frequency of a serial or of the updates to an integrating resource even if the frequency is apparent from the rest of the description.

Allergy quarterly. —

Quarterly.

Bimonthly.

Integrating resources

Include the word "updated" or "updates" with the frequency word to clarify that the frequency is not of the resource itself but that of the updates (e.g., "updated quarterly," "Monthly updates").

12.7B4.2 - Change in title proper of integrating resources When the title proper has changed and a new ISSN is assigned, move the ISSN for the earlier title proper from the 022 fields to the 247 fields for that earlier title proper.

12.7B8a) – Continued by

12.7B8c) – Split

The notes could be very lengthy and complex. In the machine-readable records serials resulting from a split are already linked to serials, which have been split.

12.7B8d) – Absorption

The option is applied when the information is readily available.

12.7B8g) – Supplements

Serial supplements to other serials

For serial supplements represented by their own bibliographic records (see rule interpretation 21.28B), give linking notes to the related serials.

NUMBERING AREA (serials and series)

In serials, numbering ("designation") is recorded either in field 362 or in the 500 "Description based on" note. Usually, those serials that are journals or periodicals use both enumerative (strictly numbers) and chronological (year, sometimes month/day) designations, e.g. "362 0_ ‡a no. 1 (May 1980)" or "500 ___ Description based on: no. 2 (June 1999)." In some cases, the serial will only have a chronological designation, like an annual.

Monographic series are serials, but catalogers are usually working with monographic series analytics, which are books. On monographic series analytics, the numbering is recorded in 4XX/8XX ‡v. Monographic series generally have only enumerative designation, e.g. 440 ___ Studies in Civil War history ; ‡v v. 1."

Cataloging records for integrating resources do not record numbering; 362 is used only for notes about the first iteration.

Prior to the 2002 amendments, if the numbering of the serial or series re-started (i.e. went from v.1-v.35, then started to number from v.1 again) a new record (cataloging record or series authority record) was created if the new numbering sequence lacked wording (e.g. "new series," "n.s.") indicating that a new numbering sequence had begun. Following the 2002 amendments, the cataloger does NOT create a new record if the "new series" wording is lacking. In those situations, the appropriate wording is inserted in square brackets.

EXAMPLE (Serial):

Successive designation is recorded in serial cataloging in two ways, depending on whether the first issue for the new designation is in hand.

If the first issue of the new designation is in hand, the designation is recorded in field 362 only:

362	0	_	$a No. 1 (May 1980)-No. 8 (Feb. 1988); [new ser.], no. 1 (Mar. 1988)-

If the first issue of the new designation is not in hand, the old designation is left as is in field 362 and the old designation is recorded in field 515:

362	0	_	$a No. 1 (May 1980)-

515	_	_	$a Issues for <Feb. 1989> called <[new ser.], no. 2 (Feb. 1989)>

EXAMPLE (monographic series):

Last volume of original numbering sequence:

440	_	0	$a Civil war history; $v v. 35

First volume of new numbering sequence:

440	_	0	$a Civil war history; $v [new ser.], v. 1

12.7B10 – Numbering and issuing peculiarities

For serials reproduced in microform, if some issues are missing, give the issues filmed. If these cannot be determined easily, give notes in general terms.

Issues reproduced: May 1980-. Publisher's catalogue.

Issues reproduced: July 1981-Oct. 1984; Aug. 1985-.

LINKING NOTES

Serial catalogers have always used fields 780 and 785 to refer to the earlier and later title respectively on serial records. Now you may start to see these fields on monograph and integrating resource records. One case would be if papers from a conference for one year were cataloged as a monograph and the cataloger decided to catalog subsequent conference collections as serial issues. The last conference collection cataloged as a monograph would have a 785 field with the title of the serial; the serial record would have a reciprocal 780 linking field with the title of the monograph. If you receive a conference papers collection and you find a monograph record with an earlier publication date and with a 785 field, you need to search Voyager, LCDB, and the utilities for a serial record, or pass the volume to a serial specialist.

UPDATING LOOSE-LEAFS AND OTHER INTEGRATING RESOURCES

Latest iteration is the basis for description. Look for the qualifier "(loose-leaf)" in field 300 to identify an updating loose-leaf.

300	_	_	$a v. (loose-leaf); $c 25 cm.

Record is *updated* if the title changes on a later iteration (*new record is not created*). The title for the earlier iteration is recorded in field 247.

EXAMPLE:

Existing record for updating loose-leaf.

245	0	0	$a Scholarship opportunities for future math teachers.
300	_	_	$a v. (loose-leaf) ; $c 25 cm.
500	_	_	$a Description based on: release 5, published 2001.

Same record after change in title proper with the later iteration:

245	0	0	$a Future math teachers' scholarship opportunities.
247	1	0	$a Scholarship opportunities for future math teachers $f <release 5, published 1999>
300	_	_	$a v. (loose-leaf) ; $c 25 cm.
500	_	_	$a Description based on: release 9, published 2001.

CAUTION: serials cataloged under preAACR2 "latest entry" rules may have field 247; don't confuse with integrating resources records. (Serials won't have "300 __ $a v. (loose-leaf)")

21.2A2 - Minor changes in title proper of continuing resources other than integrating resources

21.2C1b - Changes in titles proper. Integrating resources

Note that if the title proper change is accompanied by an edition statement change creates a new bibliographic record.

21.3B1b - Changes of persons or bodies responsible for a work. Integrating resources.

PART-I: DESCRIPTION

CHAPTER 1
General Rules for Description

CONTENTS

1.0 GENERAL RULES

Categories of Material: The categories of material identified in the libraries are:

i) Monographs (Book): Textual material that is monographic in nature.

ii) Continuing resources (Serials): Textual items with a recurring pattern of publication, e.g., periodicals, newspapers, and yearbooks.

iii) Electronic resources (computer file): Electronic resources used for computer software, numeric data, computer-oriented multimedia, online systems or services. Material may be monographic or serial in nature.

iv) Maps: All types of cartographic materials, including sheet maps and globes in printed, manuscript, electronic, and microform.

v) Music: Printed and manuscript notated music.

vi) Sound recordings: Nonmusical sound recordings, and musical sound recordings.

vii) Motion pictures and Video-recording: Projected media, two-dimensional graphics, three-dimensional artifacts or naturally occurring objects, and kits. Used for archival visual materials when format or medium is being emphasized.

viii) Mixed materials: Primarily archival and manuscript collections of a mixture of forms of material. Material may be monographic or serial in nature.

Type of bibliographic record [06]: A one-character code that indicates the characteristics of and defines the components of the record.

i) Language material [a]. This code is used for printed, microforms and electronic language material.

ii) Notated music [c]. This code is for microforms and electronic printed music.

iii) Manuscript notated music [d]. This code is used for microforms of manuscript music.

iv) Cartographic material [e]. This code is used for maps, atlases, globes, digital maps and other cartographic items.

v) Manuscript cartographic material [f]. This code is used for microforms of manuscript maps.

vi) Projected medium [g]. The described item is a motion picture, video recording, filmstrip, slide, transparency, or material specifically designed for overhead projection.

vii) Nonmusical sound recording [I]. It's including speech.

viii) Musical sound recording [j]. It's including phonodiscs, compact discs, or cassette tapes.

ix) Two-dimensional nonprojectable graphic [k]. This code is used for items such as activity cards, charts, collages, spirit masters, study prints, computer graphics, drawings, duplication masters, flash cards, paintings, photonegatives, photo prints, pictures, postcards, posters, prints, technical drawings, transparency masters, photomechanical reproductions, and reproductions of any of these.

x) Electronic resources [m]. The described item is numeric or textual data, computer software, or a combination of these types of information that are encoded for computer processing.

xi) Kit [o]. The described item contains a mixture of components from two or more types of items, no one of which is the predominant constituent of the kit.

xii) Mixed material [p]. Indicates that there are significant materials in two or more forms that are usually related by virtue of their having been accumulated by or about a person or body. Includes archival fond and manuscript collections of mixed forms of materials, such as text, photographs, and sound recordings.

xiii) Three-dimensional artifact or naturally occurring object [r]. This code is used for such man-made objects as models, dioramas, games, puzzles, simulations, sculptures and other three-dimensional art works and their reproductions, exhibits, machines, clothing, and toys. It also includes such naturally occurring objects as microscope specimens and other specimens mounted for viewing.

xiv) Manuscript language material [t].

Bibliographic level: It indicates the bibliographic level of the record.

i) Monographic component part [a]. A monographic bibliographic unit that is physically attached to or contained in another unit such that the retrieval of the component part is dependent on the identification and location of the host item or container. The record contains fields that describe the component part and data that identify the host, field 773 (Host Item Entry).

ii) Serial component part [b]. A serial bibliographic unit that is physically attached to or contained in another serial unit such that the retrieval of the component part is dependent on the physical identification and location of the host item or container. The record contains fields that describe the component part and data that identify the Host Item Entry (field 773).

iii) Collection [c]. A made-up multipart group of items that were not originally published, distributed, or produced together. The record describes units defined by common provenance or administrative convenience for which the record is intended as the most comprehensive in the system.

iv) Subunit [d]. A part of a collection, especially an archival unit described collectively elsewhere in the system. The record contains fields that describe the subunit and data that identify the Host Item Entry (field 773).

v) Integrating resource [i]. A bibliographic resource that is added to or changed by means of updates that does not remain discrete and are integrated into the whole. Examples include: Updating loose-leafs and updating Web sites.

vi) Monograph/item [m]. An item either complete in one part or intended to be completed in a finite number of separate parts.

vii) Serial [s]. An item issued in successive parts bearing numerical or chronological designations and intended to be continued indefinitely.

Levels of Details in Description: The AACR2R has prescribed three levels of description; First level provides the minimum information, which is necessary to identify a given document. Second level description provides all the data, which may be considered necessary for description of documents forming part of the main collection of medium to large libraries in the context of libraries in developed countries. The third level provides information covering every descriptive element described in the code, given as below:

Main Entry	[tag 1XX]
Title proper [GMD] = Parallel Title: Other title information/first Statement of responsibility; each Subsequent statement of responsibility	[tag 2XX]
Edition statement/first statement of Responsibility relating to the edition	[tag 250]
Material specific details	[tag 255/256]
First place of publication, First Publisher, date of publication etc	[tag 260]
Extent of Item; other physical details, Dimensions	[tag 300]
Title proper of series/statement of Responsibility relating to series, ISSN of series, numbering within the series. Title of sub series, ISSN of sub series, numbering within the series	[tag 4XX]
Notes	[tag 5XX]
Subject Added Entry	[tag 6XX]
Added Entry Name	[tag 7XX]
Series Added Entry	[tag 8XX]
Local Entry	[tag 9XX]

Punctuation: For spacing in the full stop within the descriptive portion is applicable is given below:

1) Leave no space after a full stop used to separate one initial from another.

245	1	_	$a Library automation / $c R.S. Aswal.
260	#	#	$a New Delhi: $b I.L.A. Publication, $C 2005.

2) Leave one space after a full stop used to separate an abbreviation or initial from a word, a number, or another abbreviation.

300	#	#	$a no. 27
500	#	#	$a Ph. D.

3) Separate an abbreviation from a following initial, or to separate one *set* of initials from another.

100	1	#	$a M. J.P. Rabaut (i.e. Monsier J.P. Rabaut.

4) Leave two spaces after a full stop used to separate sentences within the same area or to separate discrete units within an element or area (e.g. to separate the title of the main work from the title of a part, or to separate the title of a series from the title of a sub-series).

400	#	0	$a Publication series. Monograph series

5) Leave no space between separate letters that are not followed by full stops, e.g. XYZ

Exception

1) If the forenames and/or surnames are not followed by full stops, insert the full stops as given below:

On source: by R S Aswal

Transcription: by R.S. Aswal

2) If a colon, a slash, or an equals sign occurs within an element, no spacing is used as given below:

   Dinner at 10:00

   Study/workbook for knitting

   2x2=5 : a farce in one act

3) Otherwise substitute a comma, dash, or some other mark that is not a prescribed mark of punctuation for the area in which the element occurs.

   On source: Symposium: Fine Arts in the 80's

   Transcription: Symposium--Fine Arts in the 80's

4) If the spacing cannot be closed up, and no satisfactory substitution can be made, simply omit the mark of punctuation.

Capitalization

1) Capitalize the first word of each heading for persons, and corporate bodies.

100	1	#	$a Aswal, Rajendra Singh.
110	1	#	$a India. $b High Court of Justice.

2) Capitalize the first word of title.

245	1	#	$a Journal of polymer science.

Exception: Capitalize the formal, or conventional, name of a document such as a charter, constitution, legislative act, pact, plan, statement of policy, or treaty.

240	1	#	$a Articles of Confederation.
245	1	#	$a Third Five Year Plan (India)
240	1	#	$a Civil Right Act of 1964.

3) Capitalize the title of sacred scripture, one of its divisions, a group of books or individual book.

130	0	#	$a Bible. $p O.T. $p Five Scrolls. $l Hebrew. $s biblioteca apostolic a Vatican. $k Manuscript. $n Urbinite Hebraicus 1. $f 1980.

4) Do not capitalize the first word of a title of it preceded by a dash (-) indicating that the beginning of the phrase from which the title was derived has been omitted.

   - and master of none

5) If a title proper consists of two or more parts, capitalize the first word of the title of the second and subsequent parts.

245	1	#	$a Advamced calculus $p Student handbook.
245	1	#	$a Journal of biosocial science $p Supplement.

6) Do not capitalize the word in GMD [music] [map]

Language and script of the description: In the following area, give information transcribed from the item itself in language and script:

1) Title and statement of responsibility
2) Edition
3) Publication, distribution, etc

4) Series

When transcribing information presented in roman script, record the letters as they are given, except as follows:

1) Convert earlier forms of letters to their modern form;
2) Separate the letters forming ligatures in English, French and other languages (except Danish, Icelandic, Norwegian); e.g. encyclopedia not encyclopedia;

Diacritical marks: Add diacritical marks as appropriate to words that are not present in the data found the source of the information in accordance with the usage of the language used in the context.

On source:	Ecole polytechnique de Montréal
Transcription:	École polytechnique de Montréal
On source:	Ecrits sur l'avenir
Transcription:	Écrits sur l'avenir

Edition or Copy: If two items are known to be two different editions, create a separate record for each. Also, consider the new manifestation to be a separate edition if any of the following conditions apply:

1) An clear indication of changes of content;
2) The bibliographic record changed to another: title and statement of responsibility area, edition area, the extent statement of the physical description area, and series area; or
3) For printed music and sound recordings, whenever two items have different publisher's or plate numbers.
4) If the difference in the copyright date; publication date; and difference in the printing date.

However, if the only variation is in the publication, distribution, etc., area or to ISBNs, consider the new manifestation to be a copy of an earlier manifestation, one or more of the following:

If minor variation in an entity's name used concurrently, e.g.,

Ess Ess Publication and Ess Ess Publication Press.

Do not consider a genuine name change, even if minor, as a variation; the addition, deletion, or change of an ISBN; or a difference in binding.

For all other variations in the publication, distribution, etc., area, consider that the item is a new edition, e.g.,

Variations involving different places or entities transcribed or any difference in an entity's name that is suggestive of either a name change or a different entity, e.g.,

Ess Ess Publication & Brothers

becomes Ess Ess Publication & Row.

1.1 TITLE AND STATEMENT OF RESPONSIBILITY

1.1A. The information recorded in this area from the chief sources of information for the material to which the item being described belongs. The MARC tag 210-247 contain the title of the item described is the bibliographic record and variant titles that also apply to the item. These fields may be used to generate access point and to display note for the various fields.

1.1B. Title proper

Transcribe the title proper exactly as to wording, order and spelling, but not necessarily as to punctuation and capitalization.

Use judgment in deciding whether a word or

phrase is part of the title proper or other title information, with language, meaning, layout, typography.

1) If any letters or symbols used in titles to indicate a trademark, a patent, copyright, etc. do not transcribe as a title proper.

   On source: (c) copyright: how to use copyright information

   Transcription: Copyright: how to use copyright information

2) When replacing a mark of omission (...) within the title proper by a dash (—), leave one space following the dash, unless the dash is at the beginning of the title.

   Nothing ventured—: investing in Canada's winners

   —and so on: new designs for teaching mathematics

If chief source of information lacking the title proper from reference source or elsewhere or any source, devise a brief descriptive title and enclose it with square brackets. Also mention in the note area.

246	#	0	$a <variant title> $g <varies lightly>

If the chief source of information bears both a collective title and the titles of individual works, give the collective title as the title proper and give the title of the individual works in contents notes.

245	0	1	$a Three notable stories.
505	0	0	$a Love and peril / $r Marquies - $t To be or not to be / $r Mr. Alexander - $t The melancholy hussar / $r Thomas.

Quotation marks: Rule 1.1B1, states that the title proper is to be transcribed "exactly as to wording, order and spelling, but not necessarily as to punctuation and capitalization," quotation marks appearing in the title proper generally are not ranscribed. If quotation marks are judged to be an integral or essential part of the title, then transcribe them and it should always be recorded as double quotation marks regardless of how they appear in the title.

245	0	0	$a Rainbow A song of "Rainy day".
245	0	2	$a "Peace, order and good government" re-examed.

If there is any doubt whatsoever as to what constitutes the "main written, spoken, or sung content of the item, prefer the title proper of the chief source of information.

Bilingual publications: In cases of bilingual publications consisting of English and French text with a predominance in one language, choose the title proper according to the order of titles on, or layout of, the chief source of information.

Supplement: Title proper of supplement to, or section of, another resource. The following are general guidelines; situations not addressed here should be left to cataloguer's judgement.

If the supplement to, or section of, has a title insufficient to identify it without the inclusion of the title common to all sections as presented on the chief source, give the common title first and consider the title of supplementary item or section as a part/section ($p/$n).

245	0	0	$a Journal of the Faculty of Science, the University of Tokyo. $n Section IV.
245	0	0	$a Advanced calculus. $p Student book.

When the supplement to, or section of, another resource has a title that can be disassociated from the title common to all sections (or the title of the main resource), consider the title of the supplementary item or section as the title proper and treat the common title (or title of the main resource) as a series if appropriate.

245	0	0	$a Valley Truss & Metal Ltd., converting on-site wood.
440	0	0	$a Biomass combustion systems

1.1C. General material designation: Add a general material designation (GMD), as instructed, to all records except those for eye-readable printed copy ("text") the GMD are desired.

The GMD [kit] is assigned to two categories of material:

1) If the item containing more than one type of material and the relative predominance of the components is not easily determinable, e.g. Picture set which includes both photographs and study prints would be considered.
2) Single medium packages sometimes called "lab kits".

   a lab kit is a set of cards, with or without manuals, largely consisting of text.

1.1D. Parallel titles: When recording parallel titles,

apply the same rules for transcription as are used for titles proper as above.

245	0	0	$a Annual report of the Minister of Supply and Service India = $b Rapport annuel du minister of Indiana.

1.1E. Other title information

If a items containing two or more works by the same author without a collective title, where the chief source of information is not unitary in nature and other title information that applies to all the works is repeated with the individual titles on various sources within the item, record such other title information once only, following the last title proper.

245	0	0	$a Rose Marie $h [round recording]; Indian love call : $b from the musical play, Rose Marie / $c words by Harbach.

If the title is in other languages, record such other title information in other languages. If the title is lengthy, it can be abridge only if this can be done without loss of essential information. Never omit any of the first five words of the other title information. Otherwise it give in the note section.

1.1F. Statements of responsibility

Definition: "statement of responsibility" given in the glossary is based entirely on the function of the person or corporate body named and has no dependence on whether that function is made explicit in the statement or not. Statements that do include an explicit indication of function will be readily identified as statements of responsibility. Names that do not carry with them an explicit indication of function must be judged on the basis of known or implied function to determine whether they qualify as statements of responsibility.

Its very clears that the person or corporate body named performs one or more of the functions defined under "statement of responsibility" found on any source within the item is sufficient to warrant the treatment of that name as a statement of responsibility on all other sources on which it appears regardless of whether the function is indicated on all sources or not.

A name appearing immediately above or below the title, or otherwise in proximity to the title, should be considered as a statement of responsibility except in cases where there is reason to doubt that the person or corporate body named performs one of the defined functions.

"statement of responsibility", consider "persons responsible for the intellectual or artistic content of the item" to include authors, editors, translators, arrangers, adaptors, etc.

Do not include under "house" editors, editorial supervisors, managing editors, sponsoring editors, book designers, cover artists, graphic designers, production managers, etc.).

If there is doubt as to whether the function performed by a particular person should be included or excluded, consider it to be excluded unless the person's name appears on the chief source of information.

245	0	0	$a How to play cricket / $c Sunil Singh.

If personal name(s), that is/are to be recorded in a statement of responsibility, appear(s) in inverted order, transcribe the name(s) as found. If any confusion with respect to the number and name(s) of the individual(s), follow the statement with a bracketed statement in direct order.

245	1	0	$a Cataloging practice / $c A. K. Singh.

If the names of two or more corporate bodies are recorded in a single statement of responsibility, and the punctuation within the names is such that it is unclear where one name ends and another begins, separate the names by inserting within square brackets the word "and" or its equivalent in the language appropriate to the context.

245	1	0	$a Indian census / $c sponsored by Ministry of Planning, Department of Statistics, [and] Department of History.

Add the statement or statements in other languages according to the Provisions.

245	0	0	$a Proceedings / $c Canadian Institute of Actuaries = Institute canadien des actuaries.

If the statements pertaining to illustration unless the statement includes the name of the illustrator or forms is generally omitted.

...; illustrations de Clarence Gagnon

If a single statement of responsibility name more than three person or corporate bodies performing the same function or with the same degree of responsibility, omit all but the first of each group of such persons or bodies. Indicate the omission by the mark of omission (. . .) and add [et al.] in square bracket.

245	0	4	$a The plays of Oscar / $c Alan Bird ... [et al.]

If there is more than one statement of responsibility, give them in the order indicated by their sequence on, or the layout of, the chief source of information. If the sequence and layout are ambiguous or insufficient to determine the order, give the statement in order that makes the most sense. If statements of responsibility appear in sources other than the chief source, record them in the order that makes the most sense.

245	1	2	$a A saint in Philadelphia / $c Raymonds C. kaminers and Carl R. Steikeck; mdade by creative sight.

The statement includes title and abbreviation of title of nobility, address, and distinction, initials of socities, qualifications date of founding, mottoes, etc., in statement of responsibility.

245	1	4	$a The play / $c Dr. Johnson.

If the relationship between the title of the item and the person(s) or body (bodies) named not clear, add the word or short phrase. e.g., edited by, illustrated by, etc,

245	1	4	$a The analysis of the games / $c edited by Mathew.

If the individual works are by different person or emanate from different bodies, or in case of doubts, follow the title information and statement of responsibility. Separate the groups of data with a full stop followed by two spaces.

245	1	4	$a The analysis of the law / $c Sir Mathew Hale. The students companion / Giles Jacob.

1.1G. Items without a collective title: If in an item lacking a collective title, no one work predominates, either describe the item as a unit or make a separate description for each separately titled work, linking the separate description with notes.

If the linking word or phrase is used between titles in the chief source of information, a comma should be inserted following the linking word or phrase only when desirable for clarity.

1.2 EDITION AREA

1.2A. The information taken from the chief source of information or from any other source prescribed for this area. If information supplied from any other source it enclose in square brackets.

1.2B. If an edition statement found on the item, record the statement as found.

250	#	#	$a 2nd ed.

If the title and/or statement(s) of responsibility have been recorded in more than one language, record the edition statement in parallel forms.

250	#	#	$a 23rd [ed.] = 3e [ed.]

Treat any phrase that calls attention to changes

from a previous issue of the item or distinguishes it from an issue in a different format as an edition statement or a statement relating to a named revision of an edition.

250	#	#	$a Teacher's ed.

However, if a word such as "edition", "issue", "version", etc., or a term indicating revision, etc., does not appear in the statement, and there is doubt that the statement is actually an edition statement or remaining portion of the title. In this cases, treat it as part of the title proper or as other title information.

Any edition information supplied by the cataloguer is given in the note area.

1.2C. Statements of responsibility relating to the edition

Give parallel statement(s) of responsibility relating to the edition in accordance with the provisions.

250	#	#	$a 4th ed. / $b revised by J.K. Kothari.

If the statement of responsibility to a named revision of an edition, transcribe a statement of responsibility relating to one or more as the order given.

250	#	#	$a Rev. ed. / $b with revisions, an introduction, and a chapter on writing by E.B White, 2nd ed. / with the assistance of Eleanor gould Packard.

1.3 MATERIAL SPECIFIC DETAILS AREA

This area is used in the description of cartographic materials, music, Electronic resources, serial publications and in some circumstances, microforms. This data may also be coded in field 034 (Coded Mathematical Data).

255	#	#	$a Scale [ca. 1:90,000]

1.4 PUBLICATION, DISTRIBUTION, ETC., AREA

1.4A. Information taken form the chief source of information or from any other source prescribed for this area. Enclose is square brackets information supplied from other sources.

1.4B. Information relating to the publication, printing, distribution, issue, release, or production of a work, etc., and dates in accordance with the provisions established under "levels of Details in Description"

If necessary to give the name of the country, state, province, etc., after the name of the place for identification or to distinguish the place from others of the same name.

260	#	#	$a Hyderabad, India : $b Ess Esss $c 2005.

If the required addition appears within the prescribed source of information in an abbreviated form, transcribe it as is.

On source: Hamilton, Ontario

Transcription: Hamilton, Ont.

On source: St. John's, Newfoundland

Transcription: St. John's, Nfld.

If the required addition does not appear within

the prescribed source of information, use the name and form prescribed as an addition to the place name under rule 23.4 and enclose it within square brackets.

On source: Moose Jaw

Transcription: Moose Jaw [Sask.]

In the cases when the required addition does not appear within the prescribed source of information and the addition has undergone a name change, use the current name of the jurisdiction (regardless of the imprint date) in the form prescribed as an addition to the place name and enclose it within square brackets.

On source: Goose Bay

Transcription: Goose Bay [N.L.]

Do not include as an addition any place name other than the one prescribed by rule 23.4.

On source: Kingston, Canada

Transcription: Kingston [Ont.]

Do not add the name of the country, state, province, etc., if the name, in noun or adjectival form, forms part of the name of the publisher, distributor, etc., and is being recorded as such.

260	#	#	$a London : $b University of Western Ontario, $c 1978.

Not

260	#	#	$a London [Ont.]: $b University of Western Ontario, $c 1978.

1.4C. If the place of publication, distribution, etc., is not named in the item, or if the place is only probable rather than certain, give the name in its well-established English form if there is one, followed by a question mark.

[Toronto?] [Drumheller, Alta.?]

For Canadian publications, if no probable place can be given, give the name of the province, if known. If the province is not certain, but probable, give it with a question mark. If the province cannot be conjectured, give "Canada".

For publications of Australia, Malaysia, United States, U.S.S.R., or Yugoslavia, if no probable place can be given, give the name of the state or territory, if known or probable. If the state or territory cannot be conjectured, give the name of the country.

For British publications, if no probable place can be given, give "England," "Ireland," "Northern Ireland," "Scotland." "Wales," "Isle of Man," or "Channel Islands," as appropriate. If this cannot be determined, give "Great Britain".

For all other publications, if no probable place can be given, give the name of the country.

When recording information in a nonroman script that has no equivalent abbreviation, use the roman "S.l." (sine loco).

260	#	#	$a [S.l.]: $b Macmillan, $c 1978.

1.4D. Name of the Publisher, distributors, etc. The elements of hierarchy retained, however, may differ from those in the heading, particularly if the heading is subordinated to the name of a government.

On source: Agriculture Canada, Research Branch, Dairy Division

Heading: Canada. Dairy Division

Transcription: Agriculture Canada, Dairy Division

Generally omit from the name of the publisher, distributor, etc., initial articles, phrases such as "and company," "and sons," etc., terms such as "incorporated," "limited," etc., and their equivalents in other languages.

On source: Ess Ess & Co.

Transcription:

260	#	#	$a New Delhi: $b Ess Ess, $c 1978.

On source: Macmillan and co.

Transcription:

260	#	#	$a London : $b Macmillan, $c 1978.

Omit the name of a parent firm if the name of a division, branch, subsidiary, etc., is sufficient to identified on its own.

On source: Harmuse Publications, a division of the Frederick Harris Music Co. Limited

Transcription:

260	#	#	$a London : $b Harmuse, $c 1971.

Omit the name of the director or founder of a publishing firm unless it forms an integral and inseparable part of the firm's name. Do not omit phrases such as "published by" and "published for" when they are used to introduce a statement naming more than one body and the names are linked grammatically by a word or phrase other than a simple "and" or its equivalent.

: Published for the Ontario Economic Council by University of Toronto Press

: Published by University of Toronto Press in association with the Medieval Academy of America

: CSSCQ et CSSQ pour l'Association des CSS du Québec

1.4D5. If required add the name and place of the distributor when the information is necessary for clarification.

1.4D6. If the name of the publisher distributor etc is unknown, give abbreviation "s.n." (sine nominee).

260	#	#	$a New Delhi : $b [s.n.], $c 1978.

1.4F. Date of publication, distribution, etc: The date of publication, distribution, etc., of a work is mentioned. It May be contain multiple dates (e.g., dates of publication and copyright).

If the date appearing in the prescribed source of information is presented as both a Gregorian and non-Gregorian date, record only the Gregorian form. If the date is presented only as a non-Gregorian date, give the date as found followed by the Gregorian date enclosed in square brackets.

, 4308 [1975]

If there is no date appearing in the prescribed source of information, and the only date appearing elsewhere in the item is presented as a non-Gregorian date, give the date as found followed by the abbreviation "i.e." and Gregorian date, enclosing the entire element in square brackets.

, [4308 i.e. 1975]

The date of distribution only may be applicable if it differs from the publication date by two years or more.

For sound recordings, record the date of

phonogram preceded by a lower case "p", regardless of the symbol, abbreviation, or other designation appearing in the prescribed source of information. Since 1971 the phonogram date has been used to indicate the copyright date for the sound content of a recording (as opposed to program notes, libretto, etc.).

If the item contains only a copyright date, give the copyright date. Always precede a copyright date with a lower case "c".

If the date of publication, distribution, etc., is not known precisely, but the probable date of publication differs from the copyright date by three years or more, precede the copyright date by the approximate date of publication.

[1980?], c1961

(Approximate date of publication based on preface dated June 1980).

If the date of manufacture can be assumed to be the date of publication, distribution, etc. (i.e. if it is the date of the first printing, etc.), give the date without the addition of the term "printing", etc., and without any indication that it is only an approximation ("?," "ca.," etc.). If the date is taken from a source other than one of the prescribed sources of information for the publication, distribution, etc., area, enclose the date in square brackets. Add the copyright date if it is different.

, 1980 (Verso of title page: "First Printing 1980").

, 1980, c1979 (Verso of title page: "Copyright 1979 // First Printing 1980").

If the date of manufacture cannot be assumed to be the date of publication, distribution, etc., and there is no copyright date, give the date of manufacture followed by the term "printing," etc.

260	#	#	London : $b Macmillan, $c (1978 print)

If the date of manufacture as it appears in the item is obviously incorrect, ignore it and give instead an approximate date of publication.

, [1976?] (Verso of title page: "Printed 1974". Preface dated "September 1976").

If the date of publication, distribution, etc., is not known precisely, but the probable date of publication differs from the copyright date by three years or more, precede the copyright date by the approximate date of publication.

[1980?], c1961 (Approximate date of publication based on preface dated June 1980).

The option is applied. If the first and/or last published issue, iteration, or part is not available, the beginning and/or ending publication date(s) separated by a hyphen will be supplied in square brackets if it can be readily ascertained.

1.4G. Place of manufacture, name of manufacturer, date

If a bracketed date of publication, etc., is followed by a bracketed place of manufacture, disregard 1.0C and put a closing bracket after the date and an opening bracket before the place.

Paris : Plans-guides Blay, [1979]

([Paris] : Imprimerie de Montligeon)

not

Paris : Plans-guides Blay, [1979

(Paris] : Imprimerie de Montligeon)

Add the place of manufacture and/or name of

manufacturer only if they are considered to be of unusual importance. Add the date of manufacture only if the library holds no copies manufactured within three years of the date of publication or copyright.

, 1976 (1981 printing)

, c1968 (1974 printing)

If the library holds at least one copy manufactured within three years of the date of publication or copyright, give only the date of publication and/or copyright, and treat later printings, etc., simply as added copies.

, 1979 ("Copy 2: 1980 printing")

1.5 PHYSICAL DESCRIPTION AREA

1.5A. A physical description of the described item, including its extent, dimensions, and such other physical details as a description of any accompanying materials and unit type and size.

The source of the information is the item itself.

1.5B. Extent of the item has giving by the number of physical units in the Arabic numerals and the specific material designation [SMD]. It contains the number of pages, volumes, cassettes, total playing time, etc., of the described item.

300	#	#	$a 11 v. : $b ill. ; $c 24 cm.
300	#	#	$a 1 sound dise (20 min.) : $b analog, 33 1/3 rpm, stereo.

1.5C. Dimensions

1.5C1. In giving the dimensions of an item requiring more than one measurement, use a lower-case "x" as the multiplication sign to separate each of the measurements.

300	#	#	$a 1 sound dise (20 min.) ; $c 48 x 30 cm, folded to 24 x 15 cm.
	300	#	# $a 1 sound dise (20 min.) ; $c in container 18 x 25 x 19 cm.

1.5E. Accompanying Material: Apply the following guidelines in determining which method to use to describe accompanying material.

1.5E1. Create a separate entry if any of the following:

1) the accompanying material is issued at a later date than the main publication; or,
2) the title and/or statement(s) of responsibility for the accompanying material are significantly different from those for the main publication; or,
3) the nature of the material is such that a separate record is required to facilitate processing and storage.

Do not use multilevel description to describe accompanying material.

Use a note to describe accompanying material if either of the following criteria apply:

1) the accompanying material is insubstantial in size/ volume/ content, and clearly of little bibliographic importance; or,
2) the criteria listed under (a) and (d) exclude the possibility of describing the accompanying material either as a separate entry or at the end of the physical description.

300	#	#	$a 1 sound dise (56 min.) : $d digital, stereo.
500	#	#	$a Accompanied by filmstrip entitled.

Record the name of the accompanying material at the end of the physical description if all the following criteria apply:

1) the accompanying material is issued at the same time and by the same publisher as the main publication, and is essentially of use only in conjunction with the main publication;
2) responsibility for the accompanying material is either the same as for the main publication, or unknown, or of a nature that does not require mention either in a note or an added entry; and,
3) the accompanying material is either untitled, or carries only a generic or dependent title that can be recorded simply.

300	#	#	$a 1 globe : $d col., wood, mounted.

1.6 SERIES AREA

1.6A. The information taken from the chief source of information or from any other source prescribed for this area. If information supplied from any other source it enclose in square brackets, within the parentheses enclosing each series statement.

Fields 440 and 490 contain series statements. Field 440 also provides an added entry for the series. A series statement is recorded in field 490 when either it is given no added entry in the record (an untraced series) or is given an added entry in a form that differs from the series statement appearing on the item. One of fields 800-830 (Series added entries) is used in conjunction with field 490 when the series is to be traced differently.

The parentheses that customarily enclose a series statement and the tracing Series., preceded by a roman numeral, in some displays for field 440 are not carried in the MARC record. They may be generated based on the field tag.

The name of a corporate body responsible for a series may be given as the title proper of the series, provided the name appears on the source in conjunction with the numbering of the item within the series and there is no other title given.

400	#	#	$a Winnipeg Art Gallery; $v 6

The name of the body need not be represented in its full or established form on the source; an initialism or acronym representing the name of the body may be treated as the title proper of the series.

400	#	#	$a AEEE; $v 2

(Full name: School of Agricultural Economics and Extension Education)

The name of a corporate body should not be given as the title proper of the series if the body is a commercial publisher. Give the name of the body as it appears and the numbering of the item within the series as a quoted note. If the name has been recorded in the publication, distribution, etc., area, give the numbering alone as a quoted note.

1.6G. Numbering within series: If the numbering of the item within the series includes a chronological designation in addition to a numeric or alphabetic designation, record the chronological designation within parentheses following the numeric/alphabetic designation.

Do not, however, construe the date of publication, distribution, etc., to form part of the series numbering.

On source: volume 3 part 2 September 1981

400	#	0	$a Publication series. $v v. 3, pt. 2

If the numbering consists of two portions, one representing the year, and the other representing the sequence of items within that year, record the two portions in the order in which they appear on the source.

On source: 1-1979

400	#	#	$a Publication series. $v 1-1979

Abbreviations, etc.: Use abbreviations as instructed in Appendix B.5B1 and numerals as instructed in Appendix regardless of how the designation appears on the source.

On source: Toronto studies in religion vol. 19

400	#	0	$a Toronto studies in religion ; $v v. 19

On source: Garland composer resource manuals numb. 21

400	#	0	$a Garland composer resource manuals; $v no. 21

If there is no standard abbreviation for the term given in the item, and the term is excessively long or complex, record only the number. When substituting

Arabic numerals for other numerals or spelled out numbers, use the ordinal form if the number on the source is in the ordinal form; use the cardinal form if the number on the source is in the cardinal form.

Numbering in more than one system of designation: If the numbering within the series is given according to more than one system of designation, and there is a one to one relationship between the item itself and each of the numbers, record the numbers in the order in which they are presented in the source. Precede the alternative numbering by an equals sign. If the alternative numbering is given in excessively lengthy or complicated terms, omit it from the series area, and record it in a note instead.

new series 5 (94)

400	#	#	$a Publication series. $v new ser. 5

If the numbering of the item within the series includes a chronological designation in addition to a numeric or alphabetic designation.

If parallel titles are being recorded and the numbering also appears in more than one language or script, but does not form an integral part of the title, record each number after the title proper/parallel title to which it relates.

400	#	#	$a Canadian meteorological history ; $v no. 4 = $a Historie de la ; $v no 4

If this criterion does not apply, record the form that appears first in the source of information for the series. Note that unless the numbering forms an integral part of the title, the numbering element follows the parallel titles of the series and is placed after other title information, statements of responsibility, and ISSN, if present. Do not place it between the title proper of the series and the parallel title. If the number appears only once, record it after the title it linguistically matches or after the last title if it matches all, more than one, or none of the titles.

1.6H. Subseries: Apply the rule for subseries only if the title of the main series and the title of the subseries appear within the same source of information. The layout of titles within the source (order, proximity, etc.) is not a factor.

If there is doubt whether a title designates a subseries (i.e. a series within a series) or a separate series (i.e. a series that may have one or more items that it contains in common with another series, but is not itself wholly contained within that series) treat the title as a separate series.

If one of the titles designates a series and the other designates a multipart item, treat each as a separate series. Treat a phrase such as "new series", "second series" as a subseries title if the items within the "new series", etc., are unnumbered. If the items are numbered, and the phrase "new series", etc., forms part of the numbering scheme, treat the phrase as part of the series numbering.

400	#	#	$a Studies in philat ; $v new ser. no 2
400	#	#	$a Papers for war ;$v second ser. no. 3

If the ISSN of the subseries does not appear in the item, but the ISSN of the main series does, record the ISSN of the main series in its appropriate position.

If a multipart being described as a unit contains parts that belong to than in the serie·, area.

Pts. 1 and 2 in series: African p·rspective.

Pts. 3 and 4 in series: Third Wcrld series.

Pt. 5 in both series

1.7 NOTE AREA

1.7A. The note recorded from any suitable source. Use square bracket only for interpolations with quoted materials. The order of the note information should be recorded in the order in which they appear in the title and statement of responsibility, edition, material specific details, publication, etc., physical description, and series areas.

Use quotations from the item or from other sources in quotation marks. Use introductory word or phrase or a standard form or words when uniformity of presentation assists in the recognition of the type of information being presented or when their use provides economy of space without loss of clarity.

Fields 500-535 contain notes relating to aspects of bibliographic items that are not specific to any particular type of material or control (e.g., archival control). Specialized note fields are used when access to the data is needed and/or the note is introduced by a distinctive word or phrase. Field 500 is used for all other note information.

Fields 536-586 contain bibliographic notes which are more specific in nature. A significant number of these note fields are used to record information relating to the archival or serial control of the bibliographic item.

The print program supplies some 5XX fields with

a display constant. Display constants are words that are supplied by the print program when it prints the cards. The 1st indicator value determines the display constant for the field. Do not include display constant in thes text of the fields.

Display constants may vary for AACR2 and pre-AACR2 records.

1.7.0. General Note [500, R]: General information.

Both Indicators # Undefined

Subfield Codes $a General note (NR)

500	#	#	$a Recast in bronze from artist's.
500	#	#	$a Caption title.

1.7.1. With Note (501, R): This is used when more than one bibliographic work is contained in a physical item at the time of publishing, release, issue, or execution. The works usually have distinctive titles and lack a collective title.

Both Indicators # Undefined

Subfield Codes $a With note (NR) Includes a relevant introductory phrase (e.g., With:, On reel with:).

505	#	#	$a With: Special bulletin.

1.7.2. Dissertation Note (502, R): The dissertation or thesis note that describes the relationship of a work to a dissertation or thesis is recorded in field 500.

Both Indicators # Undefined

Subfield Codes $a Dissertation note (NR)

502	#	#	$a Thesis-University College, New Delhi, 1995.

1.7.3. Bibliography, Etc. Note (504, R): This is used when one or more bibliographies, discographies, filmographies, and/or other bibliographic references in a described item or in accompanying material presence.

Both Indicators	#	Undefined
Subfield Codes	$a	Bibliography, etc. note (NR)
	$b	Number of references (NR)

504	#	#	$a Bibliography: p. 238-239.

1.7.4. Formatted Contents Note (505, NR): This is used when separate works or parts of an item or the table of contents of a finding aid for materials under archival control. The field may also contain statements of responsibility and volume numbers or other sequential designations. This note fields is very useful in the case of multi-volume books.

First Indicators	0	Contents: may be generated for display.
	1	Incomplete contents All parts of a multipart item are not listed because they were not available for analysis. Incomplete contents: may be generated for display.
	2	Partial contents All parts were available for analysis but only selected parts are listed. Partial contents: may be generated for display.

	8	No display constant generated
Second Indicator	#	Basic
	0	Enhanced
Subfield Codes	$a	Formatted contents note (NR) The format of the note is determined by the relevant cataloging rules.
	$g	Miscellaneous information (R)
	$r	Statement of responsibility (R)
	$t	Title (R)
	$u	Uniform Resource Identifier (R)

505	0	#	$a pt. 1. How to play – pt. 2. Record history.
505	8	#	$a Contents on sound disk: A suitable tone ; Left hand colouring.

1.7.4. Scale Note for Graphic Material (507, NR): For visual materials, this field contains the scale of architectural drawings or three-dimensional artifacts. For maps, the scale of an item is contained in this field only in pre-AACR 2 cataloging records. Scale information is contained in field 255 (Mathematical Data Area) in AACR 2 formulated records.

Both Indicators	#	Undefined
Subfield Codes	$a	Representative fraction of scale note (NR)

		$b	Remainder of scale note (NR)

507	#	#	$a Scale 1:5000,000; $b in. iquals 8 miles.

1.7.5. Creation/Production Credits Note (508, NR): The names of the persons (other than members of the cast) or organizations who participated in the artistic or technical production of the work.

Both Indicators	ḃ	Credits:
Subfield Codes	$a	Creation/production credits note (NR)

508	#	#	$a Producer, Joseph N. Ermolieff; director, Lesley Selander.

1.7.6. Citation/References Note (510, R): Citations or references to published bibliographic descriptions, reviews, abstracts, or indexes of the content of the described item.

First Indicators	0	Indexed by:
	1	Indexed in its entirety by:
	2	Indexed selectively by:
	3	References:
	4	References:
Second Indicator	#	Undefined
Subfield	$a	Name of source (NR)
	$b	Dates of coverage of source (NR)
	$c	Location within source (NR)
	$x	International Standard Serial Number (NR)

			$3 Materials specified (NR)
510	1	#	$a Education index, $b 1966.

1.7.7. Participant or Performer Note (511, R): The names of the participants, players, narrators, presenters, or performers.

First Indicators	0	No display constant generated
	1	Cast :
Second Undefined	#	Undefined
Subfield	$a	Participant or performer note (NR)

511	0	#	$a Voice: Subhash Chand Bose.

1.7.8. Type of Report and Period Covered Note (513, R)

Information on the type of report and the period covered by the report.

Both Indicators	#	Undefined
Subfield Codes	$a	Type of report (NR)
	$b	Period covered (NR)

513	#	#	$a Quarterly technical progress report $b Jan. – Apr. 1, 1977.

1.7.9. Numbering Peculiarities Note (515, R): Irregularities and peculiarities in numbering or publishing patterns, report year coverage, revised editions, and/or issuance in parts.

Both Indicators	#	Undefined
Subfield Codes	$a	Numbering peculiarities note (NR)

515	#	#	$a Vols. 50 and 51 combined.

1.7.10. Type of Electronic resources or Data Note (516, R): Specific information such as the form or genre of textual material (e.g., biography, indexes) and a file. The general type of file is coded in field 008/26 (Type of Electronic resources).

First Indicators	ƀ	Type of file :
	8	No display constant generated
Second Indicator	#	Undefined
Subfield	$a	Type of Electronic resources or data note (NR)

516	#	#	$a Computer programs.

1.7.11. Date/Time and Place of an Event Note (518, R): The date/time and/or place of creation, capture, or broadcast, associated with an event or the finding of a naturally occurring object. This information in coded form is contained in field 033 (Date/Time and Place of an Event).

Both Indicators	#	Undefined
Subfield Codes	$a	Date/time and place of an event note (NR)
	$3	Materials specified (NR)

518	#	#	$a Recorded in New Delhi in 1972.

1.7.12. Summary, Etc. (520, R): The level of detail appropriate in a summary may vary depending on the audience for a particular product. When a distinction between levels of detail is required, a brief summary is given in subfield $a and a fuller annotation is given in subfield $b.

First Indicators	ɓ	Summary :
	0	Subject :
	1	Review :
	2	Scope and content :
	3	Abstract :
	8	No display constant generated
Second Undefined	#	Undefined
Subfield Codes	$a	Summary, etc. note (NR)
	$b	Expansion of summary note (NR)
	$u	Uniform Resource Identifier (R)
	$3	Materials specified (NR)

520	#	#	$a An illustrated collection of nursery.

1.7.13. Target Audience Note (521, R): Identifies the specific audience or intellectual level for which the content of the described item is considered appropriate.

First Indicators	ɓ	Audience :
	0	Reading grade level :
	1	Interest age level :
	2	Interest grade level :
	3	Special audience characteristics
	4	Motivation interest level
	8	No display constant generated

Second Indicator	#	Undefined
Subfield	$a	Target audience note (R)
	$b	Source (NR)
	$3	Materials specified (NR)

521	ɓ	#	$a 7 - 10.

1.7.14. Supplement Note (525, R): Information of supplements or special issues (usually unnamed) that are neither cataloged as separate records nor recorded in field 770 (Supplement/Special Issue Entry).

Both Indicators	#	Undefined
Subfield	$a	Geographic coverage note (NR)

525	#	#	$a Supplements a accompanies v. 2.

1.7.15. Additional Physical Form Available Note (530, R): The information concerning a different physical format.

Both Indicators	#	Undefined
Subfield	$a	Additional physical form available note (NR)
	$b	Availability source (NR)
	$c	Availability conditions (NR)
	$d	Order number (NR)
	$u	Uniform Resource Identifier (R)

530	#	#	$a Issued also as 16 mm. filmstrip

1.7.16. Reproduction Note (533, R): The data for a reproduction of an original item when the main portion of the bibliographic record describes the original item and the data differ.

533 ## $a Microfilm. $bWashington, D.C. : $c United States Historical Documents Institute, $d [1972] $e12 reels ; 35 mm. $7 s1972####dcun#a

533	#	#	$a Microfilm. $b Washington, D.C.: $c United States Historical Documents Institute, $d [1972] $e 12 reel; 35 mm. $7 s1972 ####dcun#a

1.7.17. Original Version Note (534, R): If data for an original item when the main portion of the bibliographic record describes a reproduction of that item and the data differ.

534	#	#	$a Originally published : $c New Delhi :Ess Ess, 1972, $b ist ed.

1.7.18. Location of Originals/Duplicates Note (535, R): The name and address of the repository that has custody of the original or a duplicate copy of the described material.

First Indicators	1	Holder of originals
	2	Holder of duplicates
Second Indicator	#	Undefined
Subfield	$a	Custodian (NR)
	$b	Postal address (R)
	$c	Country (R)
	$d	Telecommunications address (R)
	$g	Repository location code (NR)

535 1# $a American Mining Congress; $b1980

1.7.19. Funding Information Note (536, R): Information concerning the sponsor or funding agency also may be included.

536	#	#	$a Sponsored by the World Health Organisation.

1.7.20. System Details Note (538, R): Technical information about an item, recording densities, parity, blocking factors, software programming language, computer requirements, peripheral requirements, etc.

Both Indicators	#	Undefined
Subfield	$a	System details note (NR)

538	#	#	$a Data in extended ASCII character.

1.7.21. Terms Governing Use and Reproduction Note (540, R): Terms governing the use of the described materials (e.g., copyrights, film rights, trade rights) after access has been provided.

Both Indicators	#	Undefined
Subfield	$a	Terms governing use NR)
	$b	Jurisdiction (NR)
	$c	Authorization (NR)
	$d	Authorized users (NR)
	$u	Uniform Resource Identifier (R)

540	#	#	$a Restricted: Coplying allowed only for non-profit organiazations.

1.7.22. Immediate Source of Acquisition Note (541, R): The immediate source of acquisition of the described materials. The field is used primarily for original or historical items or other archival collections.

Both Indicators	#	Undefined
Subfield	$a	Source of acquisition (NR)
		[The name of the person or organization that is the source of the material].
	$b	Address (NR)
	$c	Method of acquisition (NR)
		[The terms under which a transfer of physical custody occurs, e.g., by gift, loan, purchase].
	$e	Accession number (NR)
		[The identification code assigned to materials acquired in a single and separate transfer of custody].
	$f	Owner (NR)
		[The individual or organization with legal custody over the described materials].
	$h	Purchase price (NR)
	$n	Extent (R)
		The number of items acquired.
	$o	Type of unit (R)
		[The name of the unit of

			measurement, e.g., cartons].
541	#	#	$c Gift: $a William, D.W. $d 1997.

1.7.23. Location of Other Archival Materials Note (544, R): The name and address of the custodian of materials that, at a previous time, have been part of the same collection or record group as the described materials.

First Indicators	#	No information provided
	0	Associated materials
	1	Related materials
Second Indicator	#	Undefined
Subfield Codes	$a	Custodian (R)
	$b	Address (R)
	$c	Country (R)
	$d	Title (R)
	$e	Provenance (R)
	$n	Note (R)

544	#	#	$d Blurt Berner papers; $e Also located at; $a Archives of American Art.

1.7.24. Language Note (546, R): A description of the alphabet, script, or other symbol system (e.g., arabic alphabet, ASCII, musical notation system, bar code, logarithmic graphing) may also be included. Coded language information is contained in fields 008/ 35- 37 and/or 041.

Both Indicators	#	Undefined
Subfield	$a	Language note (NR)

	$b	Information code or alphabet (R)

546	#	#	$a English, French, or German.

1.7.25. Former Title Complexity Note (547, R): The complex relationship between former titles when an intelligible note cannot be generated from the data in field 247 (Former Title or Title Variations).

Both Indicators	#	Undefined
Subfield Codes	$a	Former title complexity note (NR)

547	#	#	$a Edition varies: 1950, New Delhi.

1.7.26. Issuing Body Note (550, R): Information about the current and former issuing bodies of a serial.

Both Indicators	#	Undefined
Subfield	$a	Issuing body note (NR)

550	#	#	$a Vols. For 1990—issued with: Blureau of census.

1.7.27. Cumulative Index/Finding Aids Note (555, R): Information on the cumulative indexes for serials or finding aids and similar control materials for archival and manuscripts control and visual materials.

First Indicators	ƀ	Indexes
	0	Finding aids
	8	No display constant generated
Second Indicator	#	Undefined
Subfield	$a	Cumulative index/finding aids note (NR)

$b	Availability source (R)
$c	Degree of control (NR)
$d	Bibliographic reference (NR)
$u	Uniform Resource Identifier (R)

555	#	#	$a Vols 1(1957)-10(1954) in v. 11, no.1.

1.7.28. Information About Documentation Note (556, R): The information about the documentation of a file.

First Indicators	#	Documentation
	8	No display constant generated
Second Indicator	#	Undefined
Subfield	$a	Information about documentation note (NR)
	$z	International standard book number (R)

556	8	#	$a Documentation also available LOC.

1.7.29. Ownership and Custodial History (561, R): Information concerning the history of the described materials from the time of their creation to the time of their accessioning, including the time at which individual items or group of items were first brought together in their current arrangement or collation.

Both Indicators	#	Undefined
Subfield Codes	$a	History (NR)
	$3	Materials specified (NR)

	$5	Institution to which field applies

561	#	#	$a Collected by L. McGarry, $b 1948.

1.7.30. Linking Entry and Complexity Note (580, R): A complex relationship between the described item and other items when an intelligible note cannot be generated from data in the linking entry fields 760-787.

Both Indicators	#	Undefined
Subfield Codes	$a	Linking entry complexity note (NR)

580	#	#	$a Continued in 1982 by: U.S. exports. Schedule E commondity groupings by world area and country.

1.7.30. Publications About Described Materials Note (581, R):

A information about a publication that is a study or analysis of the described materials.

First Indicators	#	Publications
	8	No display constant generated
Second Indicator	#	Undefined
Subfield	$a	Publications about described materials note (NR)
	$z	International Standard Book Number (R)

581	8	#	$a Reproduction, June 1982, p. 80.

1.8 STANDARD AND TERMS OF AVAILABILITY AREA

1.8A. Information can be taken form any source. Do not enclose ay information in brackets.

1.8B. Give the International Standard Book Number(ISBN), or International Standard Serial Number (ISSN), or any other internationally agreed standard number for the item being described. Give such numbers with the agreed abbreviation and with the standard spacing or hyphenation.

If an item bears two or more such numbers, give the one that applies to the item being described.

Optionally, give after the standard number, a brief qualification when an item bears two or more standard numbers.

Length of the ISBN String/Check Digit

Generally ISBN standard consist 10 digit in a four groups but in January 2007, the ISBN standard will expand the current 10-digit string of numbers to 13. This action is being taken to increase the availability of new numbers and to make the ISBN standard compatible with European standard numbering systems. All ISBNs in the original pool of numbers will be prefaced by the prefix "978" to accomplish this increase in digits. All new ISBNs will be given a prefix "979", allowing the agency to effectively "reuse" the current pool of ISBNs.

The check digit for the 13-digit ISBN will be updated based on the research currently being carried out by the Society of Motion Picture and Television Engineers (SMPTE—an official American National Standards Institute standards development body) for the ISAN standard.

ISBN International will continue to pursue various means of increasing the pool of ISBNs and recommends that all users of ISBNs plan for at least 32 characters in the ISBN field. Systems flexibility is essential in the ability to utilize ISBNs no matter what the subsequent developments might be.

International Standard Book Number (020, R): The ISBN assigned to a monographic publication by designated agencies in each country participating in the program. The field may include terms of availability and cancelled or invalid ISBNs. The initialism ISBN, the phrase ISBN (invalid), and the hyphens embedded in the number are not carried in the MARC record. (The ISBN is an agency-assigned data element.) If an items bears two or more such number, give the one that applies to the item being described.

Optionally, give more then one number and add a qualification.

Term of availability: Give the term on which the items is available. These terms consist of the price.

Qualification: Give, after the standard number, a terms of qualification when an item bears two or more standard numbers.

Both Indicators	#	Undefined
Subfield	$a	International Standard Book Number (NR) [The valid ISBN and any parenthetical qualifying information. ISBN and the embedded hyphens may be generated for display].
	$c	Terms of availability (NR) [The price or a brief

statement of availability and any parenthetical information qualifying the information].

$z Cancelled/invalid ISBN (R)

[A cancelled or invalid ISBN and any parenthetical qualifying information. ISBN (invalid) and the embedded hyphens may be generated for display].

020	#	#	$a 0914378260 (pbk.: v. 1) $c Rs.50

International Standard Serial Number (R): The ISSN assigned to a serial publication by a national center under the auspices of the International Serials Data System (ISDS). The initialism ISSN and the phrases ISSN (incorrect) and ISSN (cancelled) are not carried in the MARC record. (The ISSN is an agency-assigned data element.)

First Indicators

Level of international interest not designated

0 Serial of international interest; full record registered with ISSN Network Used only by the NSDP and ISDS/Canada.

1 Serial not of international interest; abbreviated record registered with ISSN Network Used only by the NSDP and ISDS/Canada.

Second Indicator	#	Undefined
Subfield	$a	International Standard Serial Number (NR)
	$y	Incorrect ISSN (R)
	$z	Canceled ISSN (R)

022	#	#	$a 0145-0808$z0361-7106

1.9 SUPPLIMENTARY ITEM AND OTHER MATERIALS

1.9B1. Choose one of the following methods of describing supplementary (including accompanying and related) items described dependently:

a) record the item as accompanying material as instructed in 1.5E1d

300	#	#	$a 200 p.; $c 27 cm. + $e 1 portfolio.

1.9C. In describing a facsimile, photocopy, or other reproduction of printed texts, maps, manuscripts, printed music, and graphic items, give the data relating to the facsimile, etc., in all area except the note area. In a note area the data relating to the original title, edition, publication, distribution, etc., and series area should be recorded.

The baby's bouquet [GMD] : a fresh bunch of old rhymes and tunes / arranged and decorated by Walter Crane ; the tunes collected and arranged by L.C.— London : Pan, 1974

56p. : col. ill., 16 x 17 cm.—(A Piccolo book)

Facsim, of: 2nd ed., rev. London : Routledge, 1877

ISBN 0330240897 : $0.60

1.9D. If the facsimile, etc. has a title different from the original, give the title of the facsimile, etc. as the title proper. Give the original title as other title information if it appears on the chief source of information of the facsimile, etc. (see 1.1D3). Otherwise, give the title of the original in the note area (see 1.11F)

1.10. FORMAT OF CATALOGE CARD

As this information is collected or assigned, record it on 3 x 5 inch pieces of paper. As the catalogue cards are typed from these slips, they are sometimes referred to as "Typing Slips" or "T-slips." A T-slip is required for each item. When completed, the cards are data processed/typed and filed. An alternative to this T-slip method is the use of one of the commercially-available systems that allows the user to generate complete card sets from the input of this initial shelf list information.

The cataloguer may also choose to work directly from the item, by penciling in the Dewey number, underlining the main entry, and writing subject headings on the reverse of the title page. This avoids the use of T-slips.

Descriptive Cataloguing

Descriptive cataloguing consists of two elements: describing the physical item, and determining the main entry and added entries. In this section, the key elements determining **main entry**, correct formatting of the entry, and physical details of the entry are shown. T

The examples provide both the card and MARC formats.

Complete Details [Figure 1]

Figure 1

1st indentation: 9 spaces from left margin
2nd indentation: 13 spaces from left margin

Added entry. (Do not leave a line space)

Main Entry.
Title proper [GMD] -- parallel title : other title Information / first statement of responsibility.— Edition statement / statement of responsibility Relating to edition. – Place of publication : pub-Lisher, date of publication.
Extent of item: other physical details : phys-Cal dimensions + accompanying material. -- (Series ; numbering).
Notes
ISBN

Subject headings. I. Added entries. II. Title. III. Series

Explanation of the Card Layout [Figure 2]

Figure 2

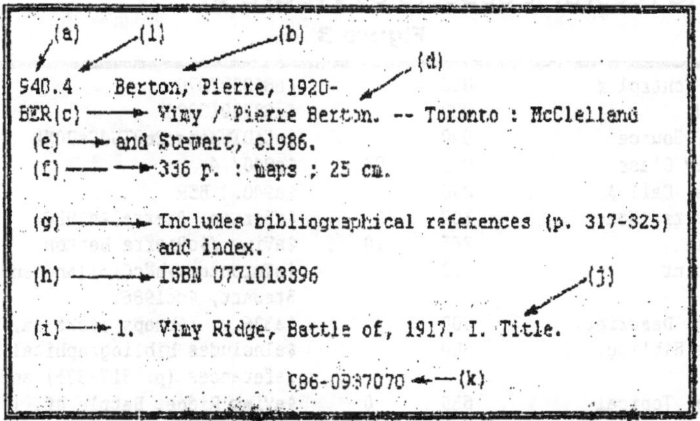

a. = Classification number (Dewey class)
b. = Main entry (person's name)
c. = Title
d. = Statement of responsibility
e. = Publishing details (imprint)
f. = Physical description (statement includes the extent of the item, the physical details, and details of accompanying materials)
g. = Notes
h. = ISBN (International Standard Book Number)
i. = Subject heading (topical)
j. = Added entries
k. = National Library of Canada Control Number or Library of Congress Card Number
l. = Call number

MARC Example of Figure 2 [Figure 3]

If the book by Pierre Berton is displayed as a MARC record, it appears as **Figure 3.**

Figure 3

NLC Control #	016		$a860937070
ISBN	020		$a0771013396
Cat. Source	040		$aCaOTUbengcCaOTUdCaOONL
Dewey Class	082	04	$a940/.4
Local Call #	090		$a940.4 BER
ME:Pers. Name	100	1_	$aBerton, Pierre,$d1920-
Title	245	10	$aVimy /$cPierre Berton
Imprint	260		$aToronto :$bMcClelland and Stewart, $cc1986.
Phys. Descript.	300		$a336 p. :$bmaps ;$c25 cm.
Note:Bibliog.	504		$aIncludes bibliographical references (p. 317-325) and
Subj. Topical	650	_0	$aVimy Ridge, Battle of, 19

In older records, you will often see the "1" and "0" follow the MARC 100 field tag. The "1" and "0" are indicators. The "1" indicates a single surname while the "0" indicates there is no relationship between the main entry and the subject of the item. This is the most common format encountered during a recon. Any book with an author follows this same format in a MARC record. In current practice, the record indicator is not used.

$a = a tag delimiter

CHAPTER 2
Books

CONTENTS

2.0 GENERAL RULES

Source of Information: This chapter cover the description of monographic printed item which published separately. The title as entered on the title page is preferred as title proper. Titles in different forms may also appear in a book, such as a title on the spine of the book. The cataloger makes added entries for these titles.

2.1 TITLE AND STATEMENT OF RESPONSIBILITY

Title proper, parallel title and statement of responsibility is transcribe as instruction 1.1.

Optional addition. General Material Designation

The general material designation "text" for eye-readable printed copy is not used unless the GMD "text" is to be further qualified. Text (large print)

If the item being catalogued has been reproduced in a form other than eye-readable print (e.g., microform), the general material designation appropriate to the reproduction is used.

Even if the term, large print, is used in the general material designation, include large print in the specific material designation [SMD] in physical description area.

245	1	0	$a Taking chage of the air travel experience $h (lage print) : $b a guide for persons with disabilities.

2.2 EDITION AREA

Edition and statement of responsibility relating edition is treated as instruction 1.2.

Edition statement. Optional addition: The option is not applied. Any edition information supplied by the cataloguer is given in the notes area.

2.3 MATERIAL SPECIFIC DETAILS AREA

This area is not used for printed monographs.

2.4 PUBLICATION, DISTRIBUTION, ETC., AREA

For publication, distribution, etc follow the instruction 1.4.

2.5 PHYSICAL DESCRIPTION AREA

For physical description area, follow the instruction 1.4. But for multiple vulume cases the following rules will be applicable:

Number of volumes and/or pagination: The option is applied selectively, e.g. for early printed books. Even if the term, large print, is used in the general material designation, include large print in the specific material designation.

245	1	0	$a Taking charge of the air travel experience $h [text (large print)]
300	#	#	$a 59 p. (lage print); $c 22 cm.

Single volumes: Give the number of pages or leaves in a terms of the numbered or lettered sequence in the volume.

300	#	#	$a 327 p.

If the numbering within a sequence changes, ignore the numbering of the first part of the sequence.

300	#	#	$a 176 p. (pages numbered : I-xii, 13-323 p.)

If the leaved or plates are available, it is recorded at the end of the sequence of pagination.

300	#	#	$a xi, 59 p., 32 p. of plates.

More than one volume: Give the number of volumes of of a printed monograph in more than one physical volume.

300	#	#	$a 3 v.

If the number of bibliographic volumes differ from the number of physical volumes, give the number of bibliographic volumes followed by is and the number of physical volumes.

300	#	#	$a 8 v. in 5.

If a set of volumes is continuously paged, give the pagination in parentheses after the number of volumes.

300	#	#	$a 3 v. (xxi, 999p.)

If the volumes in multivolume set are individually paged, give the pagination of each volume in parentheses after the number of volumes.

300	#	#	$a 2 v. (svi, 329; xx, 412 p.)

Illustrative matter: If a quick examination of the item being catalogued reveals that the illustrations appear to be all of one or two types or chiefly of one or two types, specify the type or types. In the latter case, include also the designation "ill.". In all other cases, use "ill." alone. Also, if there is doubt about specifying a type, use "ill." alone.

300	#	#	$a 327 p. $b ill.

Exception: Rare books and material in which the illustrative content is a particularly important aspect of the publication may require detailed illustration statements.

Dimensions: In giving the dimensions of an item requiring more than one measurement, use a lower-case "x" as the multiplication sign to separate each of the measurements.

300	#	#	$c 20 X 32 cm.

If the height of the item in centimeters, give the next whole centimeter up. 18 cm. (for 17.2 cm.)

If the width of the volume is either less than half the height or greater than the height, give the height x width. 20 x 8 cm.

If the volume in multipart item differ in size, give the smallest and largest size separated by hyphen. 24-28 cm.

2.5C - Accompanying material: The option is applied judiciously. It will be considered when the accompanying material is sbstantial in volume.

300	#	#	$a 271 p. : $b ill. ; $c 21 cm. + 1 disc.

For illustrative matter use "ill" as above and specific material designation [SMD] is essential to mention here as below.

300	#	#	$a 59 p. (lage print); $c 22cm.

2.6 SERIES AREA

Record each series statement instructed 1.6

2.7 NOTE AREA

Make notes as set out in the following sub rules and in the order given there. However, give the particular note first when it has been decided that note is of primary importance.

The details of notes with MACR 21 tags are already given in 1.7.

2.8 MARC 21 FORMAT WITH EXAMPLES

MARC records are composed of fixed (same place, same length) and variable fields. Fixed fields are in a Leader, and in fields 006, 007, and 008 and variable fields.

LEADER : A fixed field that comprises the first 24 character positions (00-23) of each record and provides information for the processing of the record.

00-04 - Record Length: The computer-generated, five-character numeric string that specifies the length of the entire record. The number is right justified and each unused position contains a zero.

05 - Record status: System generated. Code "n" (new) changes to "c" (corrected or revised) after record is changed and saved. Change non-MARC codes (e.g. "m" or "r") to "c".

06 - Type of record: A one-character code that indicates the characteristics of and defines the components of the record.

a Language material. This code is also used for microforms of language material.

c Printed music. This code is also used for microforms of printed music.

d Manuscript music. This code is also used for microforms of manuscript music.

- e Printed map. This code is also used for microforms of printed maps.
- f Manuscript map. This code is also used for microforms of manuscript maps.
- g Projected medium. The described item is a motion picture, video recording, filmstrip, slide, transparency, or material specifically designed for overhead projection.
- i Nonmusical sound recording.
- j Musical sound recording.
- k Two-dimensional nonprojectable graphic. This code is used for items such as activity cards, charts, collages, computer graphics, drawings, duplication masters, flash cards, paintings, photonegatives, photo prints, pictures, postcards, posters, prints, spirit masters, study prints, technical drawings, transparency masters, photomechanical reproductions, and reproductions of any of these.
- m Electronic resources. The described item is numeric or textual data, computer software, or a combination of these types of information that are encoded for computer processing.
- o Kit. The described item contains a mixture of components from two or more types of items, no one of which is the predominant constituent of the kit.
- p Mixed material.
- r Three-dimensional artifact or naturally occurring object. This code is used for such man-made objects as models, dioramas, games, puzzles, simulations, sculptures and other three-dimensional art works and their reproductions,

exhibits, machines, clothing, toys, and stitchery. It also includes such naturally occurring objects as microscope specimens and other specimens mounted for viewing.

t Manuscript language material

07 - Bibliographic level: Indicates the bibliographic level of the record.

a Monographic component part. A monographic bibliographic unit that is physically attached to or contained in another unit such that the retrieval of the component part is dependent on the identification and location of the host item or container. The record contains fields that describe the component part and data that identify the host, field 773 (Host Item Entry).

b Serial component part. A serial bibliographic unit that is physically attached to or contained in another serial unit such that the retrieval of the component part is dependent on the physical identification and location of the host item or container. The record contains fields that describe the component part and data that identify the Host Item Entry (field 773).

c Collection. A made-up multipart group of items that were not originally published, distributed, or produced together. The record describes units defined by common provenance or administrative convenience for which the record is intended as the most comprehensive in the system.

d Subunit. A part of a collection, especially an archival unit described collectively elsewhere in the system. The record contains fields that describe the subunit and data that identify the Host Item Entry (field 773).

i Integrating resource. A bibliographic resource that is added to or changed by means of updates that do not remain discrete and are integrated into the whole. Examples include: Updating loose-leafs and updating Web sites.

m Monograph/item. An item either complete in one part or intended to be completed in a finite number of separate parts.

s Serial. An item issued in successive parts bearing numerical or chronological designations and intended to be continued indefinitely.

08 - Type of control:

- No specific type of control

a - Archival control

09 - Character Coding Scheme: A one-character code that identifies the character-coding scheme used in the record.

- MARC-8 Leader

a - UCS/Unicode

10 - Indicator Count: The computer-generated number 2 that indicates the number of character positions used for indicators in a variable data field.

11 - Subfield Code Ccunt: The computer-generated number 2 that indicates the number of character positions used for each subfield code in a variable data field.

12-16 - Base Address of Data: The computer-generated, five-character numeric string that indicates the first character position of the first variable control field in a record. The number is right justified and each unused position contains a zero.

17 – Encoding Level: Indicates the fullness of the bibliographic information and/or content designation of the MARC record.

Full level : The most complete MARC level created from information derived from an inspection of the physical item.

1 **Full level, material not examined:** The information used in creating the record is derived from an extant description of the item without reinspection of the physical item. This code is used primarily in the retrospective conversion of records when all of the information on the extant description is transcribed. Certain control field coding and other data elements are based only on explicit information in the description.

2 **Less-than-full level, material not examined:** The information used in creating the record is derived from an extant description of the item without reinspection of the physical item. This code is used primarily in the retrospective conversion of records when all of the descriptive access points but only a specified subset of other data elements are transcribed. Authoritative headings may not be current.

3 **Abbreviated level:** Indicates a brief record that does not meet the National Level Bibliographic Record minimal level cataloging specifications. Headings in the records may reflect established forms to the extent that such forms were available at the time the record was created.

4 Core level

5 **Partial (preliminary) level:** A record that is not considered final by the creating agency (e.g., the headings may not reflect established forms; the record may not meet national-level cataloging specifications).

7 **Minimal level:** A record that meets the national-

level bibliographic record minimal-level cataloging specifications and is considered final by the creating agency. Headings reflect established forms. The U.S. requirements for minimal-level records can be found in National Level and Minimal Level Record Requirements (http://lcweb.loc.gov/marc/bibliographic/nlr/)

8 **Prepublication level:** Indicates a prepublication-level record. This includes records created in cataloging in publication programs.

u **Unknown:** This code is used by an agency receiving or sending data to replace a local code when the appropriate MARC encoding level code cannot be determined. Code u is not used in newly input or updated records.

z **Not applicable:** The encoding level concept does not apply to the record.

18 - Descriptive Cataloging Form: Indicates the descriptive cataloging form reflected in the record. Subfield $e (Description conventions) of field 040 (Cataloging Source) may contain additional information on the cataloging conventions used

Non-ISBD: The descriptive portion of the record does not follow International Standard Bibliographic Description (ISBD) cataloging and punctuation provisions.

a AACR 2 : The descriptive portion of the record and the choice and form of entry of the access points are formulated according to either the second edition of the Anglo-American Cataloging Rules or cataloging manuals based on AACR 2. The punctuation practices of ISBD apply.

i ISBD: The descriptive portion of the record is formulated according to the descriptive and punctuation provisions of ISBD. The heading forms are not formulated according to AACR 2. This category includes records that use ISBD punctuation but the other conventions used are unknown.

u Unknown: An organization receiving or sending data in Leader/18 cannot determine the appropriate descriptive cataloging form used in the record. Code u may be used in records converted from another metadata format.

19 - Linked Record Requirement: Indicates whether a note containing basic identification information (i.e., main entry and title, main entry and uniform title, main entry under uniform title, title, uniform title, Standard Technical Report Number, or report number) can bè generated from a Linking Entry field (76X-78X).

Related record not required: The record contains basic identification information in every Linking Entry field in the record or in a related Linking Entry Complexity Note (field 580), or the record contains no 76X-78X Linking Entry field.

r Related record required: The record contains at least one 76X-78X Linking Entry field that does not contain basic identification information and contains no related Linking Entry Complexity Note (field 580) with basic identification information.

Leader 20-23 - Entry Map: Four computer-generated, single-digit numeric characters that indicate the structure of each entry in the Directory.

20 Length of the length-of-field portion Contains a 4

21 Length of the starting-characer-position portion Contains a 5

22 Length of the implementation-defined portion Contains a 0

23 Undefined Entry map character position Contains a 0

Directory: A computer-generated index to the location of the variable control and data fields within a record. The Directory immediately follows the Leader at character position 24 and consists of a series of fixed-length (12 character positions) entries that give the tag, length, and starting character position of each variable field.

Character	Positions
2-02	Tag Three numeric or alphabetic (uppercase or lowercase, but not both) characters that identify an associated field.
6-06	Field length Four numeric characters that indicate the length of the field, including indicators, subfield codes, data, and the field terminator. The number is right justified and each unused position contains a zero.
11-11	Starting character position Five numeric characters that indicate the starting character position of the field relative to the Base address of data (Leader/ 12-16) of the record. The number is right justified and each unused position contains a zero.

006 – 006 Fixed-length Data Elements—Additional Material Characteristics—General Information (R). This field contains 18 character positions (00-17) that provide for coding information about special aspects of the item being cataloged that cannot be coded in field 008 (Fixed-Length Data Elements). It is used in cases when an item has multiple characteristics. It is also used to record the coded serial aspects of nontextual continuing resources.

The field has a tree structure, whereby the code given in 006/00 (Form of material) determines the data elements defined for subsequent character positions. Except for code s (Serial/Integrating resource), the codes in field 006/00 correspond to those in Leader/06 (Type of record). For each occurrence of field 006, the codes defined for character positions 01-17 will be the same as those defined in the corresponding field 008, character positions 18-34. Configurations of field 006 are given in the following order: books, Electronic resources/electronic resources, maps, music, continuing resources, visual materials, and mixed materials.

006 - Books

Character	Positions
00	Type of 006 code
a	Books
t	Manuscript language material

4-04 Illustrations: Up to four one-character codes (recorded in alphabetical order) that indicate the presence of types of illustrations in the item. If fewer than four codes are assigned, the codes are left justified and each unused position contains a blank (#).

#	No illustrations
a	Illustrations
b	Maps
c	Portraits
d	Charts
e	Plans
f	Plates
g	Music
h	Facsimiles
i	Coats of arms
j	Genealogical tables
k	Forms
l	Samples
m	Phonodisc, phonowire, etc.
o	Photographs
p	Illuminations
|	No attempt to code

05Target Audience: A one-character code that indicates the audience for which the item is intended.

#	Unknown or not specified
a	Preschool
b	Primary
c	Pre-adolescent
d	Adolescent
e	Adult
f	Specialized
g	General
j	Juvenile
|	No attempt to code

06 Form of Composition: A two-character code that indicates the form of composition of printed or manuscript music or a musical sound recording. The codes are based on Library of Congress subject headings. If more than one code is appropriate, the code mu (Multiple forms) is used in 008/18-19 and all appropriate specific codes are given in field 047 (Form of Composition).

07-10 Nature of Contents: Nature of Contents Up to four one-character codes (recorded in alphabetical order) that indicate whether a significant part of the item is or contains certain types of material. If fewer than four codes are assigned, the codes are left justified and each unused position contains a blank (#).

- # No specified nature of contents
- a Abstracts/summaries. The item is or contains abstracts or summaries of other publications.
- b Bibliographies
- c Catalogs
- d Dictionaries. This code is also used for a glossary or a gazetteer.
- e Encyclopedias
- f Handbooks
- g Legal articles
- i Indexes. The item is or contains an index to bibliographical material other than itself.
- j Patent document
- k Discographies
- l Legislation. The item is or contains full or partial texts of enactments of legislative bodies or texts of rules and regulations issued by executive or administrative agencies.

m Theses. Indicates that the item is a thesis, dissertation, or work identified as having been created to satisfy the requirements for an academic certification or degree.

n Surveys of literature in a subject area. The item is or contains authored surveys that summarize what has been published about a subject.

o Reviews. The item is or contains critical reviews of published or performed works.

p Programmed texts

q Filmographies

r Directories

s Statistics

t Technical reports

u Standards/specifications

v Legal cases and case notes

w Law reports and digests

z Treaties. Indicates that the item is a treaty or accord negotiated between two or more parties to settle a disagreement, establish a relationship, grant rights, etc.

| No attempt to code

11 Government Publication: Government Publication A one-character code that indicates whether the item is published or produced by or for a government agency, and, if so, the jurisdictional level of the agency.

Not a government publication

a Autonomous or semi-autonomous component

c Multilocal

f Federal/national

i International intergovernmental

l Local

m Multistate

o Government publication¾level undetermined

s State, provincial, territorial, dependent, etc.

u Unknown if item is government publication

z Other

| No attempt to code

12 Conference Publication: A one-character code that indicates whether the item OR serial consists of the proceedings, reports, or summaries of a conference.

0 Not a conference publication

1 Conference publication

| No attempt to code

13 Festschrift Festschrift: A one-character code that indicates whether the item is a festschrift.

0 Not a festschrift

1 Festschrift

| No attempt to code

14 Index: A one-character code that indicates whether the item (in the case of a Book) includes an index to its own contents, or whether accompanying material (in the case of a Map) includes a location index or gazetteer.

0 No index

1 Index present

| No attempt to code

15 Undefined; contains a blank (#) or a fill character (|)

16 Literary Form: Indicates the literary form of an item. Numeric codes 0 and 1 provide a generic identification of whether or not the item is a work of fiction. Alphabetic codes may be used to identify specific literary forms.

0 Not fiction (not further specified)

1 Fiction (not further specified)

c Comic strips

d Dramas

e Essays

f Novels

h Humor, satires, etc. Indicates that the item is a humorous work, satire, or of a similar literary form.

i Letters: Indicates that the item is a single letter or collection of correspondence.

j Short stories: Indicates that the item is a short story or collection of short stories.

m Mixed forms: Indicates that the item represents a variety of literary forms (e.g., poetry and short stories).

p Poetry

s Speech

u Unknown

| No attempt to code

17 Biography: A one-character code that indicates whether the item contains biographical material, and, if so, what the biographical characteristics are.

No biographical material

a Autobiography

b Individual biography

c Collective biography

d Contains biographical information

| No attempt to code

008 FIXED-LENGTH DATA ELEMENTS (FIXED FIELDS)

This field contains 40 character positions (00-39) that provide coded information about the record as a whole and about special bibliographic aspects of the item being cataloged. These coded data elements are potentially useful for retrieval and data management purposes.

Character positions 00-17 and 35-39 are defined the same across all types of material, with special consideration for position 06. The definition of character positions 18-34 was done independently for each type of material, although certain data elements are defined the same in the specifications for more than one type of material. When similar data elements are defined for inclusion in field 008 for different types of material, they occupy the same field 008 character positions.

5-05 Date entered on file.The computer-generated, six-character numeric string that indicates the date the MARC record was created. The date is recorded in the pattern yymmdd.

06 - Type of date: A one-character code that indicates the type of dates and the publication status.

b No dates given; B.C. date involved

c Continuing resource item currently published

d Continuing resource item ceased publication

e Detailed date

i Inclusive dates of collection

k Range of years of bulk of collection

m Multiple dates

n Dates unknown

p Date of distribution/release/issue and production/recording session when different

q Questionable date

r Reprint/reissue date and original date

s Single known date/probable date

t Publication date and copyright date

u Continuing resource status unknown

| No attempt to code

07-10 - Date 1: The determination of dates for 008/07-10 is made concurrently with choice of code for 008/06

11-14 - Date 2: The determination of dates for 008/11-14 is made concurrently with choice of code for 008/06

15-17 - Place of publication: Must match 260 |a. Add or change if required. Required if applicable or readily available in OCLC.

18-21 Illustrations

22 Target Audience

23 Form of Item

24-27 Nature of Contents

28 Government Publication

29 Conference Publication

30 Festschrift

31 Index

32 Undefined; contains a blank (#) or fill character (|)

33 Literary Form

34 Biography

35-37 language: A three-character MARC code

that indicates the language of the item. The source of the code is MARC Code List for Languages . Choice of a MARC code is based on the predominant language of the item. Three fill characters (|||) may also be used if no attempt is made to code 008/35-37.

38 Modified Record: Normally blank, but accept in derived records.

- # Not modified
- d Dashed-on information omitted
- o Completely romanized/printed cards romanized
- r Completely romanized/printed cards in script
- s Shortened. Some of the data has been omitted because the record would have exceeded the maximum length allowed by a particular system.
- x Missing characters. Characters that could not be converted into machine-readable form due to character set limitations are missing from the record.
- | No attempt to code

39 Cataloging Source: Cataloging source: Code "d" for derived and original records. Must be changed to blank when transcribing an LC bibliographic record

- # National bibliographic agency
- c Cooperative cataloging program
- d Other
- u Unknown
- | No attempt to coded from a printed source.

Other control and Variable fields

Fields 001-006 contain control numbers and other control and coded information that are used in processing MARC bibliographic records. Each control field is identified by a field tag in the Directory and contains either a single data element or a series of fixed-length data elements identified by relative character position. Variable control fields contain neither indicator positions nor subfield codes.

010	Library of Congress Control Number (NR)
020	International Standard Book Number (R)
040	Cataloging Source (NR)
050	LC classification number
080	Universal Decimal Classification Number (NR)
082	Dewey Decimal Call Number (R)
090	Locally-defined
100	Main entry – personal author (very rare)
110	Main entry – corporate body
111	Main entry – conference heading
130	Main entry – uniform title
222	Key title – (assigned by ISSN centers)
240	Uniform title (used when there is a corporate body main entry and and a uniform title is needed)
245	Title proper and statement of responsibility
245	Varying form of title (used for other forms of title and for minor changes on subsequent issues)
250	Edition statement, used only when entire serial is part of an edition
260	Publishing statement
300	Physical description
440/490	Series Statement
500	General note (for description based on note, source of title, notes are place or name of publisher, etc.)

500	With Note (R)
501	Dissertation Note (R)
504	Bibliography, Etc. Note (R)
505	Formatted Contents Note (NR)
520	Summary, Etc. (R)
521	Target Audience Note (R)
525	Supplement note
534	Original Version Note (R)
541	Immediate Source of Acquisition (Gift) Note (R)
546	Language note
547	Former Title Complexity Note (R)
556	Information About Documentation Note (R)
580	Linking entry complexity note (used for complex links, such as mergers and splits and relationships to other works.
6XX	Subject heading
700	Added Entry—Personal Name (R)
710	Added entry - corporate body (R)
711	Added Entry—Meeting Name (R)
730	Added entry - uniform title (used for related resources)
740	Added Entry—Uncontrolled Related/ Analytical Title (R)
760	Main Series Entry (R)
762	Subseries Entry (R)
765	Original Language Entry (R)
767	Translation Entry (R)
773	Host Item Entry (R)
8XX	Series added entries

Sample card:

900 S45h	Smith	, John, 1950.
  1111	 to es es no	History for beginners : introduction History / by John Smith and Tim Jon .-- 2nd ed.— New York : Smith & Jon , 1955. X, 100 p.: ill.; 23 cm.—(History text; 5) Includes bibliographical references. 1.History. I. Jones, Tim. II. Title. III. Series.

Sample MARC FOR ABOVE CARD:

LDR 00446nam 2200205 a 4500

008			050227 000 0 eng d
082			$a 900 $b S45h
100	1		$a Smith, John, $d 1950.
245	1	0	$a History for beginners : $b introduction to history / $c by John Smith and Tim Jones.
250	#	#	$a 2nd ed.
260	#	#	$a New York : $b Smith & Jones, $c 1995
300	#	#	$a x, 100 p. : $b ill; $c 23 cm.
440	#	#	$a History text; $v no. 5
504	#	#	$a Includes bibliographical references.
600	1		$a Jones, Tim.
650	#	0	$a History.
900			$a 1111

CHAPTER 3
Cartographic Materials

CONTENTS

3.0 GENERAL RULES

The following information ar: essentials for cartographic materials.

i) The cataloger should construct the title, if not given in the title page
ii) Place of publishing and name of publisher
iii) Edition and publishing date
iv) Conservation or amendment date, if fublishing date is different
v) Collation and size of sheet
vi) Mathmatical data, i.e. scale, projection

Types of Cartographic Material: Sheet maps, Globes and Atlases.

Maps: Maps are pictures of the world the embody changes in artistic depiction, scientific enquiry, and the way we view and understand the land around us. They are material objects, social documents and historical artifacts.

Maps are neither mirrors of nature nor neutral transmitters of universal truths. They are narratives with a purpose, stories with an agenda. They contain silences as well as articulations, secrets as well as knowledge, lies as we l as truth. They are biased, partial and selective.

Types of Maps: Topographic, Historical, Religious, Political

Chief Source: When an item is catalogued as a map, even if it appears with a book attached, the map remains the chief source of information.

Whole or part: Most maps occur in series, or on sheets with other maps.

Most items that include several maps can probably be dealt with under a common title, or treated as if one title subsumed the others, but there are certainly cases in which no collective title can be found, in which case the option is available of cataloging each part separately. When separate items are physically attached, it results in a few distinctive features for the record.

Globe: A model of the earth or other celestical body, depicted on the surface of a sphere.

Atlas: A volume of maps, plates, engravings, tables, etc, with or without descriptive text. It may be an independent publication or it may have been issued as accompanying material.

3.1 TITLE AND STATEMENT OF RESPONSIBILITY

Picking the right title: When there are several titles to choose from, AACR2r directs the cataloguer to consider language and script, layout and sequence, and comprehensiveness as criteria, in that order. Prefers a title within the border of the map to one outside the border to a panel title to a verso title to a cover or container title—but with presumption always going to the title that best expresses geographic coverage and subject.

Responsibility: The responsibility is frequently a vexed one with maps, whether one is dealing with a main entry heading (in which case rule 21.1B2(f) provides a lot of leeway for introducing the corporate authorship of a mapmaking company or agency), or primary statements of responsibility (again corporate authorship must often be considered, but how can one distinguish a statement of responsibility from a publication statement?), or edition/revision responsibility.

100	1	#	$a Gemmell, Arthur.
245	1	0	$a Grassington and district $h [map] $b footpaths & town maps / $c Arthur Gemmel.

3.2 EDITION AREA

Transcribe a statement relating to an edition and statement of responsibility relating edition of a cartographic items as instructed in 1.2.

3.3 MATERIAL SPECIFIC DETAILS (MATHEMATICAL DATA)

Mathematical Data: For most maps, this boils down to three items, scale, projection, and lat and long coordinates, the first of these essential if at all possible, the last an optional but desirable attempt to create an absolute means for the retrieval of geographic material.

255	#	#	$a Scale 1:22,000,000; $b Conic proj. $c 72- E 148/N 13-N180.

Scale: The scale requirement in practice usually involves a few outs, then some hard slogging. In the most common cases:

* If you are cataloging a set that includes three or more maps of different scales, you can simply say "scales vary" and be satisfied (3.3B5-6) (but if it is only two items, you have to give both of them 3.3B4, 3.3B6).

MapEasy (company)

MapEasy's Guidemap to Chicago [map]. — Scales vary.

— Amagansett, N.Y. : Mapeasy, c1995.

5 maps on 1 sheet: col., plasticized paper ; 58 x

88 cm. or smaller on sheet 61 x 91 cm folded to 23 x 12 cm.

* If it an item not drawn to scale at all, you can simply say, "not drawn to scale."
* If scale information is given on the map in the required "1:nnnnn" form, you are in luck. This is simply plugged into the record:

  AZ Leeds and Bradford street atlas. —Scale 1:15,840.
* If scale information is given in another kind of ratio, usually of the "one inch equals 16 miles" style, the ratio must be converted, and the results plugged in put placed in brackets.
* If scale information is given only in the form of a pictorial scale, the information has to be converted, and the results plugged in, prefaced by "ca.", again in brackets.

  Grassington and district [map] : footpaths & townmaps & walks guide / Arthur Gemmell. — 5th ed. / most of the paths...resurveyed for this edition by Reg and Joyce Smith and the author. Scale [ca. 1:5,760] and [1:25,000]
* If none of these apply, you may need to compare the map to a map of known scale, and arrive at a calculated scale.
* Only when all of these fail, may you give up and say "scale indeterminable" (3.3B1)

Projection: Projection is regarded as much less important and need only be given if given by the item, in the same words as given, but with all valid AACR2 abbreviations employed.

The only choice is whether to include additional projection information, especially meridians and so forth, should that happen to have been given by the item.

Scale 1:1,000,000 ; minimum error conical proj. with rectified meridians and 2 standard parallels, 59o 31' 24" and 51o 44' 06"

Coordinates: Coordinates are particularly handy things to have, since they provide an absolute reference system independent of fashions in political boundaries. They are conceptually simple, requiring one simply to give the westernmost, easternmost, northernmost, and southernmost points in order (reflecting a bias toward the North and the West?). And they can be obtained from anywhere, even if the item does not provide the information directly.

(W 3o 04' 50"—W 2o 53' 34"/N 54o 34' 18"—N54o 28' 54")

3.4 PUBLICATION, DISTRIBUTION, ETC., AREA

Give the place of publication, distribution; name of publisher, distributor and date of publication, distribution, etc., of a published cartographic item as instructed in 1.4.

Don't record a place and publisher of publication, destribution, etc., for an unpublished cartographic item. Do not record [S.l.] and [s.n.] in such cases.

3.5 PHYSICAL DESCRIPTION AREA

Physical description, in AACR2 treatment of maps ("cartographic materials" but the American GMD controversially says "maps").

Map numbering:

(i) Multiple maps on one or both sides of a sheet

300	#	#	$a 2 maps on 1 sheet : $b both sides; $c 85 X 43 cm and 104 X 36 cm.

(ii) Segments of a single map on more than one sheet

300	#	#	$a 1 maps on 2 sheet; $c 85 X 43 cm and 104 X 36 cm.

(iii) Maps sets can rely on distinctive titles of each rather than individual numbering to differentiate them.

Extra information.

If the map is multicolored, call it "col."; if not, say nothing.

If it is made of something unexpected (other than paper in the case of a map), say so, if it is un map like, add the information that fits its character.

If a globe (3.5D4) add the diameter befitting its artifactual 3d character.

If a relief, (3.5D3) add the depth of relief if desired.

If an atlas, (3.5D2, 3.5C2) add the booklike bibliographic nformation: the number of pages, maps, and height (instead of height x width).

AZ Leeds and Bradford street atlas. — Scale 1:15,840. — Borough Green, Seven Oaks, Kent, [England] : Geographers' A-Z Map Co., c1993.

1 atlas (202 p.) : 62 maps ; 20 cm.

Dimensions

Dimensions can be put off no longer, and they are a fitting place to end. Rule 3.5D1, applying to the dimensions of maps, plans, etc., is the densest rule in Chapter 3. The basic rule is simply to represent the height and width (h x w) of each map to the next nearest centimenter. If the map makes this practically difficult (specific reasons are given involving lack of borders, irregular shape, etc.,) resort to measuring the sheet instead

1 map : col. ; 98 x 76 cm.

The next commonest or at least simplest situation arises when the map size is significantly different (half the size, linearly speaking, or less) from the sheet size and/or there is substantial additional material on the sheet (e.g. text). In that case, give both map size and sheet size.

1 view ; 46 x 82 cm. on sheet 65 x 86 cm.

Common road maps and similarly designed folding maps with or without an attached cover, so long as they are clearly designed so that one panel faces the public, require that the folded size be given, and often the sheet size as well. Several of the items fall into this category, eg.

1 map : col. ; 40 x 40 cm. folded to 24 x 12 cm.
2 maps on 1 sheet : col. ; 16 x 12 cm. and 39 x 45 cm. on sheet 39 x 47 cm. folded to 20 x 12 cm.
5 maps on 1 sheet : col., plasticized paper ; 58 x 88 cm. or smaller on sheet 61 x 91 cm folded to 23 x 12 cm.

3.6 SERIES AREA

Series: Determining what kind of the series (collectively or individually)

(i) Multi-sheet single map "One complete map printed in sections on several sheets of paper which may be assembled." Map set group of distinctive maps usually published at the same time and issued as a folio or bound. Usually deal with common themes or geographic areas.

(ii) A number of maps with individual titles proper and a collective title that applies to the group as a whole relate to a defined area of the world published sequentially by the same publisher based on a common grid or projection drawn to a common scale using Common symbols.

(iii) Describe the series as a whole (with index for individual sheets)content note (individual sheets listed in note area)describe maps individually including a series statement to show the link between them provide a multi-level description identifying individual sheets and the series as a whole.

3.7 NOTE AREA

Note section of cartographic materials are recorded as instruction given in 1.7. Generally following notes are used:

i) Nature and scope of the item
ii) Language note
iii) source of title proper
iv) variation in title
v) Parralled titles
vi) Edition notes
vii) Mathematical data note

3.8 MARC 21 FORMAT WITH EXAMPLES

008 – Maps

Character Positions

01-17	for common as book
18-21	Relief
22-23	Projection
24	Undefined
25	Type of Cartographic Material
26-27	Undefined

28	Government Publication
29	Form of Item
30	Undefined
31	Index
32	Undefined
33-34	Special Format Characteristics

Variable fields:

020 (ISBN): Record the ISBN (International Standard Book Number) in field 020. spaces.

034 (Coded cartographic mathematical data): Indicate the type of scale and the scale (if indicated on the map) as shown here. The 034 field and the 255 field must be in agreement.

If a scale is stated on the map, or if one can be determined using a scale indicator, mark the first indicator **1** (one), enter **a** in subfield ,a and the denominator of the scale ratio, without commas, in subfield, b.

034	1	#	$b 2000000

If there is no scale stated on the map, and one can not be determined using a scale indicator, mark the first indicator **0** (zero), and enter **a** in subfield ,a. Do not add subfield ,b.

100/700, 110/710, or 111/711 (Main or added entry: Personal, Corporate or Conference Name):

If the map has three or fewer authors, record the first-named author in the appropriate 1XX field. If the map names no author, omit the 1XX field. If the map has three or more authors, do not input a 1XX field, and use a 7XX field for the first-named author. If there is no 1XX and there is an editor, compiler, etc., record the name in field 7XX. Treat cartographic firms (such as Hammond or Rand McNally), which are responsible for the creation of the maps they produce, as corporate authors, unless a cartographer is named specifically on the map (e.g., as with many National Geographic maps). In the latter situation, record the cartographer as main entry (100 1_), and include an added entry for the firm (710 field).

Examples:

George Philip & Son, Ltd. (form as found on map; authorized form exists)

110	2	#	$a George Philip & Son.

245, a, ,b, and ,c (Title, other title information, and statement of responsibility) Record the title in field 245 according to the following pattern:

If the record has a main entry (1XX), set the first indicator to **1** (one); if it does not, set the first indicator to **0** (zero). Transcribe the title as it appears on the map.

If a map is in a cover or has a panel title, and the cover or panel title is more comprehensive than the title on the map (e.g., "Maputo streets, monuments, and government offices" on the cover or panel vs. "Map of Maputo" on the map), transcribe the cover title in the 245 field. Capitalize the first letter of the first word and the first letter of proper nouns. Use ,b for other title information (such as subtitles, parallel titles, etc.) and precede it with space-colon (#:). Transcribe the statement of responsibility in subfield ,c, following a slash. End the field with a period.

Title and statement on map: The Ordnance Survey

map of Namibia, prepared by the Ordnance Survey.

245	1	4	$a The Ordnance Survey map of Namibia / $c prepared by the Ordinance Survey.

246 (Varying form of title) Record a varying form of the title in field.

Examples:

If the title recorded in field 245 ,a is in English and contains an ampersand (&), create a 246 field with the word "and" in place of the ampersand, using indicators as shown.

Title: Cadiz & environs

245	1	0	$a Cadoz & environs.
246	1	0	$a Cadoz and environs.

250 (Edition statement) Record edition statements in field 250.

Revised second edition

250	#	#	$a Rev. 2nd ed.

255 (Cartographic mathematical data) Record the scale, if it is stated on the map, or if it can be determined using a scale indicator. If neither is the case, enter "Scale not given

255	#	#	$a 2 maps on 1 sheet : $b both sides;

260 (Place, publisher, and date) Record the place of publication, the name of the publisher, and the date(s) of publication.

If there is more than one place of publication, record the first-named only. If there is no place of publication stated, use [S.l.]. If there is no publisher named, use [s.n.].

300 (Extent) Record the extent of the item in field 300.

300	#	#	$a 1 map on 2 sheets : $c 25 X 35 cm. and 30 X 35 cm.

440 (Series statement): A map series is not the same as a monographic series, treated here.

ISO 2709 MARC 21 Format:

00861cem 922002534a 45000010009 00000005 001 700009007000900 0260080041000 3501000 150007 603400150009104000130 0106042000 800 11 905 000260012705200140 0 153245007200167 2550038 00239260002800277300003300305 5 0000 49003385000072003876510 071004599 06004500 530955 003200575-13140708-20030331114241.0-aj|canzn-030328s2001 ii a 0 eng - a 20036 26497 -1 aab1000000- aDLCcDLC- apcc-00aG7653.U82F7 2001b.S7- a7653bU82-00aState of Uttarakhand/Uttaranchal :bGarhwal and Kumaon Hill Region.- aScale 1:1,000,000. 1 mm. to 1 km.-a[India? :bs.n.,c2001]- a1 map :bcol. ;c31 x 34 cm.-aShows districts in the state of Uttaranchal.- a"This map has been reproduced from the Atlas of Uttaranchal, 2001".- 0aUttaranchal (India)xAdministrative and political divisionsvMaps.- a7bcbcco rigcopduencipf20 gn-geogmaps- aga10 2003-03-31 sent to CMT-"

MARC 21 Format:

MARC 21 Bibliographic Records Format:

LDR **00863cem 2200253 a 4500**

001			13140708
005			20030331114241.0
007			Aj!canzn
008			030328s2001 ii a O eng
010			2003626497
034		1	$a a $b 1000000
040			$a DLC $c DLC
042			$a pcc
050	0	0	$a G7653.U82F7 2001$b .S7
052			$a 7653 $b U82
245	0	0	$a State of Uttarakhand/ Uttaranchal : $b Garhwal and Kumaon Hill Region.
255			$a Scale 1:1,000,000. 1 mm. to 1 km.
260			$a [India?: $b s.n., $c 2001]
300			$a 1 map : $b col. ; $c 31 X 34 cm.
500			$a Shows districts in the state of Uttaranchal.
500			$a "This map has been reproduced from the Atlas of Uttaranchal, 2001".
651		0	$a Uttaranchal (India) $x Administrative and political divisions $v Maps.

MARC 21 BIBLIOGRAPHIC RECORDS FORMAT:

Title	State of Uttarakhand/Uttaranchal :
Subject	Uttaranchal (India) Administrative and Political divisions
Publication	[India? : s.n., 2001]
Scale, Etc. Scale	1:1,000,000. 1 mm. to 1 km.
Description	1 map : col; 31 x 34 cm.
Note	Shows districts in the state of Uttaranchal.
Note	"This map has been reproduced from the Atlas of Uttaranchal, 2001".

CHAPTER 4
Special Cataloging Rules

CONTENTS

4.1 THESES AND DISSERTATIONS

Generally theses and dissertations are unpublished items made available through copies. A note that describes the relationship of a work to a dissertation or thesis is recorded in fields 500.

Enter a thesis note in field 502 (Dissertation Note).

If you are cataloging a copy from a commercial producer and a record exists for another copy in the same medium (photocopy or microform) from the same producer, use the existing record, even if the date of reproduction differs. Since such theses are copies, cataloging rules allow the dates to vary from earlier copies. In such cases, if date information would be the only change, do not create a new record.

Optional. If you describe a reproduced thesis in field 533 (Reproduction Note), you may enter a Ctry code for the place of reproduction in field 539 (Fixed-Length Data Elements of Reproduction Note) subfield $d (Place of publication, production or execution). You may also enter date information for the reproduced thesis in field 539 subfields $a, $b and $c. Such information is based on the data in field 533. See field 539 for more information.

Example:

100	1		$a Shankar Singh.
245	1	0	$a Understandir g the internet resources an(networking practice in academic library in Uttaranchal.
260			$a New Delhi $b Ess Ess $c 2000.
300			$a xii, 296 p.
502			$a Thesis (Ph. D.)—University of Garhwal, Uttaranchal, 2000.
504			$a Includes bibliographical reference.
533			$a Photocopy $b Ess Ess $c University Microfilms, $c 2000 $e 20 cm.
539			$s $b 2000 $d miu $e n 539.

4.2 MULTI VOLUMES

Multipart item is monograph complete, or intended to be completed, is a finite number of separate parts.

Multivolumes is a publications in more than one volume. Normally multivolume books expound collected information either relating to one subject or many subject. Reference books likes encyclopeadias, dictionaries are examples for multivolume books.

Types: Types I and Types II

Types I: Multivolumes books which have a common titles and not a separate title of individual item. All the items have no differences.

Types I are three types:

a) Complete set b) Uncompleted c) Incomplete

a) If volume have published complete set and library have a total volume. If a set of volume is continuously paged, give the pagination in parentheses after the number of volumes. Ignore separately paged sequences of preliminary matter in volumes other than the first.

Example: 3v (xxi, 800 p.)

Optional addition: If the volumes in a multivolume set are individually paged give the pagination of each volume in parentheses after the number of volumes.

Example: 2v (xvii, 329; xx, 412 p.)

b) Uncompleted: If multipart item that is not yet complete, give the specific material designation alone preceded by three spaces.

Example: ...v

c) Incomplete set: If all the multipart item have been published but library have incomplete items. Notes should be mentioned in Note Area.

500	#	#	$a Library has v. 1, w, 5 and 8 only.
500	#	#	$a Library set lacks v. 5.

If the number of bibliographic volumes differ from the number of physical volumes, give the number of bibliographic volumes followed by in and the number of physical volumes.

Example: 8 v. in 5

If two or more dates are found on the various parts of the multipart item (e.g. when an item is published in parts over a number of years)

Give the earlier and later or earliest or latest dates, separated by a hyphen.

Example: 1968-1973

Types II: If multipart have additional title of different part, inspite of general title.

As per rules the addition title of each part should be given in Note section as a contents notes.

MARC 21 FORMAT WITH EXAMPLES

Use the appropriate value in indicator 1 of the MARC 21 in field 505 (Formatted Contents note) to indicate the character of the note: e.g., "Contents:"; "Incomplete contents:"; "Partial contents:" (without quotation marks) (see also 1.7A1).

Record the title proper that appears in the source that provides the best identification; however, if the title appears on the title page, normally use the title page title; give other title information only when the title proper would be meaningless without it; another source gives a more authoritative account of the data; however, if the title appears on the title page, normally use the title page title; give other title information only when the title proper would be meaningless without it include a first statement of responsibility (cf. 1.1F) if it differs from the statement included in the title and statement of responsibility or edition areas; omit names according to 1.1F5. The statement of responsibility is preceded by a space-slash-space; Omit introductions [listed on the contents page if] already included elsewhere in the description; generally omit prefatory and similar matter;

Publications in one volume

a) omit chapter and section numbering

b) if the extent of the part being listed occupies a disporportionately large portion of the publication, include the extent within parentheses after the title (or after the title and statement of responsibility); record an unnumbered page or leaf within brackets;

c) separate the titles with a space-dash-space (see also 1.7A3)

Publications in two or more volumes

a) give the volume designation that is found on item, except use abbreviations in appendix B and substitute arabic numerals for roman; if there is no abbreviation for the term, give only the number if the term is long; if the roman numeral is required for clarity, retain it; separate the volume designation by a period-space;

b) if the number of the physical volumes differs from the number of bibliographic volumes, include the number of physical volumes within parentheses after the title (or after the title and statement of responsibility)

c) if the volumes are of different eds. (cf. LCRI 2.2) include within parentheses edition statements and dates of publication etc. after title (or title and statement of responsibility) separate each volume with a space-dash-space (see also 1.7A3)

d) if the set is incomplete, put the space-dash-space before each title (other than the first) and leave four spaces for the missing volume

e) if two or more titles are being transcribed for one volume, apply the punctuation conventions from 1.1G3 such that the title by the same person, body, etc. are separated by a space-semicolon-space and titles by different person, bodies, etc.

are separated by a period- space (or other full-stop such as dash between volumes) (see also 1.1G3)

f) when some volumes in a multipart publication have their own titles and some volumes do not, and it is decided to make a formal contents not, use the statement "[without special title]" to represent untitled volumes LC practice modifies the above as follows:

for LC original cataloging, encode contents information at the MARC 21 basic level for one-volume collections, limit contents notes to those collections containing no more than 12 titles and the title statement of responsibility area does not adequately cover the contents of the item; in case of doubt, give a contents note

First Indicators		Display constant controller Indicates the completeness of the note and which may be used to generate an introductory term or phrase.
	0	Contents Contents: may be generated for display.
	1	Incomplete contents All parts of a multipart item are not listed because they were not available for analysis. Incomplete contents: may be generated for display.
	2	Partial contents

All parts were available for analysis but only selected parts are listed. Partial contents: may be generated for display.

8 No display constant generated

Second Indicators Level of content designation

Basic

0 Enhanced

— Constantine's letter.

Each section of the Contents Note is separated by a space-dash-space (make the dash with 2 contiguous hyphens) Period (full-stop) is at the end of the Contents Note

Examples:

505	0	#	$a How these records were discovered - A short sketch of the Talmuds
505	1	#	$a pt. 1. General observations - pt. 2. Methodology - pt. 3. Initial phase
505	1	#	$a v. 1. Report - v. 3. Overseas systems of compensation

No period is at end because more are to be published

Because we don't have v. 2, no dash is after v. 1 and 4 extra spaces are inserted before the dash (2 contiguous hyphens)

505	2	#	$a Manual 1. Principles of solar geometry and otics – manual 2. Solar radiation quantitative analysis – manual 3. Heat transfer principles for solar applications – manual 4. Passive solar heating systems.

Only those titles chosen to be included are listed even though the item may contain more titles

505	0	#	$a Vol. 1. $t The history of Anne Arundel County - $g vol. 2. $t The history of... (lots of volumes) - $g vol. 3. $t The history of Prince Georges County.

505	8	#	$g Vol. 24. $t The history of Washington County beginning in 1884 - $g vol. 25. State manifest and birth record (1764-1977).

For long contents that continue to another note, end the first one with — and begin the second with 505 8

Multiple volumes and authors

505	0	#	$a Vol. 1. $t Quark models / $r J. Rosner - $t Introduction to gauge theories of the strong, weak, and electromagnetic interactions / $r C. Quigg.

When several titles are in each volume, each by a different author, separate each title/author with period-space

505	0	#	$g v. 1. Plain tales from the hills - $g v. 2-3. soldiers three and military tales –[v. 5]. The phantom rickshaw and other stories- $g v. 6. Under the deordars. The story of the Gadsbys. Wee Wille Winkie.

From the preface, title page or other sources we know these stories are by many people but they are unnamed, therefore when several titles are in one volume they are separated by period-space.

4.3 OFFPRINTS AND DETACHED COPIES

Guidelines: Use the following guidelines for offprints and detached copies:

* If a separate bibliographic record is needed for an offprint or detached copy, catalog the item as a separate bibliographic item. Do not use "In" analytic cataloging conventions for offprints, reprints or detached copies.
* Use AACR2 rule 2.5B6 to record pagination. In a field 500 note, indicate the relationship to the larger work. Begin the note with "Offprint:" or "Detached from:" as appropriate.
* If the larger work is a serial, use the title in AACR2 catalog entry form, followed by the numeric and/or alphabetic designation (preceded by a period).
* If appropriate, use the chronological designation enclosed in parentheses. If the item is detached

from another monograph, follow AACR2 rule 1.7A3 in citing the source. Under the provision of rule 21.30G, added entries may be made for the larger work.

4.4 SUPPLEMENTARY ITEMS

Guidelines Use the following guidelines for cataloging supplementary items. You may catalog supplementary items independently (i.e., in a separate record) or dependently (i.e., in the record for the main item).

If cataloging independently, include the LC card number and the OCLC number of the main item, if available, in the appropriate 7xx linking entry field.

Use the publication pattern to determine whether the supplementary item should be cataloged as a monograph or a serial. Monographs have a finite number of parts. Serials are intended to continue indefinitely.

Treat items with monograph title page (or equivalent) as monographs.

Treat subsequent parts that update the item, have different titles and are issued indefinitely as serials.

Relate any separate bibliographic record for supplements to the record for the main work (parent) via the appropriate added entry or serial linking field.

Do not create records for the updates to looseleaf publications.

Optional. Create a record for both the main work and its supplement. Such records are not duplicates.

Optional. Catalog supplements to looseleaf publications that are cataloged as serials separately as another serial in a separate record, particularly if the supplement has a separate title.

If cataloging dependently, i.e., on the same records as the main item, add 006 fields to reflect fixed-field coding of the supplementary items, especially if it is in a different format.

4.5 COPY OR INSTITUTION-SPECIFIC NOTES AND ADDED ENTRIES

You may supply copy-specific or institution-specific notes and added entries for rare and special-collections materials. However, do not create new records because single master records can have such information for more than one copy or institution.

Master records for published materials represent all copies of a work, the "universal description" of the item. MARC 21 defines subfield $5 (Institution to which field applies) for use in notes and added entries that do not apply to the universal description. Usually, only rare and special-collections materials are candidates for fields containing subfield $5.

Use subfield $5 in fields 246, 500, 501, 506, 540, 541, 561, 562, 583, 584, 585, 700, 710, 711, 730 and 740 to identify the institution to which the copy- or institution specific notes and added entries apply (by MARC Organization Code, formerly called NUC Code).

Consider the usefulness of the information in accessing and identifying the item versus the likelihood that the record will be used in copy-cataloging or found by others who will not need your copy- or institution-specific notes and added entries.

Do not include subfield $5 in master records for unpublished items and collections.

Such notes and added entries do apply to the universal description, since they are single items.

Do not include subfield $5 in master records for works that you do not own. It is difficult to confirm the validity of the information, even if the information is from LC printed copy.

If the copy- or institution-specific note or added entry is of local interest only and you want to include the information for your local processing, use the appropriate 590, 599, 790, 791, 792 or 793 field. These fields are not retained in master records.

If you add subfield $5, use the following guidelines:

Use field 501 ("With" Note) with subfield $5 for "with" notes for items bound together after publication.

Use field 710 (Added Entry–Corporate Name) with subfield $5 for an added entry for the name of a special collection.

4.6 ANALYTICS

Definition: If a separate bibliographic record is necessary for a component, you may prepare an "in" analytic entry. A component is a bibliographic unit that is physically contained in another bibliographic unit (host item) in such a way that the host item must be identified to locate the component (e.g., one article in a serial, one chapter or paper in a book or one band on a sound recording).

Do not use "in" analytic cataloging conventions for offprints, reprints or detached copies.

Element	Guidelines for "In" Analytics
BLvl	Code for the component (e.g., a for monograph, b for serial).
Ctry	If country information is available in field 773 (Host Item Entry) subfield $d (Place, publisher and

	date of publication), code accordingly. Otherwise, code Ctry as unknown (xxb/).
Dates	Use date in field 773 subfields $d or $g (Relationship information) as appropriate.
018	Use for copyright article-fee code.
580	Use for linking entry complexity notes.
773	Use for host item entries.

Analysis is the process of preparing a bibliographic record that describes a part or parts of an item. If a separate bibliographic records is necessary for a component, prepare in "In" alalytic entry. A component is a bibliographic unit that is physically contained in another bibliographic unit (host item) in such a way that the host item must be identified to locate the component (e.g., one article in a serial, one chapter or paper in a book, or one band on a sound recording). "In" analytics are made in only very ususual circumstances and used mostly for special collection material.

* Create the "In" analytic record using the guidelines found in AACR 13.5 ("In" Analytics) and OCLC Bibliographic Formats Chapter 3.4 and 773 (Host Item Entry).
* Cite the host item in the 773 field. Include the following:
    * Name and/or uniform title heading of the host item, if appropriate
    * Title proper (Omit initial articles)
    * Statement of responsibility when necessary for identification

  * Edition statement
  * Numeric or other designation (of a serial) or publication details (of a monographic item)

* If the "In" analytic is classified or shelved with the host item, create a bibliographic record for the serial, multipart item, or other type of host material. If appropriate, record the extent of holdings in the 866 field of the holdings record.

Examples:

The cowboy's warbonnet

President Roosevelt's New England and southern tour illustrated

Age and mental abilities

Native American images in advertising

* If the "In" analytic is classified by the subject of the "In" analytic, no bibliographic or holdings record is created for the host item.

  Examples:

  The beginning of bop

  Questioned imprints in the United States

Series Tracing in Analytic

Make an added entry under the name of the serial or multipart monograph, following the conventions for series added entries. If the serial has a chronological designation but no actual enumeration, use a standardized form (i.e., Year Month Day) of the chronological designation in the access point.

440		0	$a Shaw ; $v v. 5
830		0	$a Audit (Buffalo, N.Y.) ; $v v. 5, no. 1
830		0	$a Hollandia (Hague, Netherlands) ; $v 1899 Sept. 2

The fact that an item is analyzed or is an analytic is indicated in the staff/non-public note field ($x) of the 852 . The record for the serial or multipart monograph will have ANLYZ to indicate that it is analyzed, and an 866 field listing summary holdings. The record for the analytic will have ANAL to indicate that it is the analytic.

Multi-part monograph/serial:

852	7	1	$b beingen $h 1982 $i S16 $x ANLYZ.
866	4	1	$8 0 $a v.1(1981)-v.11(1991).

Analytics:

852	7	1	$b beingen $h 1982 $i S16 1 $x ANAL.
852	7	1	$b beingen $h 1982 $i S16 7 $x ANAL.

CHAPTER 5
Sound Recording

CONTENTS

5.1 TITLE AND STATEMENT OF RESPONSIBILITY AREA

The rules in this chapter cover the description of sound recordings in all media, i.e. discs, tapes (open reel-to reel, cartiridges, cassettes), piano rolls (and other rolls), and sound recordings on film (other than intended to accompany visual images. It cover all sound types, including recording of music and spoken content.

Title proper: If the chief source of information bears the name of an author or the name of a performer in a prominent position preceding the titles of individual works, and there is doubt as to whether the name is intended to serve as a collective title or as a statement of responsibility, treat the name as the title proper. If, however, the name is that of the composer of the individual works, and there is doubt as to its intended function, treat the name as a statement of responsibility.

If the chief source of information consists of two or more labels each containing the name of a different author, performer, or composer apply the guidelines above independently to each label. If each of the names is to be treated as a title proper, record each as an individual title, separated by a full stop and two spaces.

Other title information

Do not restrict the recording of other title information on the basis of language or sequence. Give other title information in the language of the title proper, the language of the parallel title(s), and in other languages as well, provided it appears on the chief source of information.

245	0	3	$a Lamer $h [sound recording] ; $b Khamma ; Rhapsody for clarinet and o-chestra / $c Claude Debuss\.

Statements of responsibility

Record statements relating to performers only if the performer is responsible for improvisation and/or arrangement of the work. Performers may also be responsible for composing, writing lyrics, script-writing, etc., in which case their names are recorded in a statement of responsibility, not because of their responsibility as performers, but because of their responsibility for the intellectual or artistic content of the work as composers, etc. The names of composers, lyricists, scriptwriters, improvisationalists, a-rangers, etc., normally are recorded only if the person named has contributed to the entire work, as defined by the title that the statement of responsibility follows. For items containing several works under a collective title, the names of composers, lyricists, etc., are recorded only if they apply to all the works covered by the item. Responsibility for individual works within the item is recorded in a note.

For items without a collective title, where the titles of the individual works are recorded separately, persons responsible for each of the works may be recorded in a statement of responsibility following the appropriate title or titles.

740	0	2	$a South Pacific $h [sound recording]

5.2 PUBLICATION, DISTRIBUTION, ETC., AREA

Record information about the place, name, and date of all types of publishing, distributing, etc., activities as instructed in 1.4B. Do not record a place of publication, distribution, etc., for a nonprocessed sound recording. Do not records [s.l.] in such a case.

Distributors often play a significant role, and may be listed in addition to the publisher.

5.3 PHYSICAL DESCRIPTION AREA

Physical description area: As mentioned at 1.5, metric measurement and writing are used in the description. Follow the instructions at 1.5 and use the metric symbols listed in B.9.

1 sound disc (45 min) : analog, 33 1/3 r/min, stereo. ; 30 cm

not

1 sound disc (45 min.) : analog, 33 1/3 rpm, stereo. ; 12 in.

1 sound cassette (60 min) : analog, 9.5 cm/s, mono. ; 19 x 9 cm

not

1 sound cassette (60 min.) : analog, 3 3/4 ips, mono. ; 7 1/4 x 3 1/2 in.

1 sound disc (56 min) : digital, stereo. ; 12 cm

not

1 sound disc (56 min.) : digital, stereo. ; 4 3/4 in.

Extent of item (including specific material designation)

Record the number of physical units of a sound recording by giving the number of in Arabic numerals and one of the following terms as appropriate:

compact disc
DVD-audio
sound cartridge
sound cassette
sound disc
sound tape reel
videocassette

If none of these terms is appropriate, give the specific name of the item as concisely as possible.

300	#	#	$a 4 audiodiscs ; $c 3 in.

If the total playing time is stated as a total on the item, its container, or its accompanying textual material, record the total in minutes or minutes and seconds as instructed.

If the total playing time is not stated for items made up of parts (individual works, sides, units), but the playing time of each part is stated, the total playing time may, if desirable, be calculated by adding the stated durations together. Do not record the total playing time if it cannot be readily calculated.

Dimensions

In giving the dimensions of an item requiring more than one measurement, use a lower-case "x" as the multiplication sign to separate each of the measurements.

; 19 x 9 cm

Accompanying material

Add the details of description when the accompanying item(s) is (are) substantial in volume or interest, important to the effective use of the recording, represents the music and/or text of a recording in printed form, and/or seems capable of being alternatively and reasonably construed as the predominant medium.

300	#	#	$a 16 sound cassettes ; $c 37/8x2 in., $e 1 booklet. (169 p. : ill. ; 23 cm.

5.4 SERIES AREA

Record each series statement as instructed in 1.6.

440	#	#	$a CD Sound recording ; $v v. 6

5.5 NOTE AREA

Nature or artistic form and medium of performance

Make notes on the form of a literary or the type of musical or other work unless it is apparent from the rest of the description. Name the medium of performance when necessary, as instructed in 5.7b1'

500	#	#	$a The 2nd - 4th works are cantons popular

Language of the spoken or sung content of a recording

Give the language(s) of the spoken or sung content of a recording unless this is apparent from the rest of the description.

500	#	#	$a English and romanized Japanes words.

Statements of responsibility

Make notes of variant names of persons or bodies named in statements of responsibility if these are considered to be important for identification. Give the names of performers and the medium in which they perform if they have not been named in the statements of responsibility and if they are judged necessary.

511	#	#	$a Marshall Moss, violin ; Neil Roberts, Harpsichord.

Edition and history

Make notes relating to the edition being described, to the edition of the work performed, or to the history of the recording.

500	#	#	$a Recorded in Eaton Aluditorium, Toronto, Oct. 1976.

For serious music and for other music known to have been published in many editions, make note of the edition of the music performed, if the information is readily available.

500	#	#	$a Ed recorded : New York : Farrar, 1937.

Make notes indicating previous or alternate releases of the recording.

500	#	#	$a Previously released as : Westminster.

Physical description

Make notes on important physical details of Specific Materials Descriptions [SMD] that are not included in the physical description area, especially if these affect the use of the item. Do not give any physical details that are standard to the item being described (e.g., assume that all analog discs are electrically recorded, laterally cut, and designed for playing from the outside inward).

500	#	#	$a Compact dise.
500	#	#	$a Duration : 35:38; 3:39.

Other formats

Give a note on other formats available only when other formats are known to exist at the time of cataloging (see 1.5A3).

Summary. Give a brief objective summary of the content of a sound recording (other than one that consists entirely or predominantly of music) unless another part of the description provides enough information.

520	#	#	$a Fonds consists of minutes of meetings, research files relating to the delivery of health case services in Nova Scotia.

Contents. List the titles of individual works contained on a sound recording. Add to each title statement of responsibility not included in the title and statement of responsibility area and the duration of the piece.

505	8	#	$a Contents on sound disk : A suitable tone; Left hand colouring.

Publishers numbers. Give the publisher's stock number, usually an alphabetic and/or numeric symbol as found on the item. Precede each number by the brand or trade name associated with it on the baled or container and a colon. If the item has two or more numbers, give the principal number if one can be ascertained, otherwise give both or all. If one of the number applies to the set as a whole, give it first and designate it as such.

028	2	#	$a RA-931001C $b ROI Roductions.

5.6 STANDARAD NUBER AND TERMS OF AVAILABILITY AREA

Optional addition. Terms of availability

The option is generally not applied, however, will be applied (i.e., include the price) to preliminary CIP items. Do not update (i.e., neither delete nor change) this information upon receipt of the item.

Qualification

The option is applied only as a qualification to the standard number whenever applicable. Terms of availability are generally not used (see rule interpretation 6.8D).

When required, use a brief qualification (see 1.8E1) and note that consistency of terminology is not necessary. Do not make up and use qualifiers additional to that found in the transcribed data.

5.7 MARC 21 FORMAT WITH EXAMPLES

007 - Sound Recording

Every sound recording should have an 007. If the 007 is not in the record it should be added. A disc, tape, film, cylinder, or wire on which sound vibrations have been registered so that the sound may be reproduced; and paper rolls on which the notes of a music composition are represented by perforations in the paper and from which sound can be mechanically produced.

00 Category of material s Sound recording

01 Specific material designation. Indicates the special class of sound recording to which the item belongs.

02 Undefined Each contains a blank (#) or fill character (|)

03 Speed. Indicates the playback speed of the sound recording.

04 Configuration of playback channels. Indicates the configuration of playback channels for the sound recording.

05 Groove width/groove pitch. Indicates the width of the groove of the recording for a disc or the pitch of the groove for a cylinder.

06 Dimensions. Indicates the diameter of an open reel or disc, or the dimensions of a cassette, cartridge, or cylinder.

07 Tape width. Indicates the width of a tape.

08 Tape configuration. Indicates the number of tracks on a tape.

09 Kind of disc, cylinder or tape. Indicates the type of disc, cylinder, or tape.

10 Kind of material. Indicates the kind of material used in the manufacture of the disc or the cylinder (both instantaneous and mass-produced).

11 Kind of cutting. Indicates the kind of cutting used to make the grooves used on a disc.

12 Special playback characteristics. Indicates the playback characteristics for the sound recording,

including special equipment or equalization necessary for proper playback. The code is not used to indicate special processes used during the making of the recording unless those processes must be applied during playback.

13 Capture and storage technique. Indicates how the sound was originally captured and stored. A re-released recording is coded for the original capture and storage technique.

MARC Record Sample – Sound Recording – CD

LDR **000** **njm a**

001			13140708
005			20030331114241.0
007			s
008			010507r20001991tnucyn d eng d
024	1		$a 724353012021
028		2	$a 7243-5-30120-2-1 $b Capital
040			$a DLC $c DLC
042			$a pcc
082	0	4	$a 782.421642 $2 21
100	1		$a William, D.W.
245	0	0	$a Summer season $h [sound recording] $c D.W. William.
250			$a 10 th anniversary special ed.
260			$a New Delhi: $b Capital, $c 2000.

300			$a 1 sound disc : $b digital ; $c 4 ¾ in.
538			$a compact disc.
511	0		$a D.W. William, vocals, guitar ; with acc.
500		0	$a Reissued from recordings.
500			$a Lyrics in container
505	0		$a Against the grain (2:20) – Rodeo (3.51) – What she's doing now (3:23)
650		0	$a Country music $y 1991-2000.
650		0	$a Country music $x Summer season.

Chapter 6
Motion Pictures, Videorecordings

CONTENTS

6.0 GENERAL RULES

Introduction: Videorecordings released on DVD are often copies of motion pictures or television shows that have been rereleased on DVD. While chapter 7 deals with both videorecordings and motion pictures, specific rules apply to both formats, so when cataloging a DVD it is necessary to understand that the object in hand is a "videorecording." Indeed, often videorecordings on DVD are copies of motion pictures, and consequently it may be difficult for catalogue users to determine the specific nature of the item. The use of the GMD "videorecording," however, may help, although the establishment of a specific GMD for DVD would go a long way towards easily clarifying this issue.

Videorecording : A recording on which visual images, usually in motion and accompanied by sound, have been registered; designed for playback by means of a television set. —*AACR2r* Appendix D

Motion picture. A length of film, with or without recorded sound, bearing a sequence of images that create the illusion of movement when projected in rapid succession. --*AACR2r* Appendix D

DVD vs CD

Both DVDs and CDs consist of 12 cm (4 ¾ in.) diameter discs containing billions of tiny pits (non-reflective holes) and lands (reflective bumps) arranged in one long spiral track. These pits and lands represent the zeros and ones of digital information, and are read by a laser. The main differences are that a DVD's pits and lands are shorter and narrower than those of a CD, and that the DVD's laser also has a shorter wavelength. In terms of storage, this means that a DVD can hold 4.7 billion bytes of information; seven times the informational capacity of a standard CD. DVDs can also hold two information layers on one side which roughly increase their storage to 9 gigabytes. Unlike CDs, DVDs can also hold information on both sides of a single disc.

DVD Types:

* **DVD-A (DVD-Audio)** — Equivalent to an standard audio CD which uses Pulse Code Modulation (PCM) for recording sound, except that it holds some seven times the information of a regular CD.
* **DVD-V (DVD-Video)** — What most people think of when referring to the DVD. Usually used to store video recordings.
* **DVD-R (DVD-Recordable)** — A write-once data storage disc that is similar to CD-Rs. It can record around 4.7 gigabytes, and is used mainly for the archiving of information and the storage of video recordings.
* **DVD-RAM (DVD-Re-writable)** — An erasable, re-recordable version of the DVD-ROM. Provides random access to its 4.7 gigabytes of recorded information, and is best suited for use in computers. May be rewritten some 100,000 times.
* **DVD-ROM** — Equivalent to the CD-ROM, a commercially produced read-only disc containing computer programs, data or both. Can hold anywhere between 4.7 and 17 gigabytes of information.
* **DVD-RW (DVD-Re-writable)** — A re-writable version of the DVD-R that is compatible with most DVD video players. It can sequentially record almost 4.7 gigabytes of data, and can be rewritten about 1,000 times.

* **DVD+RW (DVD-Re-writable) —** Competing standard to DVD-RAM and DVD-RW developed by Sony, Philips and Hewlett-Packard. It also sequentially records almost 4.7 gigabytes of data and can be rewritten some 1,000 times. DVD-RAMs, DVD-RWs, and DVD+RWs are incompatible with each other.
* **SACD (Super Audio CD) —** Competing audio standard to DVD-A that utilizes Direct Stream Digital (DSD) recording technology instead of PCM.

Future:

The DVD Forum is working on something they call "DVD Multi." DVD Multi is a set of hardware specifications designed to enable disc compatibility for virtually all formats officially created by the DVD Forum. For example, a DVD Multi-compliant DVD-ROM computer drive would be able to read all of the following: DVD-V, DVD-A, DVD-ROM, DVD-RAM, DVD-RW, and DVD-R discs.

In February 2002, 9 members of the DVD Forum announced a new high-density recordable DVD standard known as Blu-Ray (it uses a blue laser to read and store the information rather than the typical red laser). The Forum is investigating many possible next-generation DVD standards, but Blu-Ray is considered to be the most likely successor because of its support by these 9 current members. While originally intended for storing video, Blu-Ray will probably be adapted for use in computer information storage and retrieval.

Chief Source of Information: As prescribed by *AACR2r* 7.0B2, unlike music CDs, the chief source of information for a DVD is "the item itself (e.g., the title frames)" or "its container." In the case of a DVD, the main menu should not be substituted for "the title frames," which are often located towards the beginning of a videorecording, and may only be viewed after the feature is "played." If the required information is not available on the chief source, other sources suggested by *AACR2r* 7.0B2

Chief source of information (in order of preference)

- Item itself (title and credit frames)
- Container (and container label) if the container is an integral part of the piece (e.g. a cassette) [they mean the actual plastic cassette container] If the information is not available from the chief source, take it from the following sources (in this order of preference)
- Accompanying textual material (e.g. scripts, shot lists, publicity material)
- Container (if not an integral part of the piece) [what they really mean is the box]
- Other sources, if possible, it is best to view the film. According to AACR2R title should be taken from the title frame or the cassette label. If the title is not taken from the title screen the source of title should be stated in a note. This is important for copy cataloging. Often the title on the cassette label or the box may be different than what is on the title screen. If the source of title is not noted if it is not the title screen, catalogers may have a hard time knowing if they have a match. Prescribed sources of information – Information taken from outside the prescribed sources of information must be enclosed in square brackets.

6.1 TITLE AND STATEMENT OF RESPONSIBILITY

Statement of Responsibility: Individuals or corporate bodies who are credited in the chief source with the production of the work, or are considered to be of major importance to the film may be included in the statement of responsibility. Other individuals should be recorded in notes. Transcribe statements of responsibility relating to those persons or bodies credited in the chief source of information with a major role in creating a film (e.g., as producer, director, animator) as instructed in 1.1F. Give all other statements of responsibility (including those relating to performance) in notes. --*AACR2r* 7.1F1

Optional addition. General material designation: The general material designation "motion picture" or "videorecording," as appropriate.

Items without a collective title

In describing as a unit a motion picture or videorecording lacking a collective title transcribe the titles of the individual parts as instructed in 1.1G3.

245	1	0	$a Facts about Korea $h [videorecording] / $c Korea Film Production ; director, Kim.

yusan. Han ok, a traditional Korean house / Korea Film Production.

6.2 EDITION AREA

Edition - Chief source of information, accompanying material, container. Many film titles are/have been available in multiple formats (film, Beta, VHS, laser disc, DVD) as well as multiple versions/releases within a format. Numerous titles have been released on DVD then followed (sometimes within the month) with another DVD release that is changed somewhat from the first release. The later release may contain supplementary materia that wasn't on the first release, and/or additional 'anguage sound tracks, or be in widescreen where the first release was in the standard format. It may carry a banner across the container "Special Edition" or be otherwise identified. Be careful to distinguish between edition statements related to the item in hand, and series statements relating to the item being part of a publisher's collection.

Examples of edition statements (which would go into a 250 field) include:

* Special edition
* Deluxe widescreen presentation
* Widescreen version

6.3 PUBLICATION, DISTRIBUTION, ETC., AREA

Name of publisher, distributor, etc.: The option is applied occasionally. Add the name and place of the distributor when the information is necessary for clarification and is readily ascertainable. Liberal use of the option is discouraged and no strict uniformity is expected.

Optional addition. Statement of function of publisher, distributor, etc.: The option is applied when the information is necessary for clarification and is readily ascertainable. Liberal use of the option is discouraged and no strict uniformity is expected.

Date of publication, distribution, etc.: The option is applied if the information is readily available.

A. Dates in field 260

Some DVDs have a copyright date on the printed

disc surface that represents the date the item was published; this date would be recorded in MARC 21 field 260, just as found (with the copyright symbol).

If there is no copyright date on the disc surface, look for the latest date of those that may be printed on the back of the container [copyright date for cover design, etc.], and use this latest date as the assumed date of publication. Record this date in brackets and without the copyright symbol because it is an assumed date. Copyright renewal dates are ignored according to LCRI 1.4F6 (CSB 92).

B. Dates in notes

Dates for the original production as a motion picture, or on television, or as a videorecording, are given in the history note.

Place of manufacture, name of manufacturer, date of manufacture.

The option is applied if such information is "considered important", i.e., rarely, and is easily found in the item.

Unpublished Items: As noted above, for locally produced DVDs, often DVD-Rs, it is not necessary to record the place or name of the publisher; however, *AACR2r* 7.4F3 explicitly notes that the date of creation is to be recorded for unedited or unpublished material.

6.4 PHYSICAL DESCRIPTION AREA

Physical Details: *AACR2r* 7.5B2 prescribes that the playing time for "videodisks" be noted as per *AACR2r* 1.5B4, for example "1 videodisk (ca. 120 min.)." Additionally according to *AACR2r* 7.5C, information such as sound and colour should be recorded as appropriate.

Extent of item (including specific material designation): The option is not applied. When a GMD is used, "film" or "video" is not omitted from the specific material designation. However, if "film" or "video" is not part of the conventional term, do not include it in the specific material designation.

In addition to, or in place of, the terms given at 7.5B1, a term in common usage is used, when appropriate, to record the specific format of the physical carrier. Terms used by the LAC include the following:

DVD-video	film cartridge	film cassette
film loop	film reel	videocartridge
videocassette	videodisc	videoreel

Extent of item (including specific material designation): Videodiscs consisting of frames of still images. The option is not applied. Videodiscs consisting of both moving images and still images.The option is not applied.

Dimensions: In giving the dimensions of an item requiring more than one measurement, use a lower-case "x" as the multiplication sign to separate each of the measurements.

Accompanying material: The option is applied on a case by case basis. The decision will be dependent on cataloguer's judgement of the importance of the detailed count and the ease of finding or making this count.

300	#	#	$a 1 videodisc (66 min.) : sd., col. ; 4 ¾ in. + $e 1 booklet ([10]) p. : col. Ill. ; 20 cm.

Notes used with the above example would include:

538	#	#	$a DVD.
500	#	#	$a Booklet (6 p.) includes list of chapters, brief essay "The hatching of Chicken run."

6.5 SERIES AREA

Record each series statement as instructed in 1.6.

6.6 NOTE AREA

Notes of relevance to videorecordings on DVDs include:

Nature of form. Make notes on the nature or form of a motion picture or videorecording unless it is apparent from the rest of the description.

Language. Give the language(s) of the spoken, sung, or written content of a motion picture or videorrecording unless this is apparent from the rest of description. Indicate captioning or singing.

Source of title proper. Make notes on the source of the proper if it is other than the chief source of information.

Variations in title. Make notes on titles born by the item other than the title proper.

Parallel titles and other title information. Give the title in another language and other title information not recorded in the title and statement of responsibility area if they are considered to be important.

Statements of responsibility: Cast members and other individuals credited may be indicated here.

Edition and history: Edition Information

including information regarding videorecordings issued in multiple releases may be recorded here.

Publication: With DVDs, often the date of production will differ from the date of publication. Such information may be recorded here.

Physical description: Details an object's physical description and other information relating to the type of equipment necessary to play the videorecording may be recorded here. This is a useful area to record that the object being catalogued is, in fact, a DVD.

500	#	#	$a Standard version on one side, widescreen version on other side.

Some DVDs are multiple-disc sets. These additional discs often contain a sequel or sequels to the movie on the first disc, or additional episodes in the same television series. For instance, if the first disc has the movie "Toy Story," the second disc has the movie "Toy Story 2."

505	#	#	$a Dis 1. Toy story – disc 2. Toy story 2.

Enhanced DVDs: Use one note stating the DVD is enhanced, and also use field 538 for the system requirements for the computer portion, though they may be combined.

538	#	#	$a Enhanced DVD.
500	#	#	$a Includes 2 computer games, links to fan sites.

Summary: Descriptions of content, such a plot summaries, may be recorded here.

6.7 MARC 21 FORMAT WITH EXAMPLES

07 - Sound Recording

A disc, tape, film, cylinder, or wire on which sound vibrations have been registered so that the sound may be reproduced; and paper rolls on which the notes of a music composition are represented by perforations in the paper and from which sound can be mechanically produced.

00 Category of material s Sound recording
01 Specific material designation
02 Undefined
03 Speed
04 Configuration of playback channels
05 Groove width/groove pitch
06 Dimensions
07 Tape width
08 Tape configuration
09 Kind of disc, cylinder or tape
10 Kind of material
11 Kind of cutting
12 Special playback characteristics
13 Capture and storage technique

MARC Record Sample – DVD

LDR			000 ngm a
001			13140708
005			20030331114241.0
007			s
008			020304s2001 vau360 g vleng d
020			$a 078063490X
024		1	$a 79405488526
028	0	0	$a B8485D $b PBS DVD Gold
082	0	4	$a 973.7092 $2 21
245	0	0	$a Abraham and MaryLincoln $h [videorecording] : $b a house divided / $c David Grubin Productions, Inc. ; written by David Grubin and Geoffrey C. Ward ; produced and directed by David Grubin.
246	3	0	$a House divided.
260			$a [Alexandria, Va.] $b PBS Home Video, $c c2001.
300			$a 3 videodisces (360 min.) : $b sd., col. With b&w seque3nces ; $c 4 ¾ in.
538			$a DVD.
511			$a Narrator, David McCullough; voices, David Morse, Hjolly Hunter.

508			$a Cinematography, James Callanan, editors, Tom Haneka, Seth Bomse; music, Michael Bacon.
520			$a Examines the Linconlns' family life and marriage, Abraham Lincoln's presicency, and the Civil War era.
505		0	$a espisode 1. Ambition – episode 2. We are elected – episode 3. Shattered – episode 4. Dearest of all things -- episode 5. This frightful war – episode 6. Blind with weeping.
600	1	0	$a Lincoln, Abraham, $d 1809-1865.
651		0	$a United States $x History $y Civil War, 1861-1865.
700	1		$a Ward, Geoffrey C.
700	1		$a Grubin, David.
730		0	$a American experience (Televisio program).
740	0	2	$a Ambition.

CHAPTER 7
Electronic Resources [Computer File]

CONTENTS

7.0 GENERAL RULES

Cataloging an electronic resource issued in a DVD-ROM format is similar to cataloging an electronic resource issued on CD-ROM; however, the Amendments 2001 resulted in several significant changes to Chapter 9, "Electronic Resources," formerly entitled "Electronic resources."

Definition of Electronic Resource

According to AACR2, 2002 revision, an electronic resource is: "Material (data and/or program(s)) encoded for manipulation by a computerized device. This material may require the use of a peripheral directly connected to a computerized device (e.g., CD-ROM drive) or a connection to a computer network (e.g., the Internet)."

TYPES OF MATERIAL COVERED

This document will be mainly concerned with Internet resources, including electronic books and "accompanying" websites. Tangible electronic material such as computer disks and CD-ROMS that do not require the use of a computer will not be covered.

The following general classes of electronic resources:

* Computer software (including programs, games, fonts)
* Numeric data
* Computer-oriented multimedia
* Online systems or services

7.1 TITLE AND STATEMENT OF RESPONSIBILITY AREA

Transcribe the title proper and parallel title or other title information and statements of responsibility as found on the chief source of information. New with Amendments 2001 is the redefined general material designation. Use "[electronic resource]" as the GMD.

245	0	0	$a Fintastic fun in Neptune bay $h [electronic resource].
245	1	0	$a How to read a film $h [electronic resource] / $c by James Monaco.
245	0	0	$a Nihon musei eiga taizen $h [electroni resource] = $b Materpieces of Japanese silent cinema.

Give any variations in title or other title information as appropriate.

245	0	0	$a Home improvement 1-2-3.
246	3	0	$a Home improvement 1 2 3.
246	3	0	$a Home improvement one-two-three.

7.2 EDITION AREA

Transcribe an edition statement as it appears on a DVD-ROM.

7.3 TYPE AND EXTENT OF RESOURCE AREA

Use one of the following terms to describe the resource being cataloged.

Electronic data.

Electronic program(s).

Electronic data and program(s).

Provide the statement of extent only if it is readily and succinctly available. Optionally, this information can be stated in a note. If the resource is in a compressed form, omit the statement of extent.

256	0	0	$a Electronic data (1 file : 2.5 gb)

It should be noted that, according to LCRI 9.3B1, it is LC practice not supply terms for the type of electronic resource in original cataloging. They will however accept such terms when found in records originally created by other cataloging agencies and used by LC in its own cataloging.

7.4 PUBLICATION, DISTRIBUTION, ETC., AREA

All commercially available electronic resources issued in DVD-ROM format are considered published.

260	0	0	$a [Paris] : $b Montparnasse Multimedia, $c c2000.

For an electronic resource produced non-commercially on a DVD format, do not record a place of publication, distribution, etc. or name of publisher, distributor, etc. Do not record "[s.l.]" or "[s.n.]" respectively in such a case.

260	0	0	$a [2001].

According to AACR2 rule 9.4F4, if there is no publication, distribution, etc., date which applies to the item as a whole, and the item has multiple copyright dates which apply to various aspects of the production, e.g., programming, sound, graphics, documentation, transcribe only the latest copyright date. Optionally, transcribe the other dates in a note or in a contents note.

7.5 PHYSICAL DESCRIPTION AREA

Use "computer optical disc" as the specific material designation; optionally, use conventional terminology as the SMD, e.g., DVD-ROM (NB: Chapter 9 includes "DVD" as an example of conventional terminology; however, our recommendation is to use "DVD-ROM" to be analogous to the distinction made between CD and CD-ROM.) Add other physical details if specified or known and give dimensions. Give information on accompanying material, if appropriate.

300	#	#	$a 1 computer optical disc : $b sd., col. ; $c 4 ¾ in.
300	#	#	$a 1 DVD-ROM : $b sd., col. ; $c 4 ¾ in. + $e 1 installation guide.

7.6 SERIES AREA

Transcribe series statements for material issued on DVD-ROM format in the same manner as for any other material.

7.7 NOTE AREA

Give the notes in prescribed order as listed below.

System requirements

Provide information on system requirements, if readily available. Begin the note with "System requirements:"

538	#	#	$a System requirements: IBM-PC or compatible; 2 MB of free hard disk space; Windows 95/98 or NT; SVGA color display capable of displaying 1024 by 768 pixels; DVD-ROM drive.

Source of title proper

Always give the source of the title proper. Consider the disc label to be any information that is affixed, printed or stamped on the disc surface.

500	#	#	$a Title from the title screen.
500	#	#	$a Title from disc label.

Edition and history note

Provide information relating to the edition or to the history of the resource.

500	#	#	$a Previous eds, issued on CD-ROM.

Physical Description Note

Give the physical description in a note if using computer optical disc as the specific material designation in the physical description.

500	#	#	$a DVD_ROM.

Accompanying material note

Make note of any accompanying materials not detailed in the physical description area.

500	#	#	$a Accompanied by technical documentation.

Other formats note

If the content has been issued in other formats, provide that information in a note.

500	#	#	$a Issued also in print.

Summary note

Always give a brief statement of the purpose and content of resource.

520	#	#	$a Provides access to the lates information from European research in informatioOn and communication technologies.

Contents note

List the contents of the resource.

505	#	0	$a disc 1. Install – dise 2. Entire U.S.

7.8 MARC 21 FORMAT WITH EXAMPLES

Nature of the resources and how it should be cataloged

Monographs (BLvl=m)

The following types of resources are currently coded as monographs, whether issued individually or as component parts of a collection:

* digitized texts
* Web sites
* databases (including directories, A&I services, etc.)
* electronic discussion groups
* OPACs
* online services (e.g., America Online)

Serials (BLvl=s)

The following types of resources are considered serials, whether issued individually or as component parts of a collection:

* electronic journals
* electronic newsletters
* electronic editions of newspapers

Following two way of cataloging of electronic resources:

A- Single record cataloging

When adding electronic version information to an existing local bibliographic record for a traditional format, the following fields are added:

* 530 note: Use this field to focus all the information about the electronic resource in one place
* 740 title: use this field as necessary to trace any differences in title for the electronic version; or, if the titles are identical to add a title tracing with the qualifier "(Online)" to distinguish the two editions
* 856 link

Example of single record cataloging:

245	0	4	$a The dictionary of art / $c editor, Jane Turner.
530	#	#	$a Also available on the World Wide Web as The Grove dictionary of art.
740		4	$a The Grove dictionary of art.
740		4	$a The dictionary of art (Online)
856	4	1	$3 Available via UNC-CH Libraries Web $u http://eresources.lib.unc.edu/eid/description.cfm?EIDID=247 $x http://www.groveart.com.

B- Separate record cataloging

Electronic edition: What this basically amounts to is cataloging the electronic edition as though it were the only edition, with a few additional fields as needed, usually 530 and 7XX fields.

Print or microformat edition: Generally, add only an 856 field with the URL and a $3 note indicating that this is the electronic edition.

Example of separate record cataloging: Electronic edition

245	0	4	The Cambridge history of English and American literature$h [electronic resource] : $b an encyclopedia in eighteen volumes.
530			$a Contents originally issued as The Cambridge historyof Englishliterature and The Cambridge history of American literature.
730	0	2	$a Cambridge history of English literature.
730	0	2	a Cambridge history of American literature.
856	4	0	$u http://www.bartleby.com/cambridge.

245	0	4	$a The Cambridge history of English literature, $ c ed. by A. W. Ward and A. R. Waller.
856	4	0	$3 Contents also available online $ u http://www.bartleby.com/cambridge.

"Type of record" (Leader/06) code "m"

A new definition of "type of record" code "m" was implemented in February 1998, which restricted the use of the computer file 008 to "computer file software (including programs, games, fonts), numeric data, computer-oriented multimedia, and online systems and services." Under the revised definition, electronic serials that are primarily textual by nature are coded as "type of record" code "a" (language material). This means that the majority of serials once again are cataloged using the serials 008 fixed field. However, electronic serials that fit into one of the categories in the code "m" definition are cataloged using the computer file 008. (For further explanation of these categories, see "type of record" (leader/06) and "type of computer file" (008/26).

Field 006 electronic serials and integrating resources

Field 006 is mandatory in all records for electronic serials and integrating resources, whether it contains the computer file characteristics when the continuing resources 008 is used, or the continuing resources characteristics when the computer file, cartographic or other 008 is used.

The mandatory use of field 006 for computer file characteristics is a means of identifying the carrier of the item. With the redefinition of leader/06 code "m", the presence of field 006 with code "m" in the first byte ("form of material" 006/00) allows OCLC and other systems to identify records for electronic resources for purposes of searching and duplicate detection. Note that the definitions for the two "m" codes differ. The definition of code "m" in the leader is very specific to the content, as noted above. The definition of code "m" in 006/00 reads: "Code m is used to identify field 006 as containing coded data elements relating to a computer file." For current purposes, interpret this statement as applying to any resource whose carrier is electronic, regardless of the nature of the content.

For example, a separately-cataloged online version of a journal whose content is primarily textual would be coded "a" in the "type of material" because it does not fit into one of the categories in the definition of "type of record" code "m". The presence of field 006 with code "m" in the first byte identifies this record as representing the electronic version and distinguishes the record from the record for the print version.

Interim practice for coding type of record and field 006, electronic integrating resources Bibliographic level "i," was developed to identify integrating resources in anticipation of the 2002 AACR2 rule revisions. Used in conjunction with type of record code "a" (language material) it generates a continuing resources 008. (When appropriate, it can also be used in conjunction with type of record code "m" for electronic integrating resources that meet the strict computer file definitions specified for code "m," to generate a computer file 008). Since bibliographic level code "i" will not be available until at the earliest, mid-2003, an interim coding practice has been established. Electronic integrating resources that are mainly textual, are coded type of record "a," and bibliographic level "m." A continuing resource 006 and a computer file 006 are also added to the record to assure that the record contains fixed field elements for continuing resources and computer files. Integrating resources that meet the definition of record code "m" contain only the continuing resource 006. See CEG B.7 for further information.

Form of item (008/23) code "s" electronic

Code "s" in the continuing resource 008 was implemented in the spring of 2000 for both "form of item" (008/23) and "form of original item" (008/22). OCLC also added the new code "s" to the 008/23 of existing records in the spring of 2000. The current practice for coding records for textual electronic serials is to use code "s" in field 008/23 and code "m" in field 006/00. [N.B.: OCLC and other systems still use the 006 form codes for retrieval, record matching, and duplicate detection.]

Field 007

Field 007 is mandatory in records for electronic serials and electronic integrating resources

Guidelines for the use of 856 fields

March 2003 Revision. This document gives guidelines on the use of field 856 and is current as of March 2003. It includes all changes made to the field through the midwinter ALA conference held in January 2003. This field may be used in bibliographic or holdings records for resource when it or a subset of it is available electronically. In addition, it may be used to locate and access an electronic version of a non-electronic resource. The data in field 856 may be a Uniform Resource Identifier (URI), which is recorded in subfield $u.

Field 856 (R) contains the following elements

Indicators

First Indicator	**Access method**
#	No information provided
0	Email
1	FTP
2	Remote login (Telnet)
3	Dial-up
4	HTTP
7	Method specified in subfield $2
Second Indicator	**Relationship**
#	No information provided
0	Resource
1	Version of resource
2	Related resource
8	No display constant generatec
Subfield Codes	
$a	Host name (R)
$b	Access number (R)
$c	Compression information (R)
$d	Path (R)
$f	Electronic name (R)

$h	Processor of request (NR)
$i	Instruction (R)
$j	Bits per second (NR)
$k	Password (NR)
$i	Logon (NR)
$m	Contact for access assistance (R)
$n	Name of location of host (NR)
$o	Operating system (NR)
$p	Port (NR)
$q	Electronic format type (NR)
$r	Settings (NR)
$s	File size (R)
$t	Terminal emulation (R)
$u	Uniform Resource Identifier (R)
$v	Hours access method available (R)
$w	Record control number (R)
$x	Nonpublic note (R)
$y	Link text (R)
$z	Public note (R)
$2	Access method (NR)
$3	Materials specified (NR)
$6	Linkage (NR)
$8	Field link and sequence number (R)

Example:

LDR 02233cam 22003854a 4500

001			13140709
005			20030331114241.0
007			Co! ! ! !
008			010501s2000 ilu s 000 0deng
010			$a 2001561466
020			$a 0252025660
043	0	0	$a n-us-
082	0	4	$a 340.092 s2 21
245	0	4	$a The law practice of Abraham Lincoln $h [computer file] : $b complete documentary edition / $c [Martha L. Benner, Cullom Davis, editors].
260	#	#	$a New York : $b University of Illinois Press, $c c2000.
300	#	#	$a 3 computer optical discs ; $c 4 ¾ in. – $e user's manual (18 p. : ill. ; 23 cm.).
538	#	#	$a System requirements: Pentium PC; 32 MB RAM; windows 95 or windows NT 4.0; 130 MB free hard disk space; Adobe Acrobat Reader (included on disc 1); 8-bit, 256-color display with 640x480 resolution; DVD-ROM drive.
500			$a Title from disc label.

500			$a Project sponsored by Illinois.
520			$a First publicaticn of the Lincoln Legal Paapers to documents the law practice of Abraham Lincoln Legal Papers to document the law practice of Abraham Lincoln from 1836 to 1861. Includes documents for more than 5,600 cases and legal matters in which Lincoln participated. Users may search for cases by case name, participant, date, court, legal action, subject; or documents by document type, date, author or singer.
590	#	#	$a MSS84815
600	1	0	$a Lincoln, Abraham, $d 1809-1865 $x Career in Law.
600	1	0	$a Lincoln, Abraham, $d 1809-1865 $x Knowledge.
700	1		$a Benner, Martha L.
700	1		$a Davis, Clullom, $d 1935.
710	2		$a Lincoln Legal Papers (Project).
710	2		$a Illinois Historic Preservation Agency.
856	4	2	$3 Finding aid $u http://lcweb2.gov/ammem/ead/jackson.sgm
856	4	#	$3 Table of contents $u http://www.loc.gov/catdir/toc/93-3471.html

CHAPTER 8
Microform

CONTENTS

8.0 GENERAL RULES

A microform may be an original publication or a reproduction of existing textual or graphic material. For microform reproductions of previously existing materials that are made for preservation purposes and for microform dissertations and other microform reproductions.

In microform, the bibliographic data transcribe the original work to being reproduced in the following areas:

* title and statement of responsibility
* edition
* material (or type of publication) specific details
* publication, distribution, etc.
* physical description
* series
* note
* standard number and terms of availability

8.1 TITLE AND STATEMENT OF RESPONSIBILITY AREA

The title proper and statement of responsibility relating to person or bodies in transcribe as instructed in general rules for description. The microform includes microfilms, microfiches or microopaques. The information sources and general material description as per AACR2R given below.

Chief source of information

1. Title frame
2. Eye-readable data at the top of the fiche (if no title on title frame)
3. Accompanying eye-readable materials or the

container (if title is a shortened form on the "header")

For reproductions on microfilm the chief source of information is the title frame, unless: there is no title frame; the information on the title frame is insufficient or is presented in such a way so as to cause doubt as to its reliability or accuracy.

If either of these criteria apply, treat the rest of the item (including the reproduced title page or reproduced title page substitute of the original) as the chief source of information.

For reproductions on microfiche, the chief source of information is the title frame, unless: there is no title frame; the information on the title frame is insufficient or is presented in such a way so as to cause doubt as to its reliability or accuracy.

If either of these criteria apply, treat the "header" as the chief source of information unless the title appears in a shortened form on the "header" and appears in a fuller form on the accompanying eye-readable materials or container. In such a case, treat the accompanying eye-readable materials or container as the chief source of information.

However, if the information on the "header" or accompanying eye-readable materials is insufficient or is presented in such a way so as to cause doubt as to its reliability or accuracy, treat the rest of the item (including the reproduced title page or reproduced title page substitute of the original) as the chief source of information.

Information on title frame:

Title: Chemical processing

Microfilmed by: Micromedia Ltd. Hull, Quebec 1986

Information on caption of the original (i.e. reproduced title page substitute): Canadian chemical journal Published monthly by the Biggar Press, Toronto, Canada, 1917

Transcription: Canadian chemical journal [microform]. —

Hull, Quebec : Micromedia Ltd., 1986-

For this serial microreproduction, as the title frame information is considered to be inaccurate for the transcription of the title, the rest of the item becomes the chief source of information. The title is, therefore, taken from the reproduced title page substitute (i.e. caption) of the original. The publication information is taken from the title frame i.e. the micropublisher is the publisher of this microreproduction).

Optional addition. General material designation

Use the general material designation "microform".

245	0	0	$a Oklahoma $h [microform] ; $b Carousel ; South Pacific ...

Items without a collective title

The option is applied occasionally. However, always apply the option in the following situation. For serials reproduced in microform, if the title of a serial changes within a microform item, make a separate description for each title.

8.2 EDITION AREA

The option is not applied. Any edition information supplied by the cataloguer is given in the notes area.

Edition statement: Give parallel edition statements in accordance with the provisions established under "Levels of Detail in Description".

8.3 MATERIAL SPECIFIC DETAILS

For serials reproduced in microform, give the numbering of the first issue of the original. This designation may or may not represent the designation of the first available issue of the microreproduction.

8.4 PUBLICATION, DISTRIBUTION, ETC., AREA

The option is applied occasionally. Add the name and place of the distributor when the information is necessary for clarification and is readily ascertainable. Liberal use of the option is discouraged and no strict uniformity is expected. A source note is preferred if the distributor is Canadian.

Optional addition. Statement of function of publisher, distributor, etc.

The option is applied when the information is necessary for clarification and is readily ascertainable. Liberal use of the option is discouraged and no strict uniformity is expected.

8.5 PHYSICAL DESCRIPTION AREA

Apply this rule, whenever possible, to express the fractional extent of a serial reproduced in microform which changes its title within a microform item.

on reels 1-2 of 5 microfilm reels

on reels 2-5 of 5 microfilm reels

on reels 10-12 of microfilm reels

Dimensions: In giving the dimensions of an item requiring more than one measurement, use a lower-case "x" as the multiplication sign to separate each of the measurements.

; 9 x 19 cm ; 11 x 15 cm-12 x 17 cm

8.6 SERIES AREA

Series recorded as instruction in 1.6

8.7 NOTE AREA

5xx Note Field (in order if applicable)

500 Nature, scope, or artistic or other form of an item

546 Language

500 Source of title proper

500 Edition and history

500 Physical description: reduction ratio, reader, film,

500 Dissertations

500 Audience

520 Summary

505 Contents

533 Reproduction Note (R) Give in a single note (533 field) all other details relating to the reproduction and its ublication/availability. Include in the note the following bibliographic data in the order listed:

* specific material designation of the microform
* place and name of the agency responsible for the reproduction
* date of the reproduction
* physical description of the microform series statement of the reproduction (if applicable)

Descriptive data for a reproduction of an original item when the main portion of the bibliographic record describes the original item and the data differ.

Examples :

533	#	#	$a Microfilm. $b Washington, D.C. : $c United States Historical Documents Institute, $d [1972] $e 12 reeks; 35 nn, $7 s1972####dcun#a.

Note: Consider the "agency responsible for the reproduction" to be the agency that selected the material to be filmed, arranged for filming, exercised control over production formats, has overall responsibility for quality, etc. If the agency is unknown, give "[s.n.]." Transcribe also the name of the agency from which to secure copies or the agency that made the microform if the agency is named in one of the prescribed sources for the publication, distribution, etc., area (11.0B2).

8.8 STANDARAD NUBER AND TERMS OF AVAILABILITY AREA

The option is generally not applied. The option, however, will be applied (i.e., include the price) to preliminary CIP items. Do not update (i.e., neither delete nor change) this information upon receipt of the item.

Qualification: The option is applied only as a qualification to the standard number whenever applicable. Terms of availability are generally not used (see rule interpretation 11.8D). When required, use a brief qualification (see 1.8E1) and note that consistency of terminology is not necessary. Do not make up and use qualifiers additional to that found in the transcribed data.

8.9 MONOGRAPH CATALOGING CHEAT SHEET (for microfiches, microfilms)

007 – Microform

A transparent or opaque medium bearing microimages that are too small to be read without magnification. A microform may be an original publication or a reproduction of existing textual or graphic material.

Character Positions

00	Category of material h Microform
01	Specific material designation. Indicates the special class of microform to which the item belongs.
02	Undefined
03	Positive/negative aspect. Indicates the positive/negative polarity of the microform.
04	Dimensions. Indicates the dimensions of the microform, not the dimensions of the image.
05	Reduction ratio range. Indicates the reduction ratio range of the microform. The specific reduction is recorded in 007/06-08 (Reduction ratio).
06-08	Reduction ratio. The specific reduction ratio of the microform, recorded as three digits. The number is right justified and each unused position contains a zero. A hyphen is used for any unknown portion of the reduction ratio.
09	Color. Indicates the color of the image.
10	Emulsion on film. Indicates the type of light-sensitive material on the film.
11	Generation. Indicates the generation of the microform.
12	Base of film. Indicates the base of the film.

Example of a master negative microfilm reel:

LDR 01157cas 22003257a 4500

007			H d afb —baca
007			H d bfb — baaa
008			780911d19241930cu qr p ꝛ 0 b0spa d
010			$a 78646871
043			$a nwcu
050	0	0	$a Microfilm 32980 GR
245	0	0	$a Archivos del folklore cubano $h [microform]
260			$a La Habana, $b Cultural S.A. [etc.]
300			$a 5 v. $b ill. $c 24 cm.
310			$a Qyarterktm $b 1928-30
321			$a Irregular, $b 1924-27
362			$a v, 1-5m no. 3; enero 1924-jul./set. 1930
515			$a No more published
550			$a Published for the Sociedad del Folklore Cubano
500			$a Edited by Fernando Ortiz
533			$a Microfilm.$m v. 1-3 (1924-1930) $b Washington, D.C. : $c Library of Congress Preservation Microfiming Program : $c Availabvle from Library of Congress Photoduplication Services. $e microfim reels ; 35 mm.

650		0	$a Folklore $z Cuba $v Periodicals
651		0	$a Cuba $x Social life and customs $v Periodicals
700	1		$a Ortiz, Fernando, $d 1881-1969, $e ed
710	2		$a Sociedad del Folklore Cubano
776	1		$a Original $w (DLC) 28010134

CHAPTER 9
Continuing Resources

CONTENTS

9.A INTRODUCTION

Continuing Resources has been expanded to include resources that have now encompasses:

* Successively issued resources (i.e., serials);
* Ongoing integrating resources (e.g., updating loose-leafs, updating web sites);
* Some categories of finite resources (i.e., reprints of serials, resources with characteristics of serials but whose duration is limited, and finite integrating resources).

Definition

Continuing Resource: A continuing resource is defined as 'A bibliographic resource that is issued over time with no predetermined conclusion. Continuing resources include serials and ongoing integrating resources.'

" A bibliographic resource that consists of a base volume(s) updated by separate pages, which are inserted, replaced, removed, and/or substituted".

— *Hirons and Kawkins, 2003*

" A bibliographic resource issued over time with no predetermined conclusion".

Serial: The provisions for the descriptive cataloging of serials are included in revised Chapter 12, "Continuing Resources," but the categories of materials to be cataloged as serials have been expanded to include unnumbered monographic series and some publications of limited duration that have the characteristics of serials (e.g., a daily bulletin issued during a non-recurring meeting, a quarterly activities report of a project, an annual report of an expedition)

A serial is defined as 'A continuing resource issued in succession of discrete parts, usually bearing numbering, that has no predetermined conclusion. Examples of serial include journals, magazines, electronic journals, continuing directories, annual reports, newspapers, and monographic series.'

Integrating Resource: An integrating resource is defined as 'A bibliographic resource that is added to or changed by means of updates that do not remain discrete and are integrated into the whole. Integrating resources can be finite or continuing. Examples of integrating resources include updating loose-leafs and updating web sites.'

9.B GENERAL RULES

Cumulations: The publication pattern of some issued have in cumulation and it has been rearranged, corrected, and perhaps expanded and reissued as a cumulation for a certain periods. These cumulations may or may not have the same title as the individual issues but usually the contents of both the individual issues and the cumulation are basically the same.

Create separate records for cumulation in following cases:

1) If the individual issues and the cumulation have the same title but different designation systems, e.g., the individual issues have volume numbering but the cumulation has only a date designation; e.g.

   Law book guide. — Vol. 1, no. l(Jan. 1973)-

   (Monthly, except July and August)

   International law book. — 1993-(Annual)

2) If the individual issues and the cumulation have different titles.

   Index medicus. — New ser., v. l, no. 1(Jan. 1960)-

   (Monthly)

Cumulated Library Index. — Vol. 1 (1980)- (Annual)

Quarterly cumulative index medicus. Quarterly, with every

2nd issue cumulative for 6 months, Began with: Jan.-Mar. 1927.

Generally, do not create separate records:

1) If the individual issues and the cumulation have a continuous numeric designation; e.g.

International nursing index. — Vol. 1, no. 1(Jan. 1966)-

(Quarterly; the first three issues called v. I, no. 1-3; the fourth issue, an annual cumulation, called v. I, no. 4)

2) If the individual issues and the cumulation have the same title and are identified by date designations only.

Library of Congress

Library of Congress name headings with references.

-- Jan./Mar. 1974- (Quarterly; the first three issues called Jan./Mar. 1974-July/Sept. 1974; the fourth issue, an annual cumulation, called 1974). When in doubt, prefer separate records.

Serials issued in parts: A serial bibliographic unit that is physically attached to or contained in another serial unit such that retrieved of the component part is dependent on the physical identification and location of the host item or container. The record container fields that describe the component part and data that identify the host item Entry (fields 773)

Create separate records:

1) If the individual parts are unnumbered or otherwise undesignated as parts of one publication;

Singapore Airlines. Annual report. Operating review

Singapore Airlines. Annual report. Financial report

(The operating review and financial report are two parts that make up the airline's annual report) the individual parts have their own numbering system or date designation;

Chemical abstracts. Chemical substance index. — 101 CS1 (Jan.-June 1984)-

Chemical abstracts. Formula index. — 101 F1 (July-Dec. 1984)-

Journal of polymer science. Part A,General papers.— Vol. 1, no. 1 (Jan. 1963)-

Journal of polymer science. Part B, Polymer letters. — Vol. 1, no. 1 (Jan. 1963)-

Generally, do not create separate records if:

1) the individual parts do not have a numbering system or date or designation of their own;

U.S. physicians reference listing. — 1974-

(Each directory is published in ten volumes with a reference volume and numbered v. 1-11)

Who's who in computers and data processing. — 1971-

(Issued in three volumes:

v. 1, Systems analysts and programmers;

v. 2, Data processing managers and directors;

v. 3, Other computer professionals)

2) the parts have a continuous pagination or enumeration;

Journal of the Indian Institute of Science.

(Issued in three sections: Section A = Vol. 59, no. 1, 3, 5, 7, 9; Section B = Vol. 59, no. 2, 6, 10; Section C = Vol. 59, no. 4, 8, 12)

Inorganica chimica acta.

(Issued in three sections:Articles and letters = Vols. 96-105; Bioinorganic chemistry articles and letters = Vols. 106-108;F-block elements articles and letters Vols. 109-110)

3) the parts are not available separately;

4) the parts appear to be intended to be used together.

When in doubt, prefer separate records.

9.0 CHIEF SOURCE OF INFORMATION

The chief source is the title page or its substitute: Analytical title page (for series), Cover, caption, masthead, editorial page, colophon, preliminaries, other pages.

Note when chief source is not the title page, e.g.

500			$a Title from cover.

Direct access electronic resources

The provision for electronic resources use the physical carrier or its labels for direct access electronic resources takes precedence over provisions in chapter electronic resources for chief source of information.

Prescribed sources of information

Consider that the prescribed source for the Numbering area is the whole resource.

Fields 100-130 contain a name or a uniform title heading used as a main entry in bibliographic records.

100 - Main Entry—Personal Name (NR)

110 - Main Entry—Corporate Name (NR)

111 - Main Entry—Meeting Name (NR)

130 - Main Entry—Uniform Title (NR)

Main entry under Personal Name (100)

Main entry is the primary access pint under which a serial will be cited. Some have argued that there is no need for main/added entry designations in the online environment. But, the main entry is used for single entry citations, such as check-in files, union lists, ISSN registry, indexing & abstracting services, etc.

For serials, the choice of main entry is important because changes in the main entry may require a new record. Main entry under personal authorship is rare in serials ,e.g.

100	1	0	$a Gresham, Don.
245	1	4	$a The country music newsletter.

Main entry corporate body is common (110)

Works of an administrative nature about the body itself, its policies, procedures, finances (e.g. annual reports); most common category for serials. Works of legal nature, many are serials. Works recording the collective thought of body (reports of committees & commissions). Conference proceedings are often catalogued as serials, e.g.

110	2		$a International Centre for Settlement of Investment Disputes.
245	1	0	$a Annual report / $c ICSID.

Main entry under title is the most common for serials, e.g.

245	0	0	$a Serials librarian.

Main entry Uniform titles (130)

If the title is not unique, may need uniform title with a qualifying phrase, e.g.

130	0	0	$a Georgia straight (Vancouver, B.C.: 1982).
222			$a Georgia straight $b (1982).
245	0	0	$a Georgia straight.

130	0	0	$a Atlantic monthly (Boston, Mass.: 1993).
222		4	$a The Atlantic monthly $b (1993).
245	0	4	$a The Atlantic monthly.

Items with several chief sources of information: For the purposes of cataloging printed serials, the description is based on the first issue or first available issue. If that issue has maore than one chief source of information, prefer (in this order)

a) the right hand (recto) of two facing sources;

b) the first of two or more sources, both or all of which are on the recto;

c) the source that occurs first in the following list: English, French, German, Spanish, Latin, any other language using the roman alphabet, Greek, Russian, any other language using the Cyrillic alphabet, Hebrew, and other language using the Hebrew alphabet, any other language.

Integrating resources: Until rule 1.0H is revised to incorporate integrating resources, apply the general principle in 12.0B of using the most current information.

9.1 ITLE AND STATEMENT OF RESPONSIBILITY

Fields 210-247 contain the title of the item described in the bibliographic record and variant titles that also apply to the item. These fields may be used to generate access points and to display notes for the various titles.

210 - Abbreviated Key Title (NR)

222 - Key Title (R)

240 - Uniform Title (NR)

242 - Translation of Title by Cataloging Agency (R)

243 - Collective Uniform Title (NR)

245 - Title Statement (NR)

246 - Varying form of Title (R)

247 - Former Title or Title Variations (R)

Title: If the chief source of information for the first issue or first available issue bears no title and no name of a person or corporation body that could be used as title record as the title proper, enclosed in square brackets, a title derived from outside the first issue, preferably from the chief source of information for the first subsequent issue that does bear a title.

If the title proper appears in two or more languages or scripts on the chief source of information, choose the title proper by reference to the order of titles on, or layout of, the chief source of information. If one title is given prominence, prefer that as the title proper.

Most serials entered under title proper includes subfields $a (title), $n (numbering of section), and $p (name of section).

e.g.

245	0	4	$a The bookman. $n Part B.
245	0	4	$a Country profile. $p China, Mongolia.

Other title information

Include other title information if it includes an initialism, or contains a statement of responsibility, or when title proper is just the name of the corporate body. Otherwise include as a quoted note. e.g.

On serial ER Economic Reform

In record

245	0	0	$a Economic reform : $b ER.
245	0	4	$a Focus : $b a journal of legal studies.

Or

245	0	0	$a Camera obscura.
500			$a "A journal of feminism and film history."

Title proper in full and as initialism or acronym (210)

If the chief source of information gives as the title both an initialism or acronym and the full form of the initialism or acronym give the full form as the title proper even when:

* the initialism or acronym alone, without the full from, is consistently given on other sources in the item (cover, caption, masthead, editorial pages, colophon, etc.; or
* the initialims or acronym is consistently given noticeably greater prominence than the full form through layout, size, typeface, itc., on other colophon, etc.

Record the initialism or acronym as other title information, e.g.

210			$a Surg. clin. North Am.
210			$a Annu. rep. - Dep. Public Welfare $b(Chic.).

Variant title (246)

A form of the title appearing on different parts of an item or a portion of the title proper, or an alternative form of the title when the form differs significantly from the title contained in field 245.

Provide additional access, if other titles such as cover title, parallel tittles, portions of title, variations of title (initialisms, title with &, etc.), or minor title changes.

Indicator values determine whether or not an added entry is generated and the wording of a display constant, such as "Cover title" or "Spine title", e.g.

245	0	4	$a The miner & workman's advocate.
246	3		$a Miner and workman's advocate.

Change in title proper. Integrating resources (247)

Generally, change the title and, if appropriate, the statement of responsibility to reflect the current iteration when the title proper changes on a subsequent issue or part.

A former title proper when one cataloging record represents several titles associated with an entity.

Existing record:

245	0	0	$a Resources for Library Information Science.

Same record updated:

245	0	0	$a Resources for Library Information Science.
247	0	0	$a $a Library information resources $fMar. 10, 2000.

Same record updated again:

245	0	0	$a Resources for Library Information Science.
247	0	0	$a Library information resources $fMar. 10, 2000.
247	1	0	$a Library information resources $fSept. 14, 2001.

If, however, the change in title is accompanied by an edition statement change, refer to guidelines at rule interpretation 21.2B for treatment of the integrating resource(s).

General Material Designation: Add a general material designation to all records for serials except those for eye-readable printed copy (text), unless the "GMD" is to be further qualified.

Statement of responsibility

For serials, a statement of responsibility is usually a prominently placed corporate body appearing on the chief source along with the title. Editors are not given in statement of responsibility, e.g.

245	0	0	$a New and events / $c Art Institute of Pune.

9.2 EDITION AREA

Information relating to the edition of a work. Edition statements indicating volume numbering or designation, or chronological coverage in the numeric and/or alphabetic. If edition statement appears in more than one language or script, transcribe the statement that is in the language or script of the title proper. If necessary, add an appropriate word or abbreviation to the statement.

If there is no indication of edition given in the prescribed sources of information for the edition area, an edition statement may be supplied provided the conditions.

Change in edition information. Integrating resources

For change(s) in edition information, refer to rule 21.2B and 21.3B1b for treatment of the integrating resource(s).

Edition Statement for serials differ from monographs because they must apply to all issues of the serials. The edition statement often reflects the audience for that serial and there are often editions published simultaneously, e.g.

250	0	0	$a Northwest ed.

9.3 MATERIAL SPECIFIC DETAILS AREA

It contains the beginning/ending date(s) of an item and/or the sequential designations used on each part. The numeric and/or alphabetic designation of the first issue of a serial as given in that issue should be given in abbreviation as instructed. The 362 field contains data about the first and/or last issue of a serial. This data may be numeric, chronological or both, e.g.

362	0		$a Vol. 8 (1995)-
362	0		$a Vol. 8, no. 3 (Mar. 1998).

Record terms such as "bulletin," etc., (in an abbreviated form if appropriate) as part of the numeric and/or alphabetic designation provided the term is clearly presented as such in the prescribed sources of information. If the numeric and/or alphabetic designation for the first issue spans two or more sequential numbers and/or letters, use a diagonal slash to separate the numbers and/or letters regardless of the punctuation given on the item itself.

On source: Volume 4, Numbers 1 & 2

Transcription: Vol. 4, no. 1/2-

On source: Issue 3-4

Transcription: Issue 3/4-

If the numeric and/or alphabetic designation appears in two or more languages or scripts, record only the form that is in the language o the title proper and mention in notes area.

Chronological designation

If the first issue is identified by a chronological designation covering more than one calendar year, month, day, etc., use a diagonal slash to separate the years, etc., regardless of the punctuation given on the item itself.

On source: 1967-68

Transcription: 1967/68-

On source: 1976-77-78

Transcription: 1976/77/78-

On source: Aug.-Sept. 1978

Transcription: Aug./Sept. 1978-

If the first issue is identified by a chronological designation that includes the name of a day of the week, omit the name of the day when recording the designation.

On source: Volume 1, number 1. Wednesday, July 1, 1953

Transcription: Vol. 1, no. 1 (July 1, 1953)-

No designation on first issue

If the first issue of a serial lacks a numeric, alphabetic, chronological, or other designation, give [No. 1]- or its equivalent only if the description is based on the first issue of the serial.

Completed serials (ceased serials)

If the serial completed, give the designation of

the first issue followed by the designation of the last issue; e.g.

Vol. 3, no. 6 (Aug./Sept. 1970) – v. 5, no. 3 (Mar. 1972)

9.4 PUBLICATION, DISTRIBUTION, ETC., AREA

The publishing statement and the 260 field is used in much the same way as for monographs when recording place of publication (subfield a) and publisher (subfield b). The former rule that allowed for abbreviating the name of the publisher has been dropped from AACR2R. This is because online catalogues allow searching on the publisher field. The dates of publication are only entered if the first and/or last issues the title are in hand. If neither are in hand the subfield c is left blank, e.g.

260			$a Boston : $b Atlantic Monthly Co., $c 1993-
260			$a Delft, Netherlands: $bNationalTranslations Centre, $c 1978-1986.

The option is applied occasionally.

Add the name and place of the distributor when the information is necessary for clarification and is readily ascertainable. Liberal use of t he option is discouraged and no strict uniformity is expected.

Optional addition. Statement of function of publisher, distributor, etc.

The option is applied when the information is necessary for clarification and is readily ascertainable. Liberal use of the option is discouraged and no strict uniformity is expected.

Place of manufacture, name of manufacturer, date of manufacture.

The option is applied if such information is "considered important", i.e. rarely.

9.5 PHYSICAL DESCRIPTION AREA

Physical Description: A physical description of the described item, including its extent, dimensions, and such other physical details as a description of any accompanying materials and unit type and size.

Extent of item (including specific material designation) For printed serials completed in less than one volume, use the abbreviation "v." as the specific material designation.Do not use "no." or "pt." Also do not use "v. in," etc.

Fields – 300 Indicator – Undefined

Subfield Codes - $a Extent (R)
$b Other physical details (NR)
$c Dimensions (R)
$e Accompanying material (NR)
$f Type of unit (R)
$g Size of unit (R)

300			$a 11 v. : $bill. ; $c24 cm.

Dimensions

In giving the dimensions of an item requiring more than one measurement, use a lower-case "x" as the multiplication sign to separate each of the measurements, e.g.

300			$a v. :$b ill.; $c 20 x 32 cm.

Accompanying material

The option is applied judiciously. It will be considered when the accompanying material is substantial in volume.

300			$a v. : $b ill. (some col.);$c 35 mm. + booklets.

9.6 SERIES AREA

Series statement are handled in serials records in the same was as in monographic records with one exception : recording series numbering. Since the serial record represents the entire run of the serial, and the series numbering is likely to change with each issue, series numbering is normally omitted.

9.7 NOTE AREA

Notes should be informative and most optional. The notes area is used to record many pieces of information that do not fit elsewhere and to record some of those many changes that can occur in serials over a period of time. Some notes are as follows:

Frequency

Make notes on the frequency of the serial unless it is apparent from the content of the title and statement of responsibility area or is unknown, e.g. Annual, Quarterly, Monthly.

Current Publication Frequency: The current stated frequency of either an item or an update to an item. Dates are included when the beginning date of the current frequency is not the same as the beginning date of publication. These data are related to coded data in field 008/18 (Frequency) and 008/19 (Regularity), e.g.

310	#	#	$a Monthly, including annual cumulation.

Former Publication Frequency: Physical description information for an item that requires technical equipment for its use or an item that has special conservation or storage needs, e.g.

321	#	#	$a Monthly, $bMar. 1972-Dec. 1980.
321	#	#	$a Semiannual, $b1981-1982.

Integrating resources: Always make a note on the known frequency of a serial or of the updates to an integrating resource even if the frequency is apparent from the rest of the description.

Allergy quarterly. — Quarterly.

Dolls, dolls, dolls (New Westminster, B.C.)

Dolls, dolls, dolls. — Bimonthly.

Include the word "updated" or "updates" with the frequency word to clarify that the frequency is not of the resource itself but that of the updates (e.g., "updated quarterly," "Monthly updates").

Relationship note with other serials (580)

In referring to another serial, use the title proper, uniform title, name-title proper, name-uniform title (or whatever combination of elements that uniquely identifies the serial) under which the serial has been entered in the catalogue.

If the heading in that record is in pre-AACR 2R form, change the heading in the record to AACR 2R form and use the revised form in the citation. Do not however, revise the choice of entry.

If the serial referred to has not been entered in

the catalogue, attempt to formulate the citation according to AACR 2R rules for choice and form of entry. If it is impossible to determine from the information available the choice and form of entry that would be required under AACR 2R, use in the citation as close an approximation as is possible to the title proper.

A description of the complex relationship between the described item and other items when an intelligible note cannot be generated from data in the linking entry fields 760-787.

Example:

580			$a Continued in 1980 by: Indian Library Journal.
580			$a Cumulates: Indian Bibliographie. Chemical.
580			$a Merged with: Index chemicus (Philadelphia, Pa. : 1977), to form: Current abstracts of chemistry and index chemicus (Philadelphia, Pa : 1978).
580			$a Continued by: Ionospheric predictions issued by the laboratory under its later name: Institute for Telecommunication Sciences and Aeronomy.
580			$a Continues: Nova Scotia Library Association. Members handbook.
580			$a Continued by: News/views (Ontario Real Estate Association : 1984).

580			$a Split into: Report on research and development / Department of Energy, and: Report on research and Development / Department of Industry.

Indexes (555)

Information on the availability of cumulative indexes for serials or finding aids and similar control materials for archival and manuscripts control and visual materials.

Do not give a note for an index to a single volume or single year of a serial publication unless the index is issued separately and is not intended to be bound with the volume it indexes.

In general, make notes on the presence of cumulative indexes. If, however, the index is published separately and is not issued by the entity responsible for the serial being indexed, create a separate bibliographic record (monograph or serial as appropriate) for the index.

If an index is represented by its own bibliographic record, make a linking note to the related work being indexed on the bibliographic record for the separately catalogued index.

As well, make a reciprocal linking note to the bibliographic record for the serial being indexed.

For the treatment of an index which is represented by its own bibliographic record and catalogued as a monograph.

555			$a Vols. 1 (1925)-10 (1955) in v. 11, no. 1.
555	8		$a Finding aid available in the Manuscript Reading Room and on Internet. $u http://hdl.loc.gov/locmss/eadmss/ms996001.

Copy being described, library's holdings, and restrictions on use

The following rules of archiving:

a) earlier titles of electronic serials that do not retain those earlier title(s);

b) earlier iterations of integrating resources will be accommodated by multiple 856s reflecting the appropriate URL.

a) electronic serial that does not retain earlier title existing record

245	0	0	$a Asian age $h[electronic resource].
856	4	0	$u [URL of serial]
856	4	0	$u [URL of archived serial(NLC's website)].

Same record updated

245	0	0	$a Asian age online $h [electronic resource].
247	1	1	$u Asian age.

547	#	#	$a All issues originally published with titleAsian age have been reformatted with the new the new title: Asian age online.
856	4	0	$u [URL of serial with new/ current title (Publisher's website)].
856	4	0	$u [URL of archived serial, issues under original title] $z Vols. 1-15 under original title: Asian age.
856	4	0	$u[URL of archived serial, issues under new/current title]$zVols. 16-under new title: Asian age online.

b) integrating resource existing record

245	0	0	$a Scholarship opportunities for future math teachers $h [electronic resource].
246	1	3	$a Math education scholarships.
500	#	#	$a Description based on: Release 5, published 1999.
856	4	0	$u [URL of integrating resource].
856	4	0	$u [URL of archived iterations of integrating resource (NLC's website)].

Same record updated

245	0	0	$a Future math teachers' scholarshipopportunities $h [electronic resource].
246	1	#	$i Title in HTML header, release 5 published 1999:$a Math education scholarships.
247	1	0	$a Scholarship opportunities for future math teachers $f release 5, published 1999.
500	#	#	$a Description based on: Release 9, published 2001.
856	4	0	$u [URL of integrating resource with new/current title (Publisher's website)].
856	4	0	$u [URL of archived integrating resource (NLC's website), iterations under original title] $z -release 5 under original title: Scholarship opportunities for future math teachers.
856	4	0	$u [URL of archived integrating resource (NLC's website), iterations under new/current title] $z release 9- under new title:Future math teachers' scholarship opportunities.

Item described

Textual information on the language of the described materials. A description of the alphabet, script, or other symbol system (e.g., arabic alphabet, ASCII, musical notation system, bar code, logarithmic graphing) may also be included. Coded language information is contained in fields 008/35- 37 and/or 041.

When referring to the issue on which the description is based, give the numbering as given in that issue, following the recording conventions.

If the numbering appears in two or more languages or scripts in the issue on which the description is based, record only the form that is in the language of the title proper (or if not applicable, the form appearing first) regardless of the language of description used in the notes area. For serials reproduced in microform, if the numbering of the first issue of the original does not represent the designation of the first available issue of the microreproduction, give the item described.

546	#	#	$a English, French, or German.
546	#	#	$a Latin; $bRoman alphabet.

Numbering Peculiarities Note (515)

An unformatted description of irregularities and peculiarities in numbering or publishing patterns, report year coverage, revised editions, and/or issuance in parts.

515	#	#	$a Vols. 50 and 51 combined.
515	#	#	$a Suspended 1936-1939, 1946.

Supplement Note (525)

Information on the existence of supplements or special issues (usually unnamed) that are neither cataloged as separate records nor recorded in field 770 (Supplement/Special Issue Entry).

525	#	#	$a Supplements accompany some issues.
525	#	#	$a Separately paged supplement accompanies v. 3.

Issuing Body Note (550)

Information about the current and former issuing bodies of a serial.

550	#	#	$a Vols. for 1880-1900 issued by the Bureau of Statistics (Dept. of Finace); 1901-21 by the Bureau of Statistics (Dept. of Commerce); 1922-30 by the Bureau of Economic; 1931- - by the Bureau of the Census.

Preceding Entry (780)

Immediate predecessor of the target item (chronological relationship). When a note is generated from this field, the introductory term or phrase may be generated based on the value in the second indicator position.

Indicators: First	0	Display note
	1	Do not display note
Second	0	Continues
	1	Continues in part

2	Supersedes
3	Supersedes in part
4	Formed by the union of ... and ...
5	Absorbed
6	Absorbed in part
7	Separated from

Subfields:

$a	Main entry heading (NR)
$b	Edition (NR)
$c	Qualifying information (NR)
d	Place, publisher, and date of publication (NR)
$g	Relationship information (R)
$h	Physical description (NR)
$i	Display text (NR)
$k	Series data for related item (R)
$m	Material-specific details (NR)
$n	Note (R)
$o	Other item identifier (R)
$r	Report number (R)
$s	Uniform title (NR)
$t	Title (NR)
$u	Standard Technical Report Number (NR)
$w	Record control number (R)
$x	International Standard Serial Number (NR)

$y	CODEN designation (NR)
$z	International Standard Book Number (R)
$6	Linkage (NR)
$7	Control subfield (NR)
0	Type of main entry heading
1	Form of name
2	Type of record
3	Bibliographic level
$8	Field link and sequence number (R)

Examples:

780	0	0	$a American Hospital Association. $t Bulletin of the American Hospital Association $w (OCoLC)1777831.
780	0	1	$t Annales scientifiques de l'Universite de Besancon $w OCoLC)6179013.
780	0	4	$t Annales de geophysique $x 0003-4029 $w (OCoLC)1481255 $w (DLC)###52016346.

Succeeding Entry (785)

Immediate successor to the target item (chronological relationship). When a note is generated from this field, the introductory phrase may be generated based on the value in the second indicator position.

Indicators: First	0	Display note
	1	Do not display note
Second	0	Continued by
	1	Continued in part by
	2	Superseded by
	3	Superseded in part by
	4	Absorbed by
	5	Absorbed in part by
	6	Split into ... and ...
	7	Merged with ... to form ...
	8	Changed back to
Subfields:	$a	Main entry heading (NR)
	$b	Edition (NR)
	$c	Qualifying information (NR)
	$d	Place, publisher, and date of publication (NR)
	$g	Relationship information (R)
	$h	Physical description (NR)
	$i	Display text (NR)
	$k	Series data for related item (R)
	$m	Material-specific details (NR)
	$n	Note (R)
	$o	Other item identifier (R)
	$r	Report number (R)
	$s	Uniform title (NR)
	$t	Title (NR)
	$u	Standard Technical Report Number (NR)

$w	Record control number (R)
$x	International Standard Serial Number (NR)
$y	CODEN designation (NR)
$z	International Standard Book Number (R)
$6	Linkage (NR)
$7	Control subfield (NR)
0	Type of main entry heading
1	Form of name
2	Type of record
3	Bibliographic level
$8	Field link and sequence number (R)

Examples:

785	0	0	$t TEIC quarterly seismological bulletin x0741-1898 $w (OCoLC)8978559 $w (DLC)sc#83007721.
785	0	1	$a Southeastern College Art Conference. $t SECAC newsletter $w (OCoL-C)4973820.

9.8 STANDARD NUMBER (020/022)

Do not give an ISBN for an issue or part of a serial.

ISSN: The ISSN, a unique identification number assigned to a continuing resource, e.g.

020	0	#	$a 0145-0808 $z 0361- 7106.

ISSN recorded in field 022 by national centers under the auspices of the ISSN Network for key title. A note formatted as ISSN [number] = [Key Title] may be generated from data in field 022 (International Standard Serial Number) and field 222.

Terms of ISSN

ISSN may be assigned to on-line continuing resource, which meets requirements of the following definition:

* It is published periodically under the same title indefinitely, with no predetermined conclusion
* It is published
  a. in discrete parts, bearing numbering, or
  b. in form of edited web page (pages) containing full text articles, while new articles are amended/updated with specific predetermined periodicity.
* Archive of previously published articles is available/accessible.

If the publication is published simultaneously on two or more media, each version is assigned a separate ISSN.

ISSN is not assigned to following types of Internet resources:

* personal, advertising and promotional web pages, on-line bulletins of municipalities and schools, resources containing information for limited audience. At present, such resources are not among ISSN priorities.
* resources containing only article abstracts without access to full texts
* resources suspected to fall under definition of §§

198, 198a a 205 of Penal Law (Act No. 412/2002 Coll.)

Integrating resources

If an integrating resource has both an ISSN and an ISBN, give both.

Optional addition. Terms of availability

The option is generally not applied, however, will be applied (i.e., include the price) to preliminary CIP items. Do not update (i.e., neither delete nor change) this information upon receipt of the item.

9.9 MARC 21 FORMAT WITH EXAMPLES

LEADER - A fixed field that comprises the first 24 character positions (00-23) of each record and provides information for the processing of the record.

00-04 - Record Length: The computer-generated, five-character numeric string that specifies the length of the entire record. The number is right justified and each unused position contains a zero.

05 - Record status: System generated. Code "n" (new) changes to "c" (corrected or revised) after record is changed and saved. Change non-MARC codes (e.g. "m" or "r") to "c".

06 - Type of record: A one-character code that indicates the characteristics of and defines the components of the record.

a Language material. This code is also used for microforms of language material.

c Printed music. This code is also used for microforms of printed music.

d Manuscript music. This code is also used for microforms of manuscript music.

e Printed map. This code is also used for microforms of printed maps.

f Manuscript map. This code is also used for microforms of manuscript maps.

g Projected medium. The described item is a motion picture, video recording, filmstrip, slide, transparency, or material specifically designed for overhead projection.

i Nonmusical sound recording.

j Musical sound recording.

k Two-dimensional nonprojectable graphic. This code is used for items such as activity cards, charts, collages, computer graphics, drawings, duplication masters, flash cards, paintings, photonegatives, photo prints, pictures, postcards, posters, prints, spirit masters, study prints, technical drawings, transparency masters, photomechanical reproductions, and reproductions of any of these.

m Electronic resources. The described item is numeric or textual data, computer software, or a combination of these types of information that are encoded for computer processing.

o Kit. The described item contains a mixture of components from two or more types of items, no one of which is the predominant constituent of the kit.

p Mixed material.

r Three-dimensional artifact or naturally occurring object. This code is used for such man-made objects as models, dioramas, games, puzzles, simulations, sculptures and other three-dimensional art works and their reproductions, exhibits, machines, clothing, toys, and stitchery. It also includes such naturally occurring objects as microscope specimens and other specimens mounted for viewing.

t Manuscript language material

07 - Bibliographic level: Indicates the bibliographic level of the record.

a Monographic component part. A monographic bibliographic unit that is physically attached to or contained in another unit such that the retrieval of the component part is dependent on the identification and location of the host item or container. The record contains fields that describe the component part and data that identify the host, field 773 (Host Item Entry).

b Serial component part. A serial bibliographic unit that is physically attached to or contained in another serial unit such that the retrieval of the component part is dependent on the physical identification and location of the host item or container. The record contains fields that describe the component part and data that identify the Host Item Entry (field 773).

c Collection. A made-up multipart group of items that were not originally published, distributed, or produced together. The record describes units defined by common provenance or administrative convenience for which the record is intended as the most comprehensive in the system.

d Subunit. A part of a collection, especially an archival unit described collectively elsewhere in the system. The record contains fields that describe the subunit and data that identify the Host Item Entry (field 773).

i Integrating resource. A bibliographic resource that is added to or changed by means of updates that do not remain discrete and are integrated into the whole. Examples include: Updating looseleafs and updating Web sites.

m Monograph/item. An item either complete in one part or intended to be completed in a finite number of separate parts.

s Serial. An item issued in successive parts bearing numerical or chronological designations and intended to be continued indefinitely.

08 - Type of control:

- No specific type of control

a - Archival control

09 - Character Coding Scheme: A one-character code that identifies the character-coding scheme used in the record.

- MARC-8 a - UCS/Unicode

17 – Encoding Level

18 – Item Information in Record

006 - FIXED-LENGTH DATA ELEMENTS - ADDITIONAL MATERIAL CHARACTERISTICS - Serials Do not use for accompanying material.

Field 006 is used when the Acquisitions Librarian requests that a monograph record (e.g. a record for an electronic database) be included in the journal title index. The 006 is coded to bring out the serial aspects of the electronic monograph record so that the title will be included in the MORRIS journal title index.

007 - PHYSICAL DESCRIPTION FIXED FIELD - GENERAL INFORMATION:

Do not use for serials in print format.

Do not code for accompanying material.

Code for microform. (See " MICROFORM")

008 - FIXED-LENGTH DATA ELEMENTS (FIXED FIELDS) - Serials

This field contains 40 character positions (00-39) that provide coded information about the record as a whole and about special bibliographic aspects of the item being cataloged. These coded data elements are potentially useful for retrieval and data management purposes.

Character positions 00-17 and 35-39 are defined the same across all types of material, with special consideration for position 06. The definition of character positions 18-34 was done independently for each type of material, although certain data elements are defined the same in the specifications for more than one type of material. When similar data elements are defined for inclusion in field 008 for different types of material, they occupy the same field 008 character positions.

5-05 Date entered on file

The computer-generated, six-character numeric string that indicates the date the MARC record was created. The date is recorded in the pattern yymmdd.

06 - Type of date: A one-character code that indicates the type of dates and the publication status.

- b No dates given; B.C. date involved
- c Continuing resource item currently published
- d Continuing resource item ceased publication
- e Detailed date
- i Inclusive dates of collection
- k Range of years of bulk of collection
- m Multiple dates
- n Dates unknown
- p Date of distribution/release/issue and production/recording session when different

q Questionable date

r Reprint/reissue date and original date

s Single known date/probable date

t Publication date and copyright date

u Continuing resource status unknown

| No attempt to code

07-10 - Date 1: The determination of dates for 008/07-10 is made concurrently with choice of code for 008/06

11-14 - Date 2: The determination of dates for 008/11-14 is made concurrently with choice of code for 008/06

15-17 - Place of publication: Must match 260 |a. Add or change if required. Required if applicable or readily available in OCLC.

18 - Frequency: A one-character code that indicates the frequency of the serial.

- No determinable frequency.

a Annual

b Bimonthly

c Semiweekly

d Daily

e Biweekly

f Semiannual

g Biennial

h Triennial

i Three times a week

j Three times a month

m Monthly

q Quarterly

s Semimonthly

t Three times a year

u Unknown

w Weekly

z Other

| No attempt to code

19 - Regularity: A one-character code that indicates the intended regularity of the serial.

n Normalized irregular

r Regular

u Unknown

x Completely irregular

| No attempt to code

20 - ISSN Center : (US, Canada, International, etc.)

21 - Type of continuing resource: A one-character code that indicates the type of serial.

None of the following (This code is also used for yearbooks and annual reports).

m Monographic series

n Newspaper

p Periodical

| No attempt to code

22 - Target Audience: A one-character code that indicates the audience for which the item is intended.

- Unknown or not specified

a Preschool

b Primary

c Pre-adolescent

d Adolescent

e Adult

f Specialized

g General

j Juvenile

| No attempt to code

23 - Form of Original Item: A one-character code that indicates the form of material in which the serial was originally published.

- None of the following

a Microfilm

b Microfiche

c Microopaque

d Large print

e Newspaper format

f Braille

s Electronic

| No attempt to code

24 - Nature of Entire Work: A one-character code that indicates the nature of the serial if it consists entirely of a certain type of material. If more than one code is applicable, 008/24 contains a # and up to three codes may be recorded in 008/25-27 (Nature of contents).

- No specified nature of entire work

a Abstracts/summaries. The item consists of abstracts or summaries of other publications.

b Bibliographies

c Catalogs

d Dictionaries

e Encyclopedias
f Handbooks
g Legal articles
h Biography
i Indexes
k Discographies
l Legislation
m Theses
n Surveys of literature
o Reviews
p Programmed texts
q Bibliographies
r Directories
s Statistics
t Technical reports
u Standards/specifications
v Legal cases and case notes
w Law reports and digests
z Treaties
| No attempt to code

25-27 - Nature of contents: Code as indicated in MARC coding manual. Code for nature of entire work first, then the nature of the contents. Optional field in OCLC.

28 - Government publication: Code as indicated in MARC coding manual for government documents. Delete for all others, including those regarded in derived records as government publications.

- Not a government publication

a Autonomous or semi-autonomous component

c Multilocal

f Federal/national

i International intergovernmental

l Local

m Multistate

o - Government publication - level undetermined

s State, provincial, territorial, dependent, etc.

u Unknown if item is government publication

z Other

| No attempt to code

29 - Conference publication: A one-character code that indicates whether the item OR serial consists of the proceedings, reports, or summaries of a conference.

0 Not a conference publication

1 Conference publication

| No attempt to code

30-32 - Undefined

33 - Original Alphabet or Script of Title: A one-character code that indicates the original alphabet or script of the language of the title on the source item upon which the key title (field 222) is based.

- No alphabet or script given/no key title

This code may relate to the title proper in field 245 when no key title is present.

a Basic roman (Includes no diacritics or special characters)

b Extended roman (Includes diacritics and special characters)

c Cyrillic

d Japanese

e Chinese

f Arabic

g Greek

h Hebrew

i Thai

j Devanagari

k Korean

l Tamil

u Unknown

z Other

| No attempt to code

34 - Entry Convention: A one-character code that indicates whether the serial was cataloged according to successive entry or latest entry cataloging conventions.

0 **Successive entry.** A new bibliographic record is created each time a title changes or a corporate body used as a main entry or uniform title qualifier changes. The earlier or later title or author/title is recorded in a linking 780/785 field in each record.

1 **Latest entry.** The item is cataloged under its most recent title or issuing body (pre-AACR cataloging rules). All former titles and/or issuing bodies are given in notes (fields 247, 547, and 550).

2 **Integrating entry.** A record is cataloged under its latest (most recent) title and/or responsible person or corporate body. It is used for integrating resources and electronic serials that do not retain their earlier titles.

| No attempt to code

37-37 language: A three-character MARC code that indicates the language of the item. The source of the code is MARC Code List for Languages . Choice of a MARC code is based on the predominant language of the item. Three fill characters (|||) may also be used if no attempt is made to code 008/35-37.

38 - Modified Record: Normally blank, but accept in derived records.

Not modified

d Dashed-on information omitted

o Completely romanized/printed cards romanized

r Completely romanized/printed cards in script

s Shortened. Some of the data has been omitted because the record would have exceeded the maximum length allowed by a particular system.

x Missing characters. Characters that could not be converted into machine-readable form due to character set limitations are missing from the record.

| No attempt to code

39 - Cataloging Source: Cataloging source: Code "d" for derived and original records. Must be changed to blank when transcribing an LC bibliographic record

National bibliographic agency

c Cooperative cataloging program

d Other

u Unknown

| No attempt to coded from a printed source.

Other control and Variable fields

022 ISSN (number assigned by ISSN centers)

040	Authentication field
050	LC classification number
100	Main entry – personal author (very rare)
110	Main entry – corporate body
111	Main entry – conference heading
130	Main entry – uniform title (frequently used for conflicting title)
210	Abbreviated title (used in A & I Services – assigned by ISSN)
222	Key title – (assigned by ISSN centers)
240	Uniform title (used when there is a corporate body main entry and and a uniform title is needed)
245	Title proper and statement of responsibility
246	Varying form of title (used for other forms of title and for minor changes on subsequent issues)
250	Edition statement, used only when entire serial is part of an edition
260	Publishing statement
300	Physical description
310	Current frequency
321	Former Publication frequency
362	Designation of first and last issue (first indicator "O") or data on when serial began or ceased (1st indicator "1")
440/490	Series Statement
500	General note (for description based on note, source of title, notes are place or name of publisher, etc.)
515	Numbering peculiarities – when considered important

525	Supplement note
533	Reproduction note
546	Language note
550	Issuing bodies note (used for changes of issuing body, etc.)
580	Linking entry complexity note (used for complex links, such as mergers and splits and relationships to other works.
6XX	Subject heading - usually kept broad for serials; from subdivision sub tag added: $v Periodicals
710	Added entry – corporate body (frequently used)
730	Added entry – uniform title (used for related resources)
752	Hierarchical place name (used in records for newspapers)
8XX	Series added entries

Linking Entry Fields (760-787)

Important fields used to show various link between serials

760	Main Series Entry (R)
762	Sub-series Entry (R)
765	Original Language Entry (R)
767	Translation Entry (R)
770	Supplement/Special Issue Entry (R)
772	Supplement Parent Entry (R)
773	Host Item Entry (R)
774	Constituent Unit Entry (R)
775	Other Edition Entry (R)

776	Additional Physical Form Entry (R)
777	Issued with Entry (R)
780	Preceding Entry (R)
785	Succeeding Entry (R)
786	Data Source Entry (R)
787	Nonspecific Relationship Entry (R)

Example 1.

LDR **02339cas 2200505 4500**

001			11210080
005			20020817053211.0
008			771130d19771977sz mr bc i0 0eng
010			$a 77643666
035			$a (OCoLC)ocm03454402
041	0		$a engfre
042			$a lc
043			$a e-sz---
050			$a Z949 \b .G34
082			$a 017/.1/094945
110	2		$a United Nations Library (Geneva, Switzerland).
245	1	0	$a Monthly bibliography - United Nations, Library. $b Bibliographie mensuelle - Nations Unies, Bibliotháeque.
246	3	1	$a Bibliographie mensuelle - Nations Unies, Bibliotháeque.

249	0		$i ACQUIRE Title: $a Monthly Bibliography / United Nations. Library.
260			$a Geneva [Switzerland] $b United Nations, Library.
300			$a 1 v. \c 21 cm.
310			$a Monthly.
362	0		$a 50th year; Jan.-Dec. 1977.
500			$a "A subject compilation of newly acquired books, official documents and periodicals."
590			$a SERBIB/SERLOC merged record.
592			$a ACQN: aq 98005738
610	2	0	$a United Nations Library (Geneva, Switzerland) $x Catalogs $vPeriodicals.
650		0	$a World politics $v Bibliography $v Periodicals.
650		0	$a International relations $v Bibliography $v Periodicals.
710	2		$a United Nations Library (Geneva, Switzerland). $t Bibliographie mensuelle.
780	0	0	$a United Nations Library (Geneva, Switzerland). $t Liste mensuelle d'ouvrages cataloguâes áa la Bibliotháeque des Nations Unies $w(DLC)sn 87020748 $w (OCoLC)9107059.

785	0	0	$a United Nations Library (Geneva, Switzerland). $t Monthly bibliography. Part I, Books, official documents, serials $x 0251-6616 $w (DLC) 87658391 $w (OcoLC) 5022250.
850			$a CU-I $a DLC $a InU $a MH Sa MH-L $a MiU $a PPiU $a ViU.
890			$a United Nations. Library, Geneva. Monthly bibliography - United Nations, Library. Bibliographie mensuelle - Nations Unies, Bibliotheáque. Geneva, Switzerland. \i 77-643666.

MARC21 CARD FORMAT:

Author	United Nations Library (Geneva, Switzerland)
Title	Monthly bibliography - United Nations, Library.
Subject	United Nations Library (Geneva, Switzerland) Catalogs
Subject	World politics
Subject	International relations
Publication	Geneva [Switzerland] United Nations, Library.
Description	1 v.
Frequency	Monthly
Note	Bibliographie mensuelle - Nations Unies, Bibliotháeque
Note	"A subject compilation of newly

	acquired books, official documents and periodicals."
Added Entry	United Nations Library (Geneva, Switzerland).
Prec. Entry	United Nations Library (Geneva, Switzerland).
Succ. Entry	United Nations Library (Geneva, Switzerland).

Example 2:

LDR **01528cas 2200445 a 4500**

001			11345636
005			20030802105048.0
008			880225c19uu9999ii mr w 0 0eng
010			$a 88648770
022			$a 0970-1060
037			$b Eastern Book Co., 34, Lal Bagh, Lucknow, India.
042			$a lc
043			$a a-ii—
082	0		$a 342.54/068/02648$a 345.4026802648 $ 2 19
210	0		$a Adm. trib. Cases.
245	0		$a Administrative tribunals cases : $b a monthly journal reporting judgments of central administrative tribunals and of the Supreme Court of India on service matters.

260			$a Lucknow [India] : $b Eastern Book Co.
300			$a v. ; $c 25 cm.
310			$a Monthly.
500			$a Description based on: Vol. 1, pt. 4 (Oct. 1986); title from cover.
590			$a SERBIB/SERLOC merged record.
650		0	$a Civil service $z India $v Cases.
710	1		$a India. $b Supreme Court.
850			$a DLC $a MH-L
852			$x universal pattern.
853		0	$8 1 $a v. $b pt. $i (year) $j (month).
863		4	$8 1 $a <1>- $i <1986>- $x provisional.
853		3	$8 2 $a v. $i (year).
863		4	$8 2 $a <5>- $i <1987>- $x provisional.
890			$a Administrative tribunals cases. $i 88-648770.

MARC21 CARD FORMAT:

Title	Administrative tribunals cases :
Subject	Civil service
Publication	Lucknow [India] : Eastern Book Co.
Key Title	Administrative tribunal cases

Description	v.;
Frequency	Monthly
Note	Description based on: Vol. 1, pt. 4 (Oct. 1986); title from cover.
Added Entry	India.

PART-II: HEADINGS AND REFERENCES

CHAPTER 10
Choice of Acces Points

CONTENTS

10.0 INTRODUCTORY RULES

Main and added entry: The rules for determining the choice of access points (heading) under which a bibliographic description is entered in a catalogue. Heading is a name, word, or phrase placed at the head of a catalogue entry or reference to provide an access point. A heading may represent a bibliographic identity for a person or corporate body, a work or a series of creation, modification, performance, compiling or editing, emanation, etc.

Consider the entire run of serial before entering it under the heading for a person. If different issues of the serial are known to have been or are likely to be created by different persons, do not enter the work under the heading for a person. In general, enter a serial under the heading for a person only in instances in which one person is so closely connected to or involved with the serial that the publication seems unlikely to continue without that person. Some types of serials that might sometimes be considered to be unlikely to continue without the person named as author are:

1) serials for which the same person is named as both author and publisher;
2) serials that carry the whole name or part of the name of the person in the title;
3) serials that do not emanate from a corporate body that might assure that the serial is continued.

The chief source of information for the item or any part of the item that is being used as its substitute only in the content of an item.

Optional addition. In the cases noted below, add an abbreviated designation of function to an added entry heading for a person.

FUNCTION PERFORMED	MARC CODE
Author	aut
Annotator	ann
Arranger	arr
Artist	art
Compiler	com
Editor	edt
Translator	trl

10.1 GENERAL RULES

Works of personal authorship: A personal author is the person chiefly responsible for the creation of the intellectual or artistic content of a work. For example, writers of books and composers of music are the authors of the works they create; compilers of bibliographies are the authors of those bibliographies; cartographers are the authors of their maps; and artists and photographers are the authors of the works they create. In addition, in certain cases performers are the authors of sound recordings and video recordings.

Entry under corporate body: A corporate body is an organization or group of persons that is identified by a particular name that acts, or may act, as an entity. For examples of corporate bodies are associations, institutions, business firms, nor profit enterprises, governments, government agencies, religious bodies, local churches.

Conferences : A meeting of individual representative of various bodies for the purpose of discussing and acting of topics of common interest or a meeting of representatives of a corporate body that constitutes its legislative or governing body.

Entry under title: A uniform title as the particular title by which a work that has appeared under varying titles is to be identified for cataloging purposes.

10.2 CHANGES IN TITLES PROPER

Changes in titles proper: A title proper to have changed if any word other than an article, preposition, or conjunction is added, deleted, or changed, or if the order of the first five words (the first six words if the title begins with an article) is changed.

Monographs: A non-serial item (i.e., an item either complete in one part or complete, or intended to be completed, in a finite number or separate parts).

Monographs in one physical part: If the title proper of a monograph in one physical part changes between one edition and another, make a separate main entry for each edition.

Monographs in more than one physical part: If the title proper of a monograph in more than one physical part changes between parts, give the title proper of the first part as the title of the whole monograph. If, however, another title proper appearing on later parts predominates, change the title proper of the whole monograph to the later title proper. If the title proper of multipart monograph change between editions, make a separate main entry.

Serials: If title proper of the serial changes, make the separate entry of the serial.

Changes in titles proper. Integrating resources: For integrated resources, if there is an edition statement change and/or if the publisher issues a new base volume or volumes, or if the title proper change is accompanied by an edition statement change, create a new bibliographic record according to the following guidelines. Updating loose-leafs

Create a new bibliographic record:

1) if there is a new base volume having a new date in the header/footer, etc., that is consistent throughout the base volume.
2) if there is a new base volume having pages with no revision dates but the pages in the original base volume had revision dates.
3) if the main entry/title proper of the two resources are the same and neither has an edition statement, supply in brackets an edition statement in the new record using the year of publication, distribution, etc. (e.g., "[2003]"

Do not create a new bibliographic record:

1) if a gradual replacement edition (i.e., the author or publisher considers the publication to be a new edition and issues a replacement title page with a new edition statement but does not issue a new base volume); change the edition area of the existing resource to reflect the current edition and give a note as appropriate.
2) if a new base volume with pages having various dates in the header/footer, etc., or having other indications that the same or a different publisher has just reissued the content of an existing resource as of its latest iteration. Include a "Description based on" note to clarify that the iteration being catalogued is not the first iteration of a new edition statement as appropriate.

In case of doubt, create a new bibliographic record.

Updating remote access electronic resources: Create a new bibliographic record only if the resource described in the existing record continues to exist as a resource to be catalogued.

10.2A ADDITIONAL TITLE ENTRIES

Additional title entries: Generally, make additional title added entries to titles other than title proper only under exceptional circumstances:

1) General: Make added entries for cover titles, parallel titles, spine titles, and added title page titles when they are significantly different from the title proper. Be more restrictive about differences in caption titles, half titles, running titles, and other title information; added entries for these are generally made only if one of the following conditions is met:

a) the work was also published under the title;

b) the work is cited in reference sources under the title;

c) the title is given such prominence by typography or by other means that it is reasonable to assume that the publication may be known by it or, that persons examining the item might think that it is the main title of the publication.

2) Abbreviations: When an abbreviation occurs as one of the first five words (the first six words if the title begins with an initial article) in a title proper or other title for which a title added entry is made, make an additional title added entry substituting the corresponding spelled-out form of the abbreviation if it is thought that some catalogue users might reasonably expect that the form was spelled out in the source.

245	1	0	$a Comm. on Agriculture report.
246	3	#	$a Committee on Agriculture report.

However, do not create additional title added

entries to titles which include commonly abbreviated words such as those from the following list adapted from the ALA Rules for Filing Catalog Cards:

Abp.Archbishop	Bp. Bishop
C.Celsius	Capt.Captain
Cie Compagnie	Co.Company, County
c/o Care of	Col.Colonel
Cpl. Corporal	Dr. Doctor (Docteur)
Esq. Esquire	Etc. Et cetera.
F. Fahrenheit	Hon.Honourable
Lt.Lieutenant	M.Monsieur
MlleMademoiselle	MM.Messieurs
Mme Madame	Mr.Mister
Mrs.Mrs.	Ms.,MS.Manuscript
Mss.,MSS.Manuscript(s)	Mt. Mount(ain)
N.North	N.W.Northwest
Prof.Professor	Rev. Reverend
S. South	v., vs.Versus

Exception: Make additional title added entries substituting the corresponding spelled-out form of the abbreviation to the commonly abbreviated words, St. for Saint and Ste. for Sainte. Do not, however, substitute the abbreviation to the spelled-out form.

3) Initialisms, compound words, etc: Generally, do not make additional title added entries for titles with compound words (hyphenated or unhyphenated), acronyms, initialisms, etc. occuring as one of the first five words (the first six words if the title begins with an initial article), unless such a variation is found prominently in the item itself and it is thought that some catalogue users might reasonably expect the title to appear in that form; or, as in the case of serials, the publication has used a variant form that is now no longer considered to be a title change (cf. rule interpretation 21.2C2b) and access is considered necessary.

4) Partial titles (including alternative titles): Make an entry for a portion of a title when, according to the context or layout, users would consider the phrase alone as the title proper. This is often the case with art books whose title transcription begins with the artist's name; many users might perceive that name as a statement of responsibility rather than a title.

245	1	0	$a Emily Carr, sky paintings.
246	3	0	$aSky paintings.

245	1	0	$a Nature of porosity in Alberta subbituminous.
246	3	0	$a Porosity in Alberta subbituminous coals.

245	1	0	$a Madame Benoit's convection oven cookbook.
246	3	0	$a Convection oven cookbook.

Make added entries more or less routinely for the part of a title proper that is called "alternative title."

245	1	0	$a Redondillas, or, Something of that sort.
246	3	0	$a Something of that sort.

5) Ampersand: When an ampersand (or other symbol, e.g., +, representing the word "and") occurs as one of the first five words (the first six words if the title begins with an initial article) in a title proper or other title for which a title added entry is made, make an additional title added entry substituting the word "and" in the language of the title.

245	1	0	$a A-Z of art & artists.
246	3	#	$a A-Z of art and artists.

6) Corrected titles:

a) Titles corrected by "[i.e....]" and "[sic]". If the title proper has been corrected within the first five words (the first six words if the title begins with an initial article) by the "[i.e. ...]" or "[sic]" technique, make two added entries, one for the title proper as it appears on the item and another for the title in its corrected form.

245	1	4	$a The Paul Anthony Buck [i.e. Brick] lectures. ...
246	3	#	$a Paul Anthony Buck lectures.
246	3	#	$a Paul Anthony Brick lectures.

b) Titles corrected by bracketing missing letters. If the title proper has been corrected within the first five words (the first six words if the title begins with an initial article) by supplying in brackets a missing letter or letters, make two added entries, one for the title with the brackets and the supplied letter or letters (indicator 1 in 245 field) and another for the title as it appears on the item.

246	3	#	$a One day's d[u]ty ...
246	3	#	$a One day's d y.

7) Numbers: When a number occurs as one of the first five words (the first six words if the title begins with an initial article) in a title proper or other title for which a title added entry is made, make an additional title added entry as follows:

a) Arabic numbers (excluding dates). Make an added entry substituting the corresponding spelled-out form of the number in the language of the title proper if it is thought that some users of the catalogue might reasonably expect that the form was spelled out in words in the source.

In spelling out numbers (including numbers expressed as fractions) in English, follow the style indicated in the Chicago Manual of Style, University of Chicago Press. For other languages, follow the preferred style of the language.

101 = one hundred one

425 = four hundred twenty-five

1001 = one thousand one

1226 = one thousand two hundred twenty-six

2500 = two thousand five hundred

245	1	4	$ The 1-2-3 guide to libraries ...
246	3	#	$a One-two-three guide to libraries.

245	1	0	$a 1 and 2 Thessalonians ...
246	3	#	$a Three ten to Yuma.

245	1	0	$a 3:10 to Yuma ...
246	3	#	$a Three ten to Yuma.

b) Roman numerals (excluding dates). Make an added entry substituting the corresponding spelled-out form of the number in the language of the title proper if it is thought that some users of the catalogue might reasonably expect that the form was spelled out in words in the source.

c) Dates. Do not make an additional added entry substituting the corresponding spelled-out form for dates written in arabic or roman numerals.

d) Spelled-out form. Do not make an added entry substituting an arabic or roman numeral for the spelled-out form.

8) Signs and symbols: When a sign or symbol occurs as one or in one of the first five words (the first six words if the title begins with an initial article) in a title proper or other title for which a title added entry is made, make an additional added entry substituting the name or a written form for the corresponding sign or symbol if this can be done concisely and if it is thought that some users of the catalogue might reasonably expect that the sign/symbol would be given in that form in the source.

245	1	0	$a Transforming #1 ...
246	3	#	$a Transforming number one.

245	1	0	$a 100% cooperation with the United States ...
246	3	#	$a One hundred percentcooperation with the United States.

9) Statement of responsibility: When a title proper begins with a separable statement of responsibility that is omitted from the uniform title (cf. 25.3B(2)), make an additional added entry for the title without the initial statement of responsibility.

100	1	#	$a Shakespeare, William, $d1564-1616.
240	1	0	$a Midsummer night's dream.
245	1	0	$a Shakespeare's A midsummer night's dream.
246	3	0	$a Midsummer night's dream.

10) Uniform title: Do not make title added entries for uniform titles. There may, however, be instances in which a title added entry is the same or nearly the same as the uniform title (e.g. cf. 9) Statement of responsibility above).

11) Bilingual publications: Make added entries to parallel titles and added title page titles (cf. 1) General above) but make further additional title added entries only in the language of cataloging.

English record

245	1	0	$a Title A(E)
246	1	5	$a Title B(F)
246	1	4	$a Title C(E)

12) Items without a collective title: If items in a contents note. The 740 field is used for added entry access to:

a) items without a collective title; and

245	1	4	$a The ecclesiastical history of the English people; $b The greater chronicle ;Bede's letter to Egbert / $c Bede; edited by ...
740	4	2	$a The greater chronicle.
740	0	2	$a Bede's letter to Egbert.
740	0	2	$a Letter to Egbert.

b) items in a contents note.

245	1	0	$a Techniques and concepts of high energy physics.
505	0	#	$a Quark models—The jet phenomena—An accelerator design study.
740	0	2	$a Quark models.
740	4	2	$a The jet phenomena.
740	3	2	$a An acceleration design study.

13) Former title or title variations:

a) Minor change in title proper of a serial

If the change in title proper of a later issue or part of a serial is only a minor change (see 21.2C2b), give that title proper in a 246. Identify the issue(s) or part(s) with that title in subfield $i.

245	0	0	$a Research report on literacy efforts.
246	1	#	$I No. 17- have title: $aResearch reports on literacy efforts.

b) Change in titles of an integrating resource

i) Title proper, when there is a title change in an integrating resource and the later title proper is given in the 245 field (see 12.1B8), give an added entry for the former title proper in a 247 field.

245	0	0	$aRegistry of mutual funds.
247	1	0	$a Mutual funds registry, $fupdate 2, published 2000.
500	#	#	$a Description based on: update 5, published 2001.

ii) Other title information and titles other than the title proper When other title information or a title other than the title proper has been added, changed, or deleted on the latest iteration and it is considered important to make a note, give the other title information or the title in a 246 field and explain the situation in subfield #i.

Existing record

245	0	0	$a Barn och unga =$bChildren and young persons.
500	#	#	$a Title from HTML header (viewed Jan. 13, 2002).

Same record updated

245	0	0	$a Barn och unga.
500	#	#	$i Parallel title in HTML header, Jan. 13, 2002 : $a Children and young persons.

c) Electronic serials that do not retain earlier title(s)

If an electronic serial is reformatted so that all evidence of the earlier title is removed, give an added entry for the earlier title proper in a 247 11 field.

Existing record

245	0	0	$a Asian age$h[electronic resource].

Same record updated

245	0	0	$a Asian age online$h[electronic resource].
247	#	#	$a Asian age$fMar. 6, 2001.
547	#	#	$a All issues originally published with title Asian age have been reformatted with the new title: Asian age online.

10.2B. SERIES/SUBSERIES ADDED ENTRIES

Series: Added entries may be made for all series in the following categories:

1) series published before 1900 and later reprints of the same, without regard to the type of publisher;

440	#	#	$a Dime juveniles.

2) series and multipart items entered under a personal author, without regard to the type of publisher;

490	1	#	$aThe Canadians / Robert E. Wall ; $vbk. -
547	#	#	$aWall, Robert E.,$d1940- $tCanadians ;$vbk.

3) series published by any corporate body other than a commercial publisher (treating university presses as noncommercial publishers);

490	1	#	$a Occasional publication / Association of Canadian
830	#	0	$a Occasional publication (Association $a Canadian Universities for Northern Studies) ;$vno.-
440	#	0	$a University of Toronto geotechnical report

4) series published by small or "alternative" presses (i.e. small printing/publishing firms that, although they may be commercial, are devoted to special causes, certain branches of literature, fine printing, etc., and usually do not address a mass audience);

440	#	0	$a Fiddlehead poetry books ;Sv-

5) series published by commercial publishers with titles that provide significant information or focussing with regard to content, genre, or audience.

440	#	0	$a McGraw Hill Ryerson series in Canadian marketing and management
440	#	0	$a Gage urban studies series

Do not make added entries for series in the following categories:

1) series in which the items are related to each other only by common physical characteristics;
2) series in which the numbering suggests that the parts have been numbered primarily for stock control or to benefit from lower postage rates;
3) series published by commercial publishers with titles that convey little or no information about the content, audience, or purpose of the series, or consist primarily of the name of a literary or musical genre (with or without the name of the publisher) and lack any additional term that would narrow the focus of the genre or highlight a specialized audience (e.g. children).

On source: McGraw Hill Ryerson paperback library

490	0	#	$a McGraw Hill Ryerson paperback library

On source: Macmillan decision series

490	0	#	$a Macmillan decision series

On source: Harlequin American romance, 1

490	0	#	$a Harlequin American romance ;$v1

If a series in any one of the latter three categories also falls under one or more of the first five categories, an added entry may be made.

In case of doubt, and in special cases where it is felt that an added entry for the series would provide a useful collocation, an added entry may be made.

440	#	0	$a Oxford library of Italian classics

Series/subseries added entries

If an item belongs to a subseries (see 1.6H) include in the series added entry the title of the main series followed by the title of the subseries or make separate added entries for the main series and the subseries in accordance with the following guidelines:

1) if the main series is unnumbered, make a single added entry including both the title of the main series and the title of the subseries;

440	#	0	$a Cambridge natural science mnuals. $p Physical series

2) if the main series is numbered, make separate added entries for the main series (main series title only) and the subseries (main series title followed by the title of the subseries);

490	#	0	$a Biblioteca de arte hispanico ; $v 8. $a Artes aplicadas ;$v 1
830	#	0	$a Biblioteca de arte hispanico ; $v 8
830	#	0	$a Biblioteca de arte hispanico. $p Artes aplicadas ; $v 1

3) if there is a hierarchy consisting of main series, subseries, sub subseries, etc., make separate added entries for the main series (if numbered), for each intermediate subseries that is numbered, and for the subseries lowest in the hierarchy (numbered or unnumbered), including in the added entry for each subseries the main series

title and the title of any intermediate subseries;

4) if a main series title (numbered or unnumbered) appears on certain items without a subseries title, make an added entry only for the main series on those items, reverting to a main series subseries added entries (see (1) above) or separate main series and subseries entries (see (2)above) for subsequent items that bear both the main series title and the subseries title. Do not make a subseries added entry for an item if the subseries title does not appear on the item within the same source as the main series title even if other evidence indicates that the item is a part of the subseries (see 1.6H).

440	#	0	$a Acta Universitatis Stockholmiensis. $p Stockholm studies in the history of literature ;$v10

On the series authority record, make a reference from the subseries title in direct form to the main series subseries heading for any subseries title that is distinctive enough not to be dependent on the main series title for identification (cf. 26.4B3).

130	#	0	$a Acta Universitatis Stockholmiensis.$p Stockholm studies in the history of literature.
830	#	#	$a Stockholm studies in the history of literature.

Note that series titles that do not appear on the same source of information are not to be treated as subseries (see 1.6H), but as separate series (see 1.6J1).

Corporate name as series title

If the title proper of the series consists solely of the name of a corporate body (see 1.6B1), add to the name of the body in the series added entry the qualifier "(Series)" or other appropriate term.

490	1	#	$a Winnipeg Art Gallery ;$v6
830	#	0	$a Winnipeg Art Gallery (Series) ;$v6

Option

Add the numeric or other designation of the work within the series if it appears in the item. Record the numbering or other designation following the heading for the series, and precede it with a space semicolon space.

440	#	0	$a Papers in Indian studies ; $vno. 4

Abbreviations, etc.

Record the numbering in the terms given in the item. Use standard abbreviations (see Appendix B.5B1) * and substitute Arabic numerals for other numerals or spelled out numbers (see Appendix C). Use the ordinal form if the number on the source is in the ordinal form; use the cardinal form if the number on the source is in the cardinal form.

On source: Toronto studies in religion vol. 1

440	#	0	$a Toronto studies in religion ; $vv. 1

Not

490	1	#	$a Toronto studies in religion ;$vvol. 1
830	#	0	$aToronto studies in religion ;$vv. 1

But

On source: Toronto studies in religion 18

490	1	#	$a Toronto studies in religion ;$vvol. 1
830	#	0	$aToronto studies in religion ;$vv. 1

* If there is no standard abbreviation, and the term is excessively long or complex, record only the number.

Numbering as an integral part of series title

If the numbering or other designation as it appears in the item forms an integral part of the series title, omit it from the title in the series added entry and replace it by the mark of omission, unless it occurs at the beginning of the title proper of the series, in which case do not include the mark of omission (cf. 12.1B7). Record the number following the series title, preceded by the prescribed punctuation, as above.

490	1	#	$a The twenty-sixth L. Ray Buckendale lecture
830	#	0	$a L. Ray Buckendale lecture ;$v26th

490	1	#	$a 31. tom Biblioteki SIB
830	#	0	$a Biblioteka SIB ;$v31. t.

490	1	#	$a Contribution no. 9 of the Committee on Desert and Arid Zone Research, Southwestern and Rocky Mountain Division, A.A.A.S.
830	#	0	$a Contribution... of the Committee on Desert and Arid Zone Research, Southwestern and Rocky Mountain Division, A.A.A.S. ; $vno. 9

Numbering in more than one system of designation

If the numbering within the series is given according to more than one system of designation, record in the series added entry the numbering according to one system of designation only. Generally prefer the first system of designation as given in the source, unless the publication pattern for the series suggests that the use of one of the alternative designations would serve to provide a better and/or more consistent subarrangement of series entries.

On source: new series 5 (94)

490	1	#	$a____________ ;$vnew ser. 5 = 94
830	#	0	$a____________ ;$vnew ser. 5

Numbering including chronological designation

If the numbering within the series as given in the source includes a chronological designation in addition to a numeric or alphabetic designation, omit the chronological designation from the series added entry.

On source: volume 3 part 2 September 1981

490	1	#	$a__________ ;$v. 3, pt. 2 (Sept. 1981)
830	#	0	$a__________ ;$v. 3, pt. 2

If the numbering consists of two portions, one representing the year, and the other representing the sequence of items within that year, record in the series added entry the portion representing the year first, regardless of how the number is given in the source.

On source: 77-5

440	#	0	$a__________ ;$v. 77-5

On source: 1-1979

490	1	#	$a__________ ;$v1-1979
830	#	0	$a__________ ;$v1979-1

Numbering in more than one language

If parallel titles are being recorded and the numbering also appears in more than one language or script, but does not form an integral part of the title, record each number after the title proper/parallel title to which it relates.

490	1	#	$a Canadian meteorological history ;$vno. 4 =$aHistoire de
830	#	0	$aCanadian meteorological history ;$vno. 4

If this criterion does not apply, record the form that appears first in the source of information for the series. Note that unless the numbering forms an integral part of the title, the numbering element follows the parallel titles of the series and is placed after other title information, statements of responsibility, and ISSN, if present. Do not place it between the title proper of the series and the parallel title. If the number appears only once, record it after the title it linguistically matches or after the last title if it matches all, more than one, or none of the titles.

10.3. CHANGES OF PERSONS OR BODIES RESPONSIBLE FOR A WORK

Monographs. If a person or corporate body other than the person or body modifies a monographic work under which the work in its original edition was entered.

If there is a change in responsibility between the parts of a multipart monograph, enter the monograph under the heading appropriate to the first part. If however, a different person or corporate body responsible for later parts predominates, change the heading to that appropriate to the later parts and make an added entry under the heading for the earlier person of body.

Make a new entry for a serial when either of the following conditions arises, even if the title proper remains the same:

1) if a heading for a corporate body under which a serial is entered changes

2) if the main entry for a serial is under a personal or corporate heading and the person or body named in that heading is no longer responsible for the serial.

Changes of persons or bodies responsible for a work.

Integrating resources: If there is an edition statement change and/or if the publisher issues a new base volume or volumes, or if the change of persons or bodies responsible for a work is accompanied by an edition statement change, create a new bibliographic record as:

Create a new bibliographic record:

1) if there is a new base volume having a new date in the header/footer, etc., that is consistent throughout the base volume;
2) if there is a new base volume having pages with no revision dates but the pages in the original base volume had revision dates.
3) if the main entry/title proper of the two resources are the same and neither has an edition statement, supply in brackets an edition statement in the new record using the year of publication, distribution, etc.

Do not create a new bibliographic record:

1) if gradual replacement edition (i.e., the author or publisher considers the publication to be a new edition and issues a replacement title page with a new edition statement but does not issue a new base volume); change the edition area of the existing resource to reflect the current edition and give a note as appropriate;
2) if new base volume with pages having various

dates in the header/footer, etc., or having other indications that the same or a different publisher has just reissued the conten of an existing resource as of its latest iter ition. Include a "Description based on" note to clarify that the iteration being catalogued is not the first iteration of a new edition statement as appropriate.

In case of doubt, create a new bibliographic record.

Updating remote access electronic resources:

Create a new bibliographic record only if the resource described in the existing record continues to exist as a resource to be catalogued.

10.4. WORKS FOR WHICH A SINGLE PERSON OR CORPORATE BODY IS RESPONSIBLE

Work of single personal authorship: Enter a work, a collection of works, or selections from a work or works by one personal author (or any reprint, reissue, etc., of such a work) under the heading for that person whether named in the item being catalogued or not.

Lectures from Colombo to Almora / by Swami Vivekananda Main entry under the heading for Vivekananda, Swami.

The subject approach to Information / A.C. Foskett Main entry under the heading for Foskett, A.C.0

Entry under Corporate Body: Enter a work, a collection of works, or selections from a work or works emanating from one corporate body (or any reprint, reissue, etc., of such a work) under the heading for the body if the work or collection falls into one or more of the categories.

Constitution of the American society of Zoologists Main entry under the heading for the society.

Works erroneously or fictitiously attributed to a person or corporate body: If responsibility for a work is known to be erroneously or fictitiously attributed to a person or corporate body, enter under the actual personal author/corporate body or under title if the actual personal author is not known. Make an added entry under the heading for the person to whom the authorship is attributed, unless he or she is not a real person.

> The autobiography of Alice B. Toklas
>
> (The life of Gertrude Stein written by herself as though it were an autobiography of her secretary, Alice B. Toklas)
>
> Main entry under the heading for Stein
>
> Added entry under the heading for Toklas

Work of heads of state, other high government officials, popes, and other high ecclesiastical officials

Enter a work that falls into one of the following categories under the corporate heading for the official:

1) an official communication from a head of state, head of government, or head of an international body (e.g., a message to a legislature, a proclamation, an executive order other than one covered by 21.31)
2) an official communication from a pope, patriarch, bishop, etc (e.g., an order, decree, pastoral letter, bull, encyclical, constitution, or an official message to a council, synod, etc.).

Make an added entry under the personal heading for the person.

Proclamations and executive orders by the President, under, and by virtue of, the Food Control Act of August 10, 1917 : November 25, 1918 (Communications of President Wilson)

Main entry under the corporate heading for Wilson as president Added entry under the personal heading for Wilson

Other works: Enter all other works of such a person under the personal heading. Make an explanatory, reference from the corporate heading to the personal heading (26.3C1)

The second inaugural address of Abraham Lincoln Main entry under the personal heading for Lincoln

Collections of official communications and other works: Enter a collection of official communications and other works by one person under the personal heading. Make an added entry under the corporate heading.

The King to his people : being the speeches and messages of His Majesty King George the Fifth delivered between July 1911 and May 1935

Main entry under the personal heading for George V Added entry under the corporate heading for George V as sovereign

10.5. WORK OF UNKNOWN OR UNCERTAIN AUTHORSHIP OR BY UNNAMED GROUPS

If a work is of unknown or uncertain personal authorship or if it emanates from a body that lacks a name, enter it under title.

The secret expedition : a farce (in two acts) as it has been represented upon the political theatre of Europe (Author unknown) Main entry under title.

245	0	4	$a The secret expedition : a farce / $c ...

If the item contains more than one work, the work represented by the uniform title may be coextensive with the content of the item (i.e., the uniform title may represent the complete contents of the item by means of a collective title derived from the item it self, or by means of a conventional title such as "works" or "Selection"). However, if the item contains only two works by the author and lacks a collective title, the uniform title will represent only the first work named in the item.

The law scrutiny, or, Attornies' guide

(Variously attributed to Andrew Carmichael and William Norcott)

Main entry under title

Added entries under the headings for Carmichael and Norcott

245	0	4	$a The law scrutiny / $c ...
700	1		$a Andrew, Carmichael.
700	1		$a William, Norcott.

If reference sources indicate that a person is the probable author of such a work, enter under the heading for that person. If a work falling into one or more of the categories given in 21.1B2 probably emanates from a particular corporate body, enter under the heading for that body. Make added entries under the headings for other persons or bodies to which the work has been attributed, and under title.

A true character of Mr. Pope

(Author uncertain; generally attributed to John Dennis)

Main entry under the heading for Dennis

Added entry under title

100	1	0	$a Dennis.
245	1	2	$a A true character of Mr. Pope.

If the name of a personal author is unknown and in the chief source of information of the item being catalogued the only indication of authorship is the appearance of a characterizing word or phrase or of a phrase naming another work by the person, enter under the word or phrase in the form given in 22.11D. Make an added entry under title.

Memoir of Bowman Hendry... / by a Physician

(Name of author unknown)

Main entry under the characterizing word

100	1		$a Physicaian.
700	1		$a Memoir of Bowman Hendry / $c Physicaian.

If the only indication f authorship is a non-alphabetic and non-numerical device, enter under title. Do not make an added entry under the device.

Angry thoughts / by *!*!* (Name of author unknown) Main entry under title

245	1		$a Angry thoughts.

10.6. WORK OF SHARED RESPONSIBILITY

Apply this rule to:

1) Principal responsibility indicated (21.6B)
2) Principal responsibility not indicated (21.6C)

3) More than three personal authors (21.6C2)

Principal responsibility indicated: If heading for the entry represents a bibliographic identity established by the person represented as the principal author, as the first named or by the wording or the layout of the chief source of information of the item being catalogued.

The main entry under the heading for the principal author or first named author of a work of responsibility, if in a work, two or more personal or corporate body are represented as "joint authors" of the work or responsibility for the creation of the intellectual or artistic content of the work or works contained in the item is "shared" between those person. Make added entries under the heading for other person or bodies involved if there are not more than two.

Physical Chemistry / C.W. Wood and A.K. Holiday

100	1		$a Wood, C.W.
700	1		$a Holiday, A.K.

Principal responsibility not indicated: If responsibility is shared between two or three persons or bodies and principal responsibility is not attributed to any of them by wording or layout, enter under the heading for the one named first. Make added entries under the heading for the others.

If the persons or bodies are not named in the item, enter under the one named first in a previous edition or, if there is no previous edition, under the one whose heading comes first in English alphabetic order.

More than three personal authors: If responsibility is shared among more than three persons or corporate bodies and principal responsibility is not attributed to any one, two, or three, enter under title. Make an added entry under the heading for the first person or corporate body named prominently in the item being catalogued. If editors are named prominently, make an added entry under the heading for each if there are not more than three. If there are more than three named prominently, make an added entry under the heading for the principal editor and/ or for the one named first.

Texas country / Willie Nelson ...[et al.]

(A sound recording; three additional performers named on tables)

245	0		$a Texas country.
700	1		$a Nelson, Willie.

Entry under shared pseudonym: If two or more persons collaborate and use writing under a single pseudonym, use the pseudonym as the heading for a work produced by their collaboration.

Deadly weapon / Wade Miller

(Wade Miller is the joint pseudonym of Bill Miller and Bob Wade)

Main entry under the pseudonym

References to the pseudonym from the headings fro Miller and Wade

Social structure and personality / by a psychologist (Arthur Tracey)

Main entry under the pseudonym name A Psychologist

References entry shall be given under the real name Arthur Tracey

See reference:

Tracey, Arthur

see A psychologist

10.7. COLLECTION OF WORKS BY DIFFERENT PERSONS OR BODIES

Collection of works by different persons or bodies: If more than one author; two or more independent works or parts of works published together and not written for the same occasion or for the publication in hand. This means the festschrift volume, papers presented in the conference and seminars are not collection of works, because as they are written for the same occasion.

Apply this rule to:

1) collections of independent works by different persons or bodies
2) collections consisting of extracts from independent works by different persons or bodies
3) works consisting partly of independent works and partly of contributions by different persons or bodies
4) works consisting of contributions by different persons or bodies, produced under editorial direction.

The collection and works produced under editorial direction further sub-divided into two groups

(i) with collective title (21.7B)

(ii) without collective title (21.7C)

With collective title: Enter a work falling into one of the categories given in 21.7A under its title if it has a collective title. Make added entries under the headings for the compilers/editors if there are not more than three and if they are named prominently in the item being catalogued. If there are more than three compilers/editors named prominently, make an added entry under the heading for the principal compiler/editor and/or for the one named first.

Glimpses of Indian Ethno botany / edited by S.K. Jain

245	0		$a Glimpses of Indian Ethno botany.
700	1		$a Jain, S.K.

Without collective title: If a work falling into one of the categories given in 21.7A1 lacks a collective title, enter it under the heading appropriate to the first work named in the chief source of information of the item being catalogued. If the item lacks a collective chief source of information, enter it under the heading appropriate to the first work in the item. Make added entries for compilers/editors and for the other works as instructed in 21.7B1, insofar as it applies to works without a collective title.

History of the elementary school contest in England / Francis Adam. Together with The struggle for national education / John Morley ; [both] edited , with an introduction, by Asa Briggs

Added entry (name-title) under the heading for Morley

Added entry under the heading for Briggs

100	1		SaAdams Francis.
245	1	0	$a History of the elementary school contest in England / $c [by] Francis Adams; together with The struggle for national education [by] John Morley. Edited with an introduction by Asa Briggs.
700	1	2	$a Morley, John, $d 1838-1923. $t Struggle for national education. |f 1972.
700	1		$a Briggs, Asa, |d 1921- |e ed.
740	1		$a Struggle for national education.

10.8. WORKS OF MIXED RESPONSIBILITY

A work of mixed responsibility is one to which different persons or bodies make intellectual or artistic contributions by performing different kinds of activity, eg. Writing, adapting, editing, arragning, translating.

Adaptation of text: Enter a paraphrase, adaptation for children, or version in a different literary form (e.g., novelization, dramatization) under the heading for the adapter. If the name of the adapter is unknown, enter under title. Make a name-title added entry for the original work. In case of doubt about whether a work is an adaptation, enter under the heading for the original work.

The science of education : a paraphrase of Dr. Karl Rosenkranz / By Anna C. Brackett

Main entry under the heading for Brackett

Added entry (name-title)under the heading for Rosenkranz

100	1		$a Brackett, Anna C.
245	1	0	$a The science of education : a paraphraseDr. Karl Rosenkranz / $c by Anna C. Brackett.
700	1		$a Rosenkranz, Karl $t The science education
740	1		$a The science of education.

Illustrated text: Enter a work that consists of a text for which an artist has provided illustrations under the heading appropriate to the text. Make an added entry under the heading for the illustrator if appropriate under the provisions of 21.30K2.

British butterflies / by E.B. Ford ; with ... colour plates by Paxton Chadwick

Main entry under the heading for Ford

Added entry under the heading for Chadwick

100	1		$a Ford, E.B.
245	1	0	$a British butterflies / $c by E.B. Ford ; with ... colour plates by Paxton Chadwick.
700	1		$a Chadwick, Paxton.

Revisions of text

Original author considered responsible: Enter an edition of a work that has been revised, enlarged, updated, etc., under the heading for the original author if:

1) the original author is named in a statement of responsibility in the item being catalogued
2) the original author is named in the title proper and no other person is named is a statement of responsibility or other title information.

   Make an added entry under the heading for the reviser, etc.

   Anatomy of the human body / by Henry Gray. – 25th ed. / edited by Charles Mayo Goss

   Main entry under the heading for Gray

   Added entry under the heading for Goss

100	1		$a Gray, Henry.
245	1	0	$a Anatomy of the human / $c by Henry Gray.
700	1		$a Goss, Charles Mayo.

Original author no longer considered responsible: Enter under the heading for the reviser, etc., or under title, as appropriate, if the wording of the chief source of information of the item being catalogued indicates that the person or body responsible for the original is no longer considered to be responsible for the work (e.g., when the original author is named only in the title proper and some other person or body is named as being primarily responsible in the statement of responsibility or in the statement of responsibility relating to the edition). Make a name-title added entry under the heading for the original author using, if it can be readily ascertained, the title of the last edition to have been entered under the heading for the person or body responsible for the original. Always make a title added entry if the title begins with name of the original author and the main entry in under the name of the reviser, etc.

> Guide to reference books. – 7th e. / by Constance M. Winchell (Based on Gilbert Mudge's sixth edition of the same work)
>
> Main entry under the heading for Winchell
> Added entry (name-title) under the heading for Mudge

100	1		$a Winchell, Constance M.
245	1	0	$a Guide to reference books \c [by] Constance M. Winchell.
500			$aA revision, reorganization, and enlargement of the 7th ed. published in 1951 which was based on the Guide to reference books, by Isadore Gilbert Mudge.
700	1		$aMudge, Isadore Gilbert, \d 1875-1957. \t Guide to reference books.

Translations: Enter a translation under the heading appropriate to the original. Make an added entry under the heading for the translator if appropriate under the provisions of 21.30K1.

> Fathers and sons / Ivan Turgenev ; translated by Rosemary Edmonds.
>
> Main entry under the heading for the Turgenev
> Added entry under the heading for Edomonds

100	1		$a Turgenev, Ivan.
245	1		$a Edmonds, Rosemary.

Texts published with biographical / critical material: If a work consisting of a work or works by a writer accompanied by (or interwoven with) biographical or critical material by another person is presented in the chief source of information of the item being catalogued as a biographical/critical work. Make an added entry under the heading appropriate to the work or works included.

If the biographer/critic is represented as editor, complier, etc., enter under the heading appropriate to the work or works included. Make an added entry under the heading for the biographer/critic.

10.9. REPRODUCTION OF TWO OR MORE WORKS

Art catalogues and art exhibition catalogues

In determining main entry for art catalogues and art exhibition catalogues (for works of single or multiple artists), consider first the applicability of 21.1B2 for entry under corporate body. To qualify for inclusion under category "a" of 21.1B2, the publication must present itself as a catalogue (with or without reproductions of the items exhibited) and all items "listed" in it must belong to the corporate body from which the catalogue emanates. Restrict the amount of investigation involved in determining ownership of the items to any information rominently" displayed on the publication (i.e. information appearing on the prescribed sources for areas 1 and 2).

If it cannot be determined from prominent sources within the publication that all items "listed" belong to the corporate body from which the work emanates, revert to entry either under personal name or under title.

For works of a single artist :

In considering entry under personal name, determine first whether reproductions of art works are included, and if so, whether the catalogue should be entered under the heading for the artist or under the heading for the author of the text (if there is text) in accordance with rule 21.17.

Enter the catalogue under the heading for the author of the text (according to 21.4A or 21.6) only if that person is represented on the chief source of information as the author of the catalogue; make an added entry under the heading for the artist if the publication contains reproductions of the artist's works.

Otherwise, enter the catalogue under the heading for the artist but only if the publication contains reproductions of the artist's works; make an added entry under the heading for the person who wrote the text if the name appears anywhere in the item.

In case of doubt, enter the catalogue under the heading for the artist if the publication contains reproductions of the artist's works. If neither corporate body nor personal name entry is applicable, enter the catalogue under title, with added entries as appropriate.

For works of multiple artists :

For publications of works of multiple artists, apply the above guideline on author entry for works of a single artist (2nd paragr.) and enter the catalogue under the heading for the author of the text (according to 21.4A or 21.6) only if that person is represented on the chief source of information as the author of the catalogue. Make added entries for the headings under the artists as appropriate.

If entry under the heading for the author is not applicable, enter the catalogue under title or appropriate heading according to 21.7.

Mr. Lincoln's camera man, Mathew B. Brady / by Roy Meredith

Main entry under the heading for Meredith

Added entry under the heading for Brady

100	1		$a Meredith, Roy.
700	1		$a Brady, Mathew B.

10.10 . RELATED WORKS

Apply this rule to a separately catalogued work that has a relationship to another work. Such works include: continuations and sequels; supplements; indexes; subseries and concordances, etc.

Serial supplements to other works (monographs or serials). In general, create a separate bibliographic record for a serial supplement to another work if the supplement satisfies all of the following conditions:

- does not update that related work,
- carries its own designation system that is distinct and independent from that used by the related work,
- does not require the main work to be useable,
- is not an integral part of the main work,
- is considered to be bibliographically important,
- is of a nature that a separate record is required to facilitate processing and storage.

Make a linking note to the related work; as well, make a reciprocal linking note to the supplement on the bibliographic record for the related work.

Do not catalogue as serials any of the updates, revised pages, or supplements to loose-leaf publications treated as monographs, even though these updates, etc., are frequently issued in packages containing a numeric or chronological designation suggestive of serial publications

For serial supplements not catalogued separately, make notes on the bibliographic records for the related works and give added entries for the supplements whenever the titles are distinctive.

Indexes to serials

In general, indicate the presence of an index to a serial on the bibliographic record for the serial being indexed. Give an added entry whenever the title is distinctive. If, however, the index is published separately and is not issued by the entity responsible for the serial being indexed, create a separate bibliographic record (monograph or serial as appropriate) for the index. In the instance of an index catalogued as a monograph, give an added entry for the related serial unless the index has a common title that is identical to the title proper of the related serial.

Writers: Do not make an added entry under the heading for a prominently named writer of a serial unless the writer is so closely connected to or involved with the serial that the publication seems unlikely to continue without that writer.

10.11. SPECIAL RULES

CERTAIN LEGAL PUBLICATIONS

Apply this rule to legislative enactments and decrees of a political jurisdiction and to decrees of a chief executive having the force of law other than:

1) administrative regulations that are not law

2) constitutions and charter
3) court rules
4) treaties and similar formal agreement

Laws of governing one jurisdictions: Entry under the heading for the jurisdiction government by them. Add a uniform title as instructed in 25.15A. Make added entries under the headings for persons and corporate bodies responsible for compiling and issuing the laws.

Canada Corporation Act : chap. 53, R.S.C. 1952, as amended. – 2nd ed.- Don Mills, Ont. : CCH Canadian

Main entry under the heading for Canada

Uniform title for the law

Added entry under the heading for CCH Canadian

Laws governing more than one jurisdiction: Enter a compilation of laws governing more than one jurisdiction as collection. Make added entries under the headings for the jurisdictions governed if there are two or three. If there are four or more jurisdictions and they are named in the chief source of information of the item being catalogued, make an added entry under the heading for the one named first. If all the laws are enacted by a signle urisdiction, make an added entry under the heading for the enacting jurisdiction. Add a uniform title as instructed in 25.15A to each added entry heading.

Motor bus laws and regulations : a complete code of all motor bus regulatory laws... / compoled and edited by John M. Meighan

130	0#	$aMotor bus laws and regulations
710	1	$aMeighan, John.M.

Bills and drafts of legislation: Enter legislative bills under the heading for the appropriate legislative body. Enter other drafts of legislation as instructed 21.1-21.7.

Draft of an act relating to the sale of goods / by Samuel Williston

100	1		$aWilliston, Samuel.
245	1		$aDraft of an act relating to the sale of goods.

Ancient laws, certain medieval laws, customary laws, etc.

Enter the laws of ancient jurisdictions; laws of non-western jurisdictions before the legislative institutions based on western models; and customary laws, tribal laws, etc., under (in this order of preference)

a) a uniform title consisting of the title by which the law or early compilation of laws is known

b) the title proper of the item being catalogued.

The oldest code of laws in the world : the code of laws promulgated by Hammurabi, King of Babylon

130	4	#	$a The oldest code of laws in the world.
700	0		$a Hammurab.

Administrative regulations, etc.

Treat administrative regulations that constitute the rules governing a judicial or quasi-judicial body (courts, administrative tribunals, etc.) as court rules (see 21.34).

If the publication contains both court rules

(including administrative regulations of the type noted above) and other regulations that do not pertain to a judicial or quasi-judicial body, enter the publication under the heading for the rules or regulations named first in the title, following rule 21.32 or 21.34 as appropriate. Make added entries under the heading(s) for the other(s), provided there are no more than two.

Administrative regulations, etc., that are not laws

If administrative regulations, rules, etc., from jurisdictions in which such regulations, etc., are promulgated by government agencies or agent under authority granted by one or more laws, enter them under the heading for the agency or agent. If the regulations, etc., are issued by an agency other than the promulgating agency, make an added entry under the heading for the issuing agency. If the regulations, etc., derive from a particular law, make an added entry under the heading and uniform title for that law.

Rules and regulations for recreation areas : [Recreational Area Licensing Act rules and regulations] Department of Public Health, Bureau of Environmental Health, Division of Swimming Pools and Recreation

Administrative regulations, etc., that are laws

Note that all administrative regulations emanating jurisdictions (federal, provincial, regional, and local) are to be entered as laws, in accordance with the provisions of rule 21.31, regardless of whether the regulations are promulgated and/or issued by a government agency or agent.

Regulations governing a single jurisdiction are to be entered under the heading for the jurisdiction. Collections containing regulations governing more than one jurisdiction are to be entered in accordance with rule 21.32C.

For instructions on formulating uniform titles for administrative regulations, see 25.15A1 and 25.15A2.

Québec (Province)

[Crop Insurance Act. Regulations]

Regulation respecting seed corn insurance ....

Ontario

[Apprenticeship and Tradesmen's Qualification Act. Regulations] Regulations pertaining to refrigeration and air conditioning mechanics ... / Ministry of Colleges and Universities.

When applying rule 21.32B and formulating a uniform title according to the instructions under 25.15A1 or 25.15A2, do not make an added entry under the heading and uniform title for the law from which the regulations derive.

British Columbia

[Liquor Control and Licensing Act. Regulations]

Regulations made pursuant to the Liquor Control and Licensing Act ....

(No added entry under the heading and uniform title for act)

Do not make an added entry under the heading for the promulgating agency or agent if that agency or agent represents the executive arm of the government as a whole (e.g. Cabinet, Governor-in-Council, etc.).

British Columbia

[Automobile Insurance Act. Regulations]

An office consolidation of regulations 1-19 of the Automobile Insurance Act ....

(Promulgated by the Lieutenant-Governor in Council)

(No added entry under the heading for the Lieutenant-Governor in Council)

Do not make an added entry for the issuing agency if that agency functions solely as a publishing or distribution agent for the government (e.g. Queen's Printer).

> Québec (Province)
>
> [Consumer Protection Act. Regulations]
>
> Regulation respecting the application of the Consumer Protection Act. — Québec : Éditeur officiel, c1982
>
> (No added entry under the heading for the Éditeur officiel)

If the regulations bear an official short title or a citation title that differs significantly from the uniform title used in the main entry, make a name-title added entry under the heading for the jurisdiction followed by the short title or citation title.

> Canada
>
> [War Veterans Allowance Act. Regulations]
>
> Regulations for carrying into effect the purposes and provisions of the War Veterans Allowance Act ...
>
> (Citation title : Veterans Allowance Regulations)
>
> Added entry (name-title) : Canada. Veterans Allowance Regulations

If a law or laws and the regulations derived from it (also treated as laws) are published together, enter the item under the heading appropriate to the law or regulations named first in the title. Make added entries under the heading(s) for the other(s), provided there are no more than two.

> Ontario
>
> [Family Benefits Act]

The Family Benefits Act and regulations .... — [Toronto] : Ministry of Community and Social Services, 1974

Added entry (name-title) : Ontario. Family Benefits Act. Regulations

Collections of administrative regulations, etc.

Collections of regulations of the type covered under 21.32A (those that are not laws) are entered as a collection (21.7).

Collections of regulations of the type covered under 21.32B (those that are laws) are, by referral at 21.32B, entered as instructed in 21.31:

- regulations covered by 21.32B and governing one jurisdiction (see 21.31B1) are to be entered under the heading for the jurisdiction. (For instructions on formulating a uniform title for a collection of this type, see 25.15A1).
- regulations covered by 21.32B and governing more than one jurisdiction (see 21.31B2) are to be entered as collections according to the provisions of 21.7.

Court rules

Include within the scope of court rules administrative regulations that constitute the rules governing a judicial or quasi-judicial body (courts, administrative tribunals, etc.).

If the publication contains both court rules (including administrative regulations of the type noted above) and other regulations that do not pertain to a judicial or quasi-judicial body, or laws from which the rules or regulations are derived, enter the publication under the heading for the rules, regulations, or law named first in the title, following rule 21.31, 21.32 or

21.34 as appropriate. Make added entries under the heading(s) for the other(s), provided there are no more than two.

New South Wales [District Court Act]

District Court Act & rules ....

Added entry (name-title) : New South Wales. District Court.

Treaties, intergovernmental agreements, etc

If the treaties or any other formal agreement, etc., between two or three governments the entry will be in order of preference as:

a) the heading for the government on one side if it is the only one on that side and there are tow governments on the other

b) the heading for the government whose catalogue entry heading is first in English alphabetic order.

Make added entries under the headings for the aother government. Add uniform titles as instructed in 25.16B1 to the main and added entry headings.

Special Economic Assistance : agreement between the India and Nepal

130	0	#	$aIndia$tSpecial economic assistance.
730	0	#	$aNepal$tSpecial economic assistance.

Treaties, etc., between four or more governments. Enter a treaty, or any other formal agreement, between four or more national governments under title(either the title proper or a uniform title) Make the added entry under the heading for the home government (i.e., the government of the cataloguing agency) if it is a signatory. Make an added entry under the heading for any other government publishing the item being catalogued if that government is a signatory. Make an added entry under the heading for the government named first in the chief source of information if it is neither the home government nor the publishing government.

Court decisions, cases, etc. If reports of one court issued, enter law reports as a heading and added entrirs under the heading of an editor or compiler named prominently in the item being catalogued.

If the reports are more than one court, the entry under the heading for the reporter who is responsible for the report of all the cases reported.

Sacred scriptures. Enter a work that is accepted as sacred scripture by the religious groups or part of such a work, under title.

The Koran / translated from the Arabic by J.M. Rodwell

130	0	#	$aKoran.
700	1	#	$aRodwell, J.M.

10.12. MARC 21 FORMAT WITH EXAMPLES

Title Added Entries: Title added entries can be tagged in four different ways:

246 Variant titles

730 Related/analytical titles entered under uniform title

740 Related/analytical titles

700-711 $t Related author/title entries

Variant Titles (246 tag): The variant title of the work in hand should be recorded in this field. It is no longer necessary to create a note to justify the addition of a variant title, since a note will be created from the 246 field, as well as an added entry.

The kind of variant titles in this field include: alternative forms of the title such as spelled acronyms or symbols; access to portions of the title, or parallel titles; and variant titles such as spine titles, cover titles, and added title page titles.

Some notes are created directly from the value in the second indicator. If the indicator does not provide the exact note you wish to include, you may begin the tag with a |i subfield containing the note information you wish to include. (Note: at present, NOTIS does not properly index 246 tags using the $i subfield, so do not use this option until further notice.)]

Initial articles are not included infield 246, as there is no filing indicator. No punctuation mark is given at the end of the 246 field, unless it is needed for an abbreviation.

Examples

245	0	0	$a Science in the Soviet Union, 1917-1981.
246	1		$i At head of title: $a Science and public policy.

245	0	0	$a African semminar[!] series.
246	3	0	$a African seminar series.

245	0	0	$a Computerized engineering index.
246	1	0	$i Also known as: $a COMPENDEX.

245	0	4	$a The Facts on File dictionary of troublesome words.
246	3	0	$a Dictionary of troublesome words.

245	0	0	$a Japan report = |b Nihon.
246	3	1	$a Nihon.

Related/analytical Uniform Titles (730 tag): This field is used to make an added entry for the uniform title of a related work, or an analytical entry. The use of this field has not changed. The added entry should still usually be justified by a note.

245	0	0	$a Serials cataloging : $b modern perspectives and international developments / $c Jim E. Cole and James W. Williams, editors.
500	#	#	$a "Has also been published as The Serials librarian, volume 22, numbers 1/2 and 3/4, 1992"—t.p. verso.
730	0		$a Serials librarian.

Related/analytical Titles (740 tag): This field is used to provide title entries for works within the publication (with or without a collective title); for titles listed in the contents note; and for titles of related publications which do not require a uniform title, or author/title access.

245	0	4	$a The Covent Garden jester; $b Harris's list of Covent-Garden ladies.
740	4	2	$a The Covent Garden jester.
730	0	2	$a Harris's list of Covent-Garden ladies.

Related/analytical Author/title Entries (700-711 tag with $t):

These fields are used to provide author/title access to related works, or for works within the publication. The use of these tags has not changed.

245	0	0	$a Techniques and concepts of high-energy physics / $c edited by Thomas Ferbel.
505	0	2	$a Quark models / J. Rosner — Introduction to gauge theories of the strong, weak and electromagnetic interactions / C. Quigg — Deep inelactice leptognucleon scattering / D.H. Perkins.
700	1	0	$a Rosner, J. $t Quark models.
700	1	0	$a Quigg, C. $t Introduction to gauge theories of the strong, weak, and electromagnetic interactions.
700	1	0	$a Perkins, D. H. $t Deep ineleactice leptognucleon scattering.

CHAPTER 11
Heading for Persons

CONTENTS

11.1. GENERAL RULES

This chapter "Headings For Persons", contains rules for constructing names in AACR2R form. In general, choose, as the basis of the heading for a person, the name by which he or she is commonly known. This may be the person's real name, pseudonym, title of nobility, nickname, initials, or other appellation. Treat a roman numeral associated with a given name (as, for example, in the case of some popes, royalty, and ecclesiastics) as part of the name.

Punctuation and spacing: If the name chosen as the basis of the heading consists of or contains initials that are either known or presumed to represent forenames or surnames, place a full stop after each such initial, regardless of whether full stops are used in the sources(s) from which the name is derived. Leave a single space between the full stop following the initial and the subsequent initial or name.

Johnson, D.K. M.D. Shekhar

If the name chosen as the basis of the heading includes initials or abbreviations that form part of a title or term of address, or if an addition to the name includes initials or abbreviations denoting an academic degree, membership in an organization, etc., omit or include full stops or other punctuation according to the predominant usage of the person. Leave one space to separate an initial or abbreviation from a word, a number or another abbreviation, to separate an abbreviation from a following initial, or to separate one set from another.

Dr. Z Mr. Robert Brown, George, F.I.P.S.

If the name chosen as the basis of the heading lacks a forename, or if one or more of the forenames or portions of a compound surname are abbreviated, do not leave open space for insertion or completion of the missing or abbreviated element. Insert, as appropriate, a period and/or comma, followed by a single space to separate the preceding or abbreviated element from the element following it. If the element is the last element of the heading, omit the single space at the end.

Valmer, capitaine   not   Valmer, capitaine

In determining the name by which a person is commonly known "from the chief sources of information of works by that person issued in his or her language," include works issued both during and after the person's lifetime.

In determining the name by which a person working in a nonverbal context is commonly known, include among "reference sources" works by the person as well as those about the person issued either during or after the person's lifetime.

When establishing a name from information presented in roman script, rcord the letters as they are given, except as follows:

1) Convert earlier forms of letters to their modern form;
2) Separate the letters forming ligatures in English, French and other languages(except Danish, Icelandic, Norwegian); e.g. encyclopaedia not *encyclop@!dia*;
3) For items published after 1820, convert "v" to "u", "vv" to "w" and "i" to "j" as necessary to reflect modern usage.

Include any titles of nobility or words or phrases that commonly appear in association with the name either wholly or in part.

Sir Richard Acland Duke of Wellington

11.2. PREDOMINANT NAME

For persons working in a nonverbal context(or those not known primarily as authors), consider any works by the person to be included among "reference sources". Base the choice of name not solely on the name(s) appearing in the works, but choose the name that appears most frequently both in the works and in other reference sources.

If a person is known by more than one name, choose the name by which the person is clearly most commonly known, if there is one. Otherwise, choose one name or name of form of name according to the following order of preference:

1) The name that appears most frequently in the person's works
2) The name that appears most frequently in reference sources
3) The latest name.

With the exception of maiden names of married women, names appearing on a person's works in parentheses or quotation marks, such as nicknames, forenames of married women used in conjunction with a husband's forename(s), etc., are not to be considered as the preferred form of name and should not be used to the exclusion of the alternate form with which they appear when determining the predominant form. For example, if the name on a person's works appears predominantly as "J. M. (Greg) Husband", the should be established as "husband, J. M." with a reference from "Husband, Greg".

If a married woman's maiden name appears in parentheses preceding or following her married name, omit the parenthetical elements when formulating the heading. For example, if the name appears predominantly as "Maimie (Widbur) Steeves", the heading should be established as "Steeves, Maimie Widbur".

Contemporary authors: Contemporary authors who have written in the 20th century and/or are writing in the 21 st century.

Ducornet, Erica (Real name used in some works)

Ducornet, Rikki (Pseudonym used in some works)

Rikki (Pseudonym used in some works)

Fullness: Where the usage is not consistent, consider variations in fullness of form to include any usage falling within one of the types listed below:

1) omission of one or more forenames:

   Mary Gibbon

   not

   Mary Elezabeth Gibbon

2) omission of one or more portions of a surname;

   Anastasio Somoza

   not

   Anastasio Somoza Garcia

3) representation of one or more forenames by an initial;

   Daniel J. Koenig

   not

   Daniel Joseph Koenig

4) representation of one or more portions of a surname by initial;

   Luis G. de Valdeavellano

   not

   Luis Garcia de Valdeavellano

5) use of a fmiliar form of one or more forenames in place of proper form.

Corrie Ten Boom

not

Cornelia Ten Boom

Persons using more than one language: If the information is lacking or sources are unclear for language, choose the form of name that corresponds to the person's native language.

11.3. PERSONS ENTERED UNDER SURNAME

If the languages (excluding Hebrew and Yiddish) written in nonroman script, provided a single romanized form is clearly the preferred form in English/French language reference sources (i.e. provided that at least two-thirds of the major English/French language reference sources in which the name is found use the same form of name). Otherwise, apply the rule and systematically romanize the name: use the ALA/CLA/LC romanization tables for English forms of names and the transliteration tables used in French cataloging, usually ISO tables, for French forms of names.

For names in Hebrew and Yiddish, use the romanized form selected according to the following order of preference:

1) Use the romanized form appearing in the person's works.
2) Use the romanized form clearly preferred in English/French language reference sources (excluding the *Encyclopaedia Judaica*).
3) Use the romanized form found in the *Encyclopaedia Judaica*. (N.B. Not applicable for headings established in French).
4) Use the systematically romanized form following

the romanization tables for English (ALA/CLA/LC) and for French (ISO when available, otherwise the ALA/CLA/LC ones).

11.4. ENTRY ELEMENT

If a person's name consists of several parts, select as the entry element that part of the name, under which the person would normally be listed in authoritative alphabetic list in his or her language or country of residence or activity.

Direct order: If the entry element is the first element of the name, enter the name in direct order.

100	0	#	$a Ramgopal.

If the first element is a surname, follow it by a comma.

100	1	#	$a Fitzgerald, David.

If the surname is represented by initial, but at least one element of the name is given in full, enter under the initial that represents the surname

100	1	#	$a G., Michael.
100	1	#	$a Q., Mike.

If the name does not contain a surname but contains an element that identifies the individual and functions as a surname, enter under this element followed by a comma and the rest of the name.

100	1	#	$a Ali, Muhammad.

PREFERRED NAME

For compound surnames in Spanish, consider

the use of an initial or abbreviation representing the first of two or more proper names to be indicative of the person's preference for entry under the second or subsequent proper name and choose the first fully spelled name as the entry element.

Compound surnames: The entry of surnames, if consisting of two or more proper homes and names may or may not contain compound surnames.

100	1	#	$a Pandey Sharma, Karamchand.

Hyphenated surnames: IF the elements of a compound surname are regularly of occasionally hyphenated, enter under the first element.

100	1	#	$a Day-Lewis, C.

Other compound surnames. Married women whose surname consists of surname before marriage and husband's.

Place names added to surnames: Treat a place name added to a person's surname and connected to it by a hyphen as part of the surname.

Articles and preposition: If a surname includes an article or preposition of combination of the two, enter under the element most commonly used as entry element in alphabetically arranged directories, etc., in the person's language or country of residence or activity.

De villiers, Anna Johanna Dorothea Van Buren, Martin La Fountain, Jean de

100	1	#	$a Le Conte, John Eatton.

Form as found	**Form of the heading**
G. D'Allaire	D'Allaire, G.
Jean De Lorme	De Lorme, Jean
F.d'Aoust	Aoust, F.d'
Gilles De Ladurantaye	De Ladurantaye, Gilles

If the prefix is regularly or occasionally hyphenated or combined with the surname, enter the name under the prefix.

100	1	#	$a Mac Donald, William.
100	1	#	$a Fon-Lampe, A. A.

Enter under the proper name in a title of nobility if the person is commonly known by that title.

1) Use their title rather than surnames in their works.
2) Are listed under their titles in reference sources.

100	1	#	$a Byron, George Gordon Byron.

Enter a name that does not include a surname and that is borne by a person who is not identified by a title of nobility under the part of the name under which the person is listed in reference sources. Preced such words or phrases by a comma.

100	1	#	$a John, $c the Baptist.
100	1	#	$a Alban, $c Saint.

11.5. ENTRY UNDER INITIALS, LETTERS OR NUMERAL

Enter a name consisting of initials or separate letters, or numerals, or consisting primarily of initials, under those initials, letters or numerals in direct order.

Include typographic devices when they appear as part of multi-letter abbreviations of a name, but omit them when they follow single-letter initials. Include any words or phrases associated with the initials, letters, or numerals.

100	0	#	$a H.X.
100	0	#	$a 110908.

Entry under phrase: Enter in direct order a name that consists of a phrase or appellation that does not contain a forename.

100	0	#	$a Dr. X.
100	0	#	$a Author of The diary of a physician.

11.6. ADDITION TO NAMES ENTERED UNDER GIVEN NAME

Add, to the name of the person with the highest royal status within a state or people, a phrase consisting of a person's title and the name of the state or people in English.

100	0	#	$a Elizabeth $b II.

Consort of royal persons: Add, to the name of a consort of a person with the highest royal status within a state or people, his or her title followed by consort of Philip, Prince, consort of Elizabeth II, Queen of the United Kingdom.

100	0	#	$a John, $c Price of the United Kingdom.

Children and grandchildren of royal person: - Add, to the name of a child or grandchild of a person with the highest royal status within a state or people, the title borne by him or her. Mary, Princess royal, Countess of Hare wood

Popes, Bishops or other persons of religions vocation: If Popes, bishop, cardinal, and other religious term of address is identified by a given name, add the title.

100	0	#	$a John Paul $b II, $c Pope, $d 1920-

11.7. DATES

Add a person's dates (birth, death, etc.) in the form given below.

Optionally, add date (s) to any personal name, even if there is no need to distinguish between headings.

Smith, John, 1924-	*Living person*
Smith, John, 1900 Jan, 10-	*Same name, same year*
Smith, John, 1900 Mar. 2-	
Smith, John, 1837-1896	*Both years known*
Smith, John, 1836 or 7-1896	*Year of birth uncertain; known to be one of Two year*
Smith, John, 1837?-1896	*Probable year of birth*
Smith, John, *ca.* 1837-1896	*Year of birth uncertain by several years*

Smith, John, 1837-*ca.* 1896	*Approximate year of death*
Smith, John, *ca.* 1837-ca.1896	*Both years approximate*
Smith, John, *b.* 1825	*Year of death unknown*
Smith, John, *d.* 1859	*Year of birth unknown*
Johnson, Carl F., *fl.* 1893-1940	
Joannes, *Diaconus, fl.* 1226-1240	*Years of birth and death unknown. Some years of activity known. Do not use fl. dates within the twentieth*
Joannes, *Diaconus,* 12th cent.	*Years of birth and death unknown, years of activity unknown, century known. Do not use for the twentieth century.*
Jaonnes, *Actuarius,* 13th /14th	*Years of birth and death unknown. Years of activity unknown, but active in both centuries. Do not use for the twentieth century.*
Lin, Li, *chin shih* 1152	*Date at which a Chinese literary degree was conferred*

100	0	#	$a Smith $c Mr., $d 1990-
100	1	#	$a Churchill, Winston, $c Sir, $d1874- 1965.

11.8. FULLER FORMS

Fuller forms. If a fuller form of a person's name is known and if the heading as prescribed by the preceding rules does not include all of that fuller form, add the fuller form to distinguish between headings that are otherwise identical. Add all the fuller form of the inverted part of the heading and/ or the fuller form of the entry element, as appropriate. Enclose the addition in parentheses.

The most common instances of such additions occur when the heading as prescribed by the preceding rules contains initials and the spelled out form is known. Less common instances occur when known forenames, surnames, or initials are not part of the heading as prescribed. Refer from the fuller form of the name when appropriate.

100	0	#	$a H. D. $q (Hilda Doolittle), $d1886-1961.
100	1	#	$a Gresham, G. A. $q (Geoffrey Austin).

11.9. DISTINGUISHING TERMS

Distinguishing terms. When no other means is available for distinguishing between a musician (including using a word designating a musician's occupation, such as "violinist," "pianist," or "soprano"), and another person with the same name for whom a heading is already established (including changing the existing heading), "musician" may be used as a qualifier.

Côté, Serge, musician

London, David, musician

If the qualifier later appears to give a seriously inaccurate characterization of the person, change the heading by:

1) adding a date;
2) adding a fuller form of name; or,
3) changing the qualifier.

Preference in *AACR2 rev.* for using a personal name as main entry where possible. If, for example, a report is requested by a corporate body, but written by a specific person (or several specific people), then the *personal* name is used as the main entry. The corporate body which requested the report would appear as an added entry.

Examples :

100	1	#	$a Doiron,Jason.
245	1	4	$a The prevalence of problem gambling in Prince Edward Island / $c prepared for the Prince Edward Island Dept. of Health and Social Services ; by Jason Doiron & Richard Nicki....
700	1		$a Nicki, Richard.
710	1		$a Prince Edward Island. $b Dept. of Health and Social Services.

This is true whether the corporate author is listed

in the statement of responsibility, or simply appears as the publisher.

100	1	#	$a Jaques,A.P.
245	1	0	$aTrends in Canada's greenhouse gas emissions (1990-1995) / $c by A. Jaques, F. Neitzert and P. Boileau.
260	#	#	$a Ottawa : $b Air Pollution Prevention Directorate, Pollution Data Branch, Environment Canada, $cc1997....
700	1		$a Neitzert, F.
700	1		$a Boileau, P.
710	1		$a Canada. $b Air Pollution Prevention Directorate. $b Pollution Data Branch.

The authors may also be listed in a note, as they may not appear on the title page. However, personal authors are still preferred as the main entry.

100	1	#	$a Denham, Donna.
245	1	0	$a Two steps forward—one step back : $b an overview of Canadian initiatives and resources to end woman abuse, 1989-1997.
260	#	#	$a [Ottawa] : $b National Clearinghouse on Family Violence, $c c1999....

500	#	#	$a "Prepared by Donna Denham and Joan Gillespie for the Family Violence Prevention Unit, Health Canada"—T.p. verso....
700	1		$a Gillespie, Joan.
710	1		$a National Clearinghouse on Family Violence (Canada)

This is true for up to three personal authors. If more than three people are listed, then the work is catalogued as a title main entry, and the first author is listed as an added entry.

In the following example, the title page reads:

A Study of Resiliency in Communities

Prepared by: the Atlantic Health Promotion Research Centre in collaboration with Miriam Stewart, PhD, Graham Reid, PhD, Leonard Buckles, MA, Wayne Edgar, MPA, Colin Mangham, PhD, Neil Tilley, BA, and Susan Jackson, MA

for the: Office of Alcohol, Drugs and Dependency Issues, Health Canada.

The copy reads:

245	0	2	$a A study of resiliency in communities / $c prepared by the Atlantic Health Promotion Research Centre in collaboration with Miriam Stewart ... [et al.]...
700	1	#	$a Stewart, Miriam.
710	1	#	$a Canada. $b Office of Alcohol, Drugs and Dependency Issues.
710	1		$a Atlantic Health Promotion Research Centre.

11.10. MARC TAG FOR PERSONAL NAME HEADING

100 - Main Entry - Personal Name (NR)

The main entry of a work designates the person or body *chiefly responsible* for the intellectual or artistic content of the work. If more than one person or body is involved, the first named is assigned the main entry, and the additional names are given as added entries.

Additional names (both personal and corporate) will be given as added entries.

If no clear-cut author is determined, then the work is catalogued with a title main entry, and all authors are given as added entries.

The Main Entry - Personal Name (100 tag) of the MARC bibliographic record contains a personal name heading for the individual responsible for the creation of the intellectual or artistic content of the work. If the author writes under more than one name, choose the predominant name.

AACR2 covers main and added entries in chapter 21,"Choice of Access Points". The purpose of the main entry is to establish the form in which a work is to be uniformly cited. Using a main entry heading will make it easier for a library user to find an item that is listed in a bibliography or footnote.

In each cataloging record, one access point is chosen as the main entry heading. Main entry headings may also appear in the 110 tag (corporate body), the 111 tag (meeting name), or the 130 tag (uniform title). In addition, anonymous works, collections or works produced under editorial direction, and some publications of corporate bodies use the Title Statement (245 tag) as the main entry. Personal name headings not used as the main entry appear in the 700 tag.

Many rules cover the choice of headings for the personal name main entry. Rule 21.1A2 directs us to use the personal author, principal personal author, probable personal author, or the first person named as the main entry heading. Rules 21.4-21.28 deal with choosing the main entry heading for works with single, shared, or mixed responsibility.

In many cases there is only one author associated with an item, and the choice of the main entry heading is simple. When there is more than one author responsible for an item, the name that should be chosen for the main entry heading is usually listed first or in larger type. Some common rules are: for a classical recording use the composer as the main entry; for recordings of popular music use the principal musician or musical group as the main entry; and when a work is an adaptation, the person who adapted the work is used in the main entry heading and the original author is given an added entry.

Subfield a of the 100 tag contains a personal name, which may be a surname and/or forename; letters, abbreviations, phrases or numbers used in place of a name; or a family name. Some subfields may be used to qualify the name and distinguish persons with the same name from each other. A title such as King, Pope, Dr., Jr., etc. may be used in subfield c. A title such as I, II, III is placed in subfield c when distinguishing between two people with the same first and last name, such as John Smith I and John Smith II. Numerals that are used to distinguish kings, queens, popes, etc. are placed in subfield b. A fuller form of a name than is used in subfield a may be added as a qualifier, in parenthesis, in subfield q, or when authors use the same initials, their names can be spelled out in subfield q. Subfield d includes the years of birth and death when they are known or can be approximated. A question mark is used to indicate that a date is not certain. When only the date of birth or of death is known, the letters b. or d. respectively are used to indicate which kind of date is present.

Sometimes we are only able to establish the dates of an individual's life in a very rough approximation. We might use the century (19th cent., etc.) or fl. to designate a year or group of years the individual was known to be active.

Eighteen subfields may be used in the 100/700 tag, some of these subfields are used only with the personal name portion of the tag and others used only with a title of a work which is associated with the personal name. For a personal name, subfields a (name), b (numbers), c (titles), d (dates), e (relator term), q (fuller form of the name), and j (attribution qualifier) may be used. Numerals to distinguish between kings, queens, popes, etc. are entered in subfield b; however, numerals used with other personal names, such as John Doe III, are entered in subfield c. A title such as King, Pope, Dr., Jr., etc. may be used in subfield c. A fuller form of the name to help distinguish between the same name in subfield a may be added as a qualifier, in parenthesis, in subfield q. Subfield d includes the years of birth and death when they are known or can be approximated.

Subfield t contains the title of a work associated with the personal name in subfield a. Additional subfields that may be used to further define the identity of a work are: f (date of work), h (medium of work), k (form subdivision), m (performance medium), n (number of part/section of a work), o (arrangement), p (name of a part/section of a work), r (musical key), and s (version).

All the subfields will not necessarily be used in every record. Use only the subfields needed to complete the entry.

Indicators

First Indicators	0	Forename
	1	Surname
	3	Family name
Second Undefined	blank #	
Subfields	a	Personal name (NR)
	b	Numeration (NR)
	c	Titles and other words associated with a name(R)
	d	Dates associated with a name (NR)
	e	Relator term (R)
	q	Fuller form of name (NR)
	j	Attribution qualifier (R)
	f	Date of a work (NR)
	h	Medium (NR)
	j	Attribution qualifier (R)
	k	Form subheading (R)
	l	Language of a work (NR)
	m	Medium of performance for music (R)
	n	Number of part/section of a work (R)
	o	Arranged statement for music (NR)
	p	Name of part/section of a work (R)
	q	Fuller form of name (NR)

r	Key for music (NR)
s	Version (NR)
t	Title of a work (NR)

Punctuation

Subfield b is not preceded by any punctuation, unless the previous word is an initial.

Subfield c is usually preceded by a comma.

The information in subfield q is placed in parentheses.

Subfield q is usually preceded by the period ending the abbreviation.

Subfield d is preceded by a comma.

When the date of death in subfield d is open (the person does not have a death date), no punctuation follows the hyphen at the end of subfield d.

Subfield e is preceded by a comma.

Subfield j is preceded by a comma.

Subfield t is preceded by a period, unless it is preceded by subfield d with an open date, in which case it is preceded by a dash.

Subfield m is preceded by a comma.

Subfield n is preceded by a period when following a subfield t.

Subfield n is preceded by a comma when following a subfield m.

Subfield p is preceded by a comma when following a subfield m or n.

Subfield p is preceded by a period when following a subfield t.

Subfield r is preceded by a comma.

Subfield o is preceded by a semi-colon.

Subfields f, h, k, l, and s are always preceded by a period.

The field ends with a mark of punctuation (., !, ?, -) or a closing parenthesis.

Examples:

Title with author, translator, and editor.

Translators will generally not have an added entry.

100	1		$a Kawai, Toyako.
245	1	0	$a Colorful origami / $c by Toyako Kawai ; translated by Thomas I. Elliott ; edited by Don Kenny.
700	1		$a Kenny, Don.

Examples:

The ancient Greek author and a later author who used his name

100	0		$a Aesop.
100	0		$a Aesop, $d19th cent.

Several people known as John

100	0		$a John, $c Dr., $d 1941-
100	0		$a John, $c of Salisbury, Bishop of Chartres, $d d. 1180.
100	0		$a John $b XXIII, $c Pope, $d 1881-1963.

Two kings with the same name distinguished by their number and their dates

100	0		$a Louis $b XIV, $c King of France, $d 1638-1715.
100	1		$a Churchill, Winston, $c Sir, $d 1620?-1688.

The illustrator used a main entry when the publisher bound four picture books he illustrated together

100	1		$a Gergely, Tibor, $d 1900-$e ill

(Note: Illustrators are not frequently used as main entry)

Spelling out initials to distinguish between authors whose names appear the same on title pages

100	1		$a Johnson, Robert L. $q (Robert Leo)
100	1		$a Johnson, Robert L. $q (Robert Livingston), $d b. 1894.
100	1		$a Johnson, Robert L. $q (Robert Lynn), $d 1929-

Multiple surname

100			$a D'Avila-Latourrette, Victor-Antoine.

A family name is used as a main entry, if that is all that is listed on the title page

100	3		$a Churchill family.
100	3		$a Johnson family.

CHAPTER 12
Heading for Corporate Bodies

CONTENT

12.0. INTRODUCTION

A corporate name used as a main entry heading. A main entry heading is assigned according to various cataloging rules. Corporate names are the names of agencies, associations, businesses, firms, governments, institutions, nonprofit enterprises, performing groups, etc.

Following types of corporate names:

* Organized bodies entered directly under their own names
* Organized bodies entered under names of political jurisdictions
* Political jurisdictions standing alone
* Special corporate names, such as names of abbeys, cathedrals, churches, denominations, monasteries, missions, musical groups, parishes, priories, programs, studies and vessels (e.g., Catholic Church, Dire Straits (Musical group), Monasterio Las Descalzas (Lima, Peru), New York Philharmonic or Writers' Program)
* Names of conferences, conventions, exhibitions, expeditions, festivals and meetings entered indirectly, that is, under the name of a corporate body (e.g., Labour Party (Great Britain). Conference)

We can classified in following categories.

1) Government
2) Institution
3) Conference
4) Exhibition, Fairs and Festivals
5) Radio and Television Station

12.1. GOVERNMENTS

The word government is used here to mean the totality of corporate bodies (executive, legislative, and judicial) exercising the powers of a jurisdiction. A corporate body known by the word government, or its equivalent in other languages, or a term with similar meaning, that is an executive element of a particular jurisdiction is treated as a government agency. Usually, the government shall be arranged in the following order, Whole government, ministry(s), department(s), division(s), bureau(s), section(s) etc.

12.2. GENERAL RULE

Enter a corporate body directly under the name by which it is commonly identified, except when the rules that rules that follow provide for entering it under the name of a higher or related body (see24.13) or under the of a government.

Determine the name by which a corporate body is commonly identified from items issued by that body in its language, or, when this condition does not apply, from reference sources.

If the name of a corporate body consists of or contains initials, omit or include full stops and other marks of punctuation according to the predominant usage of the body. In case of doubt, omit the full stops, etc. do not leave a space between a full stop, etc., and an initial following it. Do not leave spaces between the letters of an initialism written without full stops, etc.

Make references from other forms of the name of a corporate body as instructed in AACR2 code 26.3.

If the name of the corporate body includes commas, quotation marks, parentheses, or any other marks of punctuation, such marks are to be included as part of the heading. Quotation marks should always be recorded as double quotation marks regardless of how they appear in the name.

111	1		$a International Symposium on "Quality Control" (1974-) $n(6th : $d1987 : $cOsaka, Japan)

Slashes separating elements of a name should be recorded without leaving spaces before or after the slash.

eg. Association/Le Vieux-Port

Romanization: If the name of the body is in a language written in a nonroman script, romanize the name according to the table for that language adopted by the cataloging agency. For those languages for which no ISO transliteration table has been developed, headings in French will follow ALA/CLA/LC romanization tables.

Systematically romanize all names written in nonroman script according to the ALA/CLA/CL romanization tables for headings established in English and the ISO transliteration tables for headings established in French.

Rule 24.1A gives priority to forms of name appearing in the body's own publications, but "in its language". To ensure the uniform presentation of headings we will follow the main rule which calls for systematic romanization.

Changes of name: If the name of a corporate body has changed (including change from one language to another), establish a new heading under the new name for items appearing under that name. Make a cross reference from the old heading to the new and from the new heading to the old.

110	1		$a National Tuberculosis Association.

For works by this body, see also the earlier heading;

Cross reference:

110	1		$a National Association for the study and Prevention of Tuberculosis.

Establish a new heading whenever there is a change in name no matter how slight the change may be, except when the change affects only an element of the name that has been omitted from the heading following the provisions of rules 24.5, 24.7A, 24.8A.

If a change in name results in the resumption of an earlier form of name used by the same body, and a heading has already been established for that name, do not establish a new heading. Revise explanatory and other references as required, and use the previously established name as the heading for new publications issued under that same name. If, however, a link between the earlier and later use of the name cannot be made (i.e. if it is not possible through a history and /or references to establish a connection between the two) treat the name as one name used by two different bodies, establishing two headings and making additions to each, as necessary, to distinguish one body from the other.

VARIANT NAMES: Apply this rule if a body uses variant names in items issued by it. When determining which of two or more variant names is to be used as the heading for a body, compare the forms found only on items issued by the body itself. Do not include forms of the body's name found on items issued by bodies which are subordinate or related to it. Consider formal presentation of a name to include presentations of the following type:

1) Names presented as part of a formal statement of responsibility (i.e. a statement indicating explicitly the role of the corporate body vis-à-vis the work);

   "Prepared by: Project Planning Branch, Ministry f Housing"

2) Names immediately preceding or immediately following the title proper, parallel title, or other title information;

   The Alberta Liquor Control Board / 55th Annual Report

3) Names incorporated in a statement of publication distribution, etc.

   "Published by Environment Council of Alberta"

Do not consider formal presentation to include names incorporated in the title proper, parallel title or other title information, or names appearing solely as part of a graphic device (logo, symbol, etc.).

To be considered the predominant form, a single form of name must represent either:

a) two-thirds of all occurences of the name appearing in formal presentations, or

b) if there is no predominant form among those presented formally, or if there are no forms presented formally at all, simply two-thirds of all occurences of the name appearing on chief sources of information.

Language: If the official language or languages of a body cannot readily be determined through statements issued by the body in its own administrative publications, consider all language forms of the name stated prominently and regularly on works emanating from the body to represent official languages of the body.

If the name of an international body appears in English on items issued by it, use the English form.

Arab League

Not Union des etats arabes

Jami 'at al-Duwal al –'Arabiyah

Conventional name: If a body is frequently identified by a conventional form of name in reference sources in its own language, use this conventional name.

India

Not

Republic of India

Religious orders and societies: Use the best-known form of name, in English, if possible, for a religious order or society. In case of doubt, follow this order of preference;

a) the conventional name by which its members are known in English

b) the English form of name used by units of the order or society located in English-speaking countries

c) the name of the order or society in the language of the country of its origin.

Franciscans

Not Ordo Fratrum Minorum

Order of St.Francis

Minorites

12.3. NAMES OF COUNTRIES, STATES, PROVINCES, ETC.

For inter-state, inter-provincial bodies, etc., and bodies that are involved with jurisdictions at different levels of government (e.g. federal-provincial agencies), add the name of the smallest jurisdiction that encompasses all the jurisdictions involved, unless the name of the body includes the name of that jurisdiction, or an understandable surrogate of it.

110	1		$a Interprovincial Advisory Council on Energy (Canada)

Local place names: When adding a local place name as a qualifier to the name of a corporate body.

Salem college (Winston-Salem, N. C)

Use the conventional name of a government, unless the official name is in common use. The conventional name of a government is the geographic name of the area (e g., country, province, state, county, municipality) over which the government exercises jurisdiction.

France

Not republique francaise

Names not conveying the idea of a corporate body: In general, add a general designation as a qualifier if the name alone does not convey the idea of a corporate body. Use an appropriate general term if there is one or take the term from the item being catalogued. If there is more than one corporate body with the same name, add a term as specific as necessary to resolve the conflict.

Ulua (Ship)

Franklin (Aircraft carrier)

Franklin (Steamship)

Performing Groups

In general, if there is doubt that the name contains a word that specifically designates a performing group or a corporate body (e.g., band, consort), or contains a collective or plural noun (e.g., Stampeders, Men of the Deep), add a designation to the name. Use the designation "(Musical group)" unless this term is inappropriate or inadequate (e.g., in cases of conflict).

Glass Tiger (Musical group)

Beau Dommage (Musical group)

Kashtin (Musical group)

Make the additions to all names belonging to one or more of the following types:

1) names used in the same form by more than one body, regardless of whether the name is chosen as the form on which the heading is based or whether it is simply a variant form from which a reference is made; University of Victoria (Victoria, B.C.)
2) names which differ from one another only by virtue of the fact that one uses an adjectival form of a word for which the other uses the noun form; one uses articles, prepositions, conjunctions, etc., not used by the other; one includes a word or two at the end of the name not included in the other, etc.;
3) names which are non-distinctive (e.g. names which simply indicate the type of body and/or its field of activity, area of interest, etc., names which lack any proper noun or adjective derived from a proper noun that would distinguish them from other similar names, etc.);

Centre for Policy and Management Studies (Ottawa, Ont.)

Institute for Small Business (Kitchener, School of Economic Science (Toronto, Ont.)

Centre for Theory in the Humanities and Social Sciences (York University (Toronto, Ont.))

4) names of government agencies (excluding institutions—see section on Government institutions below) that are entered directly and do not include either the name of the government or an understandable surrogate for the government's name as part of the name of the agency itself.

Montreal Port Corporation (Canada)

Vancouver Regional Rapid Transit Project (B.C.)

In determining whether a name falls within type 1 or type 2, comparison should be made with headings and references already in the catalogue at the time the name is being established. No further searching for identical or similar names is required. Type 3 and type 4 do not require comparison with existing headings and references; the characteristics of the name itself will determine whether or not an addition is to be made.

Do not make the additions prescribed under 24.4C2 - 24.4C7 to the names of business firms or to the names of international organizations unless the name falls under type 1 or type 2 (i.e. unless there is conflict or near conflict with another name in the catalogue at the time the name is established).

12.4. GOVERNMENT. ADDITIONS

If the application of rule 23.4B to the name of a state, province, or territory of Australia, Canada, or the United States, a place in the British Isles, a constituent state of Malaysia, the Soviet Union, or Yugoslavia results in the name being established without the addition of a larger place name, and the name of the state, etc., so established is the same as the name of a local place within its own boundaries, add to the name of the state, etc., a term indicating type of jurisdiction in order to clarify the distinction between it and the local place name.

Québec (Province) not Québec

(The addition is made to clarify the distinction between the heading for the province and that for the city by the same name located within the province, i.e. Québec (Québec)).

Jurisdiction name

Do not add a term indicating type of jurisdiction to the name of a sovereign state, even if the same name is used by another jurisdiction. Jurisdictions may be ecclesiastical entities or the jurisdiction name under which you enter a corporate name, a city section or a title of a work (e.g., *France* or *New York (N.Y.)*). Corporate names containing a name of a jurisdiction as an integral part of the name or qualified by a jurisdiction name are identified by 1st indicator value *1.*

110	1	#	$a Great Britain. $b Home Office.
110	1	#	$a Fulda (Germany : Ecclesiastical principality)
110	1	#	$a San Francisco (Calif.). $b Division of Mapping.
110	1	#	$a United States. $b President (1981-1989 : Reagan.

Do not add a term indicating type of jurisdiction to differentiate between successive governments presiding over the same (or approximately the same) territory. Use one heading only to represent each of the successive governments without differentiation.

Newfoundland not Newfoundland (Colony)

Multi jurisdictional government bodies: If a government agency is subordinate to a higher body which is entered directly under its own name, the subordinate agency is to be entered either directly under its own name or subordinately as a direct or indirect subheading of the heading for the higher body. Such agencies are not to be entered under the name of the government. Understand "higher body" to refer to any body in the corporate hierarchy above the agency in question. If subordinate entry is called for under 24.13, the agency should be entered as a subheading of the next higher body in the hierarchy that is entered under its own name.

Canadian Hydrographic Service.

Tides and Inland Water Levels Section.

not

Canada. Tides and Inland Water Levels Section

12.5. ORGAN OF GOVERNMENT

1. Executive bodies
2. Legislative bodies
3. Judicial
4. Adminstrative
5. Government official

12.5A. EXECUTIVE BODIES

Type 1. To determine whether a name belongs to this type consult dictionaries in the language of the form of name chosen as the heading for a definition of the term in question.

110	1	#	$a United States. $b Division of wildlife service.

Type 2. For government agencies at all levels of government in Canada, consider the following words to be among those which normally imply administrative subordination:

In French: administration, agencies, bureau, cabinet, committee, Commissaire, commission, ...consultative, delegation Direction, groupe, office, secretariat, service

In English: administration, administrative...(e.g. administrative office), advisory...(e.g. advisory group), agency, board, bureau, commission, committee, consultative...(e.g. consultative panel),directorate office, officer, panel secretariat service steering...(e.g. steering group), task...(e.g. task force), working...(e.g. working group)

110	1	#	$a United States. $b Central office of information.

N.B. The above lists are not exhaustive, and may be added to from time to time as warranted by the recurrent use of certain words in the naming of government agencies.

However, if the name of the subordinate body is distinctive (i.e. if it includes a proper noun or an adjective derived from a proper noun) enter the body directly under its own name regardless of whether the proper noun, etc. in its name serves to identify the government to which it is administratively ordinate. If required, add the name of the government as a qualifier (see rule interpretation 24.4C1).

110	1	#	$a Royal Commission on Newfoundland Finances (Canada)

Not

110	1	#	$a Canada. Royal Commission on Newfoundland Finances.

Type 3. The national level of government, consider that the name of the body is "general"—and enter it subordinately— if the name does not contain distinctive elements of the following types:

- proper nouns or adjectives derived from proper nouns; or,
- subject words; or
- terms indicating jurisdiction such as, "national", "federal", "state" (meaning national) or equivalents in foreign languages.

Research Centre, Library, Technical Laboratory can enter the names of all other national level bodies directly. If required, add the name of the government as a qualifier. (see rule 24.4C1).

110	1	#	$a Medical Research Council (Canada)

Not

110	2	#	$a Canada. Medical Research Council.

Type 4. Below the national level of government, consider that the name of the body is "general" — and

enter it subordinately — if the name does not contain the following:

- name (or an understandable surrogate of the name) of the government to which it is administratively subordnate; or,
- some other element tending to guarantee uniqueness (usually a proper noun or adjective derived from a proper noun).

British Columbia. Provincial Youth

Employment Program

110	2	#	$a India. $b Ministry of Education.

Type 5. For the Government of Canada, the major executive agencies will be defined as those listed in Schedule A of the Financial Administration Act. For the provincial governments, reference should be made to the Public Accounts of each of the respective governments.

Direct or indirect subheading

Consider "the lowest element in the hierarchy that will distinguish between the agencies" to be the lowest element of the hierarchy that can be entered directly under the name of the government, omitting any intervening unit in the hierarchy that is not, or is not likely to be, essential to distinguish bodies with the same name or to identify the body.

110	2	#	$a Alabama (Musical group)
110	2	#	$a United States Steel Corporation
710	2	#	$a Activity Records, Inc.

710	2	#	$a Golda Meir Library.
710	2	#	$a Society for American Archaeology. $b Meeting. $n(41st : $d 979 :$c St. Louis)

12.5B. LEGISLATIVE BODIES

Omit from the name of the committee, etc., the name in noun form of the legislature or chamber to which it is subordinate unless such an omission would result in an objectionable distortion.

110	1	#	$a Canada. $b Parliament. $b Senate. $b Special Committee on Retirement Age Policies.

In case of doubt as to whether a body is in fact a subordinate unit of the legislature, etc., or doubt as to whether it is subordinate solely to the legislature, etc., treat is as any other government agency.

110	1	#	$a Canada. $b Library of Parliamenet.

Not

110	1	#	$a Canada. $b Parliamenet $b Library

12.5C. JUDICIAL

Enter a civil or crimnal court under the heading for the jurisdiction whose authority it exercise, followed by name of the court.

110	1	#	$a India. Sb Supime court.
110	1	#	$a Rajasthan. $bHigh court.

12.5D. ADMINSTRATIVE

The administrative bodies as a direct subheading of the heading for the government.

If title is Director of college education. Ministry of education, Govt. of Rajashthan

110	1	#	$a Rajasthan. $b Director of college education.

No need to give the heading of Ministry of education because this directrated is always consider under the Ministry of Education.

12.5E. GOVERNMENT OFFICIAL

1. Head of state, etc: The subheading for a soverign, president, other head of state, governor acting in offical capacity under the heading for the jurisdiction, followed by the title of the official in English. Add the inclusive years of the reign or incumbency and the name of the person in a brief form and in the language of the heading for that person.

110	1	#	$a India. $b President (1967-1969 : Zakir Hussain)
110	1	#	$aUnited States. $bPresident (1981-1989 : Reagan)

For collection of official letter's

If title is: President speaks: A Collection of speechs of Zakir Hussain

100	0	#	$a Zakir Husain.
110	1	#	$a India. $b President (1967-1969 : Zakir Hussain)

2. Head of Government of International inter government bodies

The subheading for a head of government acting in an official capacity who is not also a head of state under the heading for the jurisdiction, followed by the title of the official in the vernacular.

Do not add the dates or names

110	1	#	$a Unite Kingdom. $b Prime Minister.
110	1	#	$a France. $b Premier Minister.

12.6. SUBORDINATE AND RELATED BODIES (INSTITUTIONS)

Do not make the additions prescribed under 24.4C2 - 24.4C7 to the names of institutions (schools, libraries, laboratories, hospitals, archives, museums, prisons, research centres, etc.) created or controlled by a government unless the name falls under type 1, 2 or 3 (i.e. unless there is conflict or near conflict with another name in the catalogue at the time the name is established, or unless the name is non-distinctive).

110	1	#	$a Forest Fire Research Institute (Canada)

But

110	1	#	$a Bedford Institute of Oceanography.

Not

110	1	#	$a Bedford Institute of Oceanography (Canada)

If a body is entered subordinately under the name of a parent or related body or under the name of a government, and the name to which it has been subordinated serves to distinguish it from others, do not make the additions to the name prescribed under 24.4C2 - 24.4C7.

110	1	#	$a British Columbia. Provincial Youth Employment Program.

but

110	1	#	$a Newfoundland. $b Arts and Culture Centre (St. John's, Nfld.)

(Arts and Culture Centres are located in other Newfoundland municipalities)

Generally, make the additions prescribed under rules 24.4C2-24.4C7 to any other name if the addition improves the heading (e.g., assists in understanding the scope of the activities of the body). In case of doubt, do not add the qualifier.

The National Library will correct previously established headings on an as encountered basis.

School districts: School districts are often not clearly defined either as a corporate body or as a place name since they are generally not found in gazetteers. It depend upon the National Policy of the Country, generally it as corporate bodies and always add the name of the province in which the school district is located as a qualifier whether there is conflict or not. District numbers are retained if they appear in the name by which the school district is commonly identified.

110	1	#	$a Silver Willow School District No. 681 (Sask.)

Subordinate and related bodies entered subordinately

Note: when rule 24.13 is applied to a government agency entered subordinately under the name of a higher body (see 24.17), the interpretations under rule 24.18 take precedence over those which follow. Provided that no objectionable distortion results, omit from the subheading any of the following:

a) the full name of the higher body under which the subordinate unit is entered;

b) the abbreviation or acronym for the higher body;

c) a shortened form of the name of the higher body.

National Library of Canada. Advisory Board.

not

National Library of Canada.National Library Advisory Board.

Type 1. To determine whether a name belongs to this type consult dictionaries in the language of the form of name chosen as the heading for a definition of the term in question.

Type 3. Include under type 3 names used in the same form by more than one body, regardless of whether the other body is an independent one entered directly under its own name, whether it is a subordinate or related body entered under the name of its parent, or whether the name is simply a variant form from which a reference has been made to the established name for the other body.

Include also under type 3, names of subordinate bodies which differ from one another only by virtue of the fact that one uses an adjectival form of a word for which the other uses the noun form; one uses articles, prepositions, conjunctions, etc., not used by the other, etc. Include also under type 3 names which are non distinctive (e.g. names which simply indicate the type of body and/or its field of activity, area of interest, etc., and which lack any proper noun or adjective derived from a proper noun).

Type 5. Include under type 5 all names of such bodies that indicate no more than a particular field of study, regardless of how precise the field of study is or how elaborately it is expressed in the name.

Type 6. Consider the "entire name" of the higher or related body to be equivalent to the name chosen as the heading for that body exclusive of any elements to which the name has been subordinated or elements which have been added as qualifiers.

12.7. JOINT COMMITTES, COMMITTES, COMMISSIONS, ETC.

A states that a body made up of representatives of two or more other bodies is entered directly under its own name and rule, if the parent bodies are entered as subheadings of a common higher body, the joint unit is entered as a subordinate body.

These committees and commissions submit reports to the government. Committee reports are vital from different angles. They are constantly sought in the libraries for reference or research work. Committee and commission reports may become popular either by the name of the committee and commission or by the names of the chaimen of these committees and commissions.

The entry either directly entered under the name of the committee or commission or the subordinate bodies of the government. Additional entries are provided for the chairman and also under the popular title with which it is often called.

110	1	#	$a India. $b Ministry of Shipping and Transport. $b Wage Revision Committee for Port and Dock Workers for Major Ports. (1974)
700	1		$a Lokur, B.N.
500			$a Chairman: B.N. Lokur.
710	2	#	$a Lokur committee Report.

If a body is composed of representatives of two or more other bodies and these other bodies are all entered as subheadings of a common higher body, enter the joint unit as a subordinate body.

110	1	#	$a Canada. $b Committee on Sexual Offences Against Children and Youths.

12.8. LOCAL CHURCHES, ETC

Choose the predominent form of name found in publications issued by a local church or parish. Only formal presentations of the name should be considered. This principle applies to both English and French forms of names for local churches and parishes. If the parish uses a French form and an English form of its name to identify itself in its publications, both forms should be used.

110	1	#	$aSt. James Church (Bronx, New York, N.Y.)
110	1	#	$a St. Theresa's Parish (Scarborough, Ont.)

If there is no predominant form of name in its publications, the order of preference in the rule should be applied in the case of French parishes. However, in the case of English parishes, a name containing the word "Church" is to be preferred over one containing the word "Parish".

110	1	#	$a St. Andrew's Church (Victoria, B.C.)

Buildings: In English, the term "Church" refers to both the building and the community of believers. In French, there are different terms for these two notions. The same heading can be used for both purposes in English, whereas two headings are needed in French: one for the parish, and one for the church building. The heading for the church building is created only when required for subject treatment.

Always add the local place name even if the place name is included in the name of the local church or parish and even if the location of the church is clear from the name itself. If the name of the local church or parish contains a partial form of the place name, an earlier name, etc., make the addition to the heading according to 24.4C3-24.4C4.

When adding a city or town as a qualifier to the local church or parish, give the qualifier in its catalogue entry form as modified by 23.4A1; 24.4C1.

110	1	#	$a Paroisse Sainte-Cécile-de-Lévrard.
110	1	#	$a Paroisse Saint-Félicien (Saint-Félicien, Québec)

If adding the name of the smallest or most specific

local political or ecclesiastical jurisdiction is not sufficient to distinguish one local church from another with the same name, formulate the addition as instructed under 24.4C3.

12.9. PERFORMING GROUPS

Armed Forces are treated as military units and not consider the local place associated with the base to be part of the name.

110	1	#	$a Canada. $b Canadian Forces Base (Gagetown, N.B.)

Military installations such as forts, airfields, training areas, are treated as local places.

110	2	#	$a United States Air Force Band.
110	2	#	$aHootie & the Blowfish (Musical Group)

12.10. MARE 21 TAG FOR MAIN ENTRY—CORPORATE NAME

The Main Entry - Corporate Name (110 tag) of the MARC 21 bibliographic record contains a name heading for the corporate body or performing group responsible for the intellectual or artistic content of the work.

Indicators

First	0	Inverted name
	1	Jurisdiction name
	2	Name in direct order
Second	#	Undefined

Subfield

	$a	Corporate name or

jurisdiction name as entry element (NR)

$b Subordinate unit (R)

$c Location of meeting (NR)

$d Date of meeting or treaty signing (R)

$e Relator term (R)

$f Date of a work (NR)

$h Medium (NR)

$k Form subheading (R)

$l Language of a work (NR)

$n Number of part/section/ meeting (R)

$p Name of part/section of a work (R)

$s Version (NR)

$t Title of a work (NR)

Punctuation

Subfield b is preceded by a period.

Subfield c is usually preceded by a space colon.

Subfield d is preceded a space colon.

Subfield e is preceded by a comma.

Subfield t is preceded by a period.

Subfield n is preceded by a period when following a subfield t.

Subfield n is preceded by no punctuation when following a subfield a or b.

Subfield p is preceded by a comma when following a subfield n.

Subfield p is preceded by a period when following a subfield t.

Subfields f, h, k, l, and s are always preceded by a period.

Subfields c, d, and n are enclosed in parentheses when containing the location, date, and number of a meeting.

The field ends with a mark of punctuation (., !, ?, -) or a closing parenthesis.

Examples:

110	2	#	$a PRONAPADE (Firm).
110	2	#	$a St. James Church (Bronx, New York, N.Y.)
110	2	#	$a United States. $b Congress. $b Joint Committee on the Library.
110	2	#	$a Catholic Church. $b Concilium Plenarium Americae Latinae $d (1899 : $c Rome, Italy)
110	2	#	$a International Labour Organisation. $b European Regional Conference $n (2nd : $d 1968 : $c Geneva, Switzerland)
110	2	#	$a United States. $ bCongress $n (97th, 2nd session : $d 1982). $b House.
110	2	#	$a New York Public Library. $k Manuscript $p Aulendorf Codex.

12.11. CONFERENCE

Conferences, congresses, meetings, etc.

If, among the variant forms of a conference name appearing in the chief source of information, there is a form that includes the name or abbreviation of the name of body associated with the meeting to which the meeting is not subordinate, use this form.

FAO Hybrid Maize Meeting...

If, however, the name is of a body to which the meeting is subordinate (e.g., the annual meeting of an association), see24.13A, type6.

If a conference has both a specific name of its own and a more general name as one of a series of conferences, use the specific name.

Symposium on protein metabolism ...

Not Nutrition symposium....

Symposium on Endocrines and Nutrition...

Not Nutrition symposium...

Local place names

When adding a local place name as a qualifier to the name of a corporate body, give the qualifier in its catalogue-entry form as modified by 23.4A1; 24.4C1, second paragraph; and appendix B.14.

111	2	#	$a Conference on Energy Conservation $n (2nd : $d 1976 : $c Ottawa, Ont.)

Year(s)

Add dates only when necessary to distinguish between two or more different bodies. If the same name is used by a single body during two or more separate periods of its history, establish only one heading for the name.

111	2	#	$a Governor's Conference on Aging (N.Y.) $d (1982 : $cAlbany, N.Y.)

Number

If numbering has been omitted from one or more of a series of conference headings because of irregularities, provide an information note explaining irregularities under a heading for the series of conferences as a whole (i.e. the heading omitting number and location). Add notes to the description of individual conference publications within the series as required.

111	2	#	$a AIC Seminar $n(15th : $d1986 July 22-24)

Location

In determining whether the location should be given as a local place name or as the name of an institution, etc., prefer the location as given on the source of information for the name of the conference. If both the name of an institution, etc., and a local place name appear on that source, prefer the name of the institution, etc. Include the local place name with the name of the institution, etc., only if it is necessary for identification. If the location is not given on the source from which the name of the conference is derived, prefer the location as given in a prominent source (see 0.8) to any given elsewhere in the item. Again, if both the name of an institution and a local place name appear prominently, prefer the name of the institution, etc., and include the local place name only as necessary for identification.

Note that a local place name is to be given in the form provided for in Chapter 23, and as a consequence it may be necessary to establish both an English and a French form of the heading. If the name of an institution, etc., is used, it is to be given in the nominative case in the language in which it is found in the item. Where variant forms appear, preference should be given to the form appearing on the source from which the name of the conference is derived. If the location is not given on that source, preference should be given to a form appearing prominently.

If within the chosen source, the name of the institution, etc., appears in different languages, prefer the form called for by the application of 24.3. Again, as a consequence of 24.3, it may be necessary to establish both an English and a French form of the heading.

111	2	#	$a Unesco Symposium on the Publication of Books in the Various Languages of Multilingual Countries $d(1976 : $cMoscow, Russia, and Alma-Ata, Kazakhstan)

111	2	#	$a Alabama Symposium on Justice and theBehavioral Sciences $b(3rd : $d 1974 :$c University of Alabama)

12.12. MAIN ENTRY—MEETING NAME [MARC STANDARD]

The Main Entry-Meeting Name (111 tag) of the MARC bibliographic record contains a name heading for the conference, exhibition, expedition or other type of event responsible for the work.

Indicators

First	0	Inverted name
	1	Jurisdiction name
	2	Name in direct order
Second	#	Undefined
Subfield	$a	Meeting name or jurisdiction name as Entry element (NR)
	$c	Location of meeting (NR)
	$d	Date of meeting (NR)
	$e	Subordinate unit (R)
	$f	Date of a work (NR)
	$g	Miscellaneous information (NR)
	$k	Form subheading (R)
	$l	Language of a work (NR)
	$n	Number of part/section/ meeting (R)
	$p	Name of part/section of a work (R)
	$q	Name of meeting following jurisdiction name entry element (NR)
	$t	Title of a work (NR)
	$u	Affiliation (NR)

$4 Relator code (R)

Punctuation

The field ends with a mark of punctuation (., !, ?, -) or a closing parenthesis.

Examples:

111	2	#	$a Symposium Internacional "Manuel Pedroso" In Memoriam $d (1976 : $c Guanajuato, Mexico)
111	1	#	$a Chicago. $q Cartography Conference.
111	2	#	$a Governor's Conference on Aging (N.Y.) $d (1982 : $c Albany, N.Y.)
111	2	#	$a Esto '84 $d (1984 : $c Toronto, Ont). $e Raamatunaituse Komitee.
111	2	#	$a World Peace Conference $n (1st : $d1949 : $c Paris, France and Prague, Czechoslovakia)
111	2	#	$a National Conference on Physical Measurement of the Disabled, $n 2nd, $c Mayo Clinic, $d 1981, $g Projected, not held.

CHAPTER 13
Uniform Title

CONTENTS

13.0 - INTRODUCTION

Uniform titles are used to bring together all catalogue entries for a work that has been published under variant titles. They may also be called "filing titles".

Uniform titles can be used for different purposes. They provide the means:

* for bringing together all catalogue entries for a work when various manifestations (e.g., editions, translations) of it have appeared under various titles;
* for identifying a work when the title by which it is known differs from the title proper of the item being catalogued;
* for differentiating between two or more works published under identical titles proper;
* for organizing the file."

Uniform titles will be used to resolve or anticipate conflicts of entry between works with identical titles proper as provided for below, as long as both bibliographic records are created at the same time. When a title proper conflict between a new and an existing record is identified, create a uniform title for the new record only.

13.1. SITUATION WHERE UNIFROM TILES ARE USED

Uniform titles are used if:

* More than one work has the same title and a qualifier is needed to distinguish one from another;
* A work is known by more than one title, or is a translation, or there are translations of it in our catalogue;

* A heading for the work is set up according to special cataloging rules;
* A work is a complicated one, divided into parts with titles of their own;
* A work is important for religious, historical, literary, or other reasons.

13.2. GENERAL RULES

Add accents as appropriate to French capital letters when it is certain that they are integral to a name but have been omitted in the source from which the name is taken. Add accents when creating a new heading or when revising an already established heading. Do *not* revise a heading for the sole purpose of adding accents.

Follow the same guidelines for recording additions to uniform titles. Uniform titles are added as required to original cataloging for the following:

1. Serial titles
2. Computer programs
3. Translations
4. Collective titles
5. Sacred scriptures, etc.
6. Manuscripts
7. Laws, treaties, liturgies, etc.
8. Collective artistic works
9. Music works

13.3. SERIAL TITLES

Authority records are sometimes made for serial titles. This is done in at least three cases.

* More than one serial has the same title. This often happens with a short or common title (and

especially with newspapers). A qualifier with the place of publication is added to the title in the 130 field, and in any 630 or 730 entries or any linking fields that may be needed. It also sometimes happens that a serial changes its title and later changes back again; in this case the qualifier would include the beginning date.

* A serial exists in multiple formats, for instance print and electronic. In this case a 130 with the qualifier (Online) at the end of the title is added to distinguish the electronic format, and used in any 630 or 730 fields *that refer to that format only*, or any linking fields, including the 776 field. A 130 with the qualifier (Print) is not yet common but may become so.

The serial title is used as an added entry for the serial. An authority record is created to provide access from variant titles, and to record publication data and other information that can help distinguish the title in hand from other, similar titles. (If the library has catalogued the serial, then this information is contained in the serial record itself.) A qualifier would not *necessarily* be added in this case.

More than one part: If the item being cataloged consists of consecutive parts of work and the parts are numbed use the designation of the parts of the parts in the singular as a subheading of the title of the whole work pollwed by the inclusive number of the parts.

110	1	#	$a Homer.
240			$aI liad $p Book 1-6
245	1	5	$a The first six books of homers Ilaid.

If the item consists of two unnumbered or non consecutively numbered parts of work, use the uniform title of the first part as the uniform title for the item. Make a name title added entry for the other part.

100	1		$a Dante, Alighiere.
240			$a Purgatoria. $l English.
245	1	4	$aThe vision of Purgatory and Paradise.
730			$a Dante Alighiere $k Paradise $l English.

If the item consist of three or more unnumbered or non consecutively numbered parts of, or if extracts from, a work use the uniform title for the whole work followed by Selections.

130			$a Vedas. $p Rgveda$lSanskrit. $k Selection.

Two work issued together. If an item consisting of two works is entered under a personal or corporate heading, use the uniform title of the work that occurs first in the item. Make a name-title added entry using the uniform title of the second work.

13.4. COMPUTER PROGRAMS

The Library of Congress originally treated the names of computer programs as subject headings. LC is gradually converting these names to uniform title format. Since this format is now being used in the subject file, the uniform title is also being used as an access point in the bibliographic records for consistency.

Authority records are made for these uniform titles to provide subject information as well.

13.5 . TRANSLATIONS

When a work (literary, historical, philosophical, scientific, etc.)

* is so well-known that other works are written about it,
* is translated, or
* is known by more than one title even in the original language, a uniform title can be used to bring together all the variants.

If the work is anonymous or has a title main entry for any reason, use tags 130 / 630 / 730. If the work has a personal or corporate author use 100 / 240, 600 $t, 700 $t, or 110 / 240 610 $t, 710 $t, tags as appropriate.

130		0	$a Gawain and the Grene Knight. $l English & English (Middle English)
245	1	0	$a Sir Gawain and the Green Knight : $b a dual-language version

Note that a 600 $t or 630 would include any $p subfields but would *not* include subfields for language, version, or date. It might of course include $v or $x subfields.

13.6. COLLECTIVE TITLES

A publication that consists of an author's complete or selected works presents a special case, since the title is assigned by the publisher and may be different from another publication with the same contents.

If the publication contains more than three works, a collective uniform title may be assigned. Choose if possible from the following list (except for music):

* Works
* Selections
* Correspondence
* Essays
* Novels
* Plays
* Poems
* Prose works
* Short stories
* Speeches

All but the first two of these may have $k Selections added if the works in the specified form are not complete.

Add a $l subfield for language if the work in hand is a translation. (If the original language and a translation are combined, add the original language last, after an ampersand). A $s subfield can be used to specify a translator or version. A $f subfield for the publication date may be added at the end.

100	1	0	$a Shakespeare, William, $d 1564-1616.
240	1	0	$a Plays. $f 1904.
245	1	0	$a Mr. William Shakespear's comedies, histories, and tragedies.

13.7. SACRED SCRIPTURES, ETC

A uniform title (main/added entry) is used for religious scriptures such as the Bible, the Talmud, and the Koran. Because these works, especially the Bible, exist in many languages and multiple translations into many of them, and also because their constituent parts are often published separately, their uniform titles can be quite long.

130	1	0	$a Bible. $l German (Middle Low German) $f 1961.

130 or 730 headings of this type could also include a subfield $k Selections, immediately before the date subfield. 630 headings would normally have only $p and |v or |x subfields.

13.8. MANUSCRIPTS

Entries are made for manuscripts which are in libraries or archives when works are published based on their contents. When there is no popular title for the manuscript, these entries are set up in tags 110 / 240, 610 $k and 710 $k in the form: corporate name + form heading + specific designation. Note the use of the $k and $n subfields.

710	2	#	$a British Library. $k Manuscript. $n Arundel.

Some old manuscripts (codexes), etc., are better known by popular names. The authority record should have a reference from the formal name if known.

130		0	$a Book of Kells.

13.9. LAWS, TREATIES, LITURAGIES, ETC

Laws, treaties, liturgical works, etc., are usually set up as corporate name-title entries in 110 / 240, 610 $t and 710 $t tags.

710	1		$a Ontario. $t Laws, etc. (Ontario acts)

There are exceptions to this as well. For example, a treaty involving up to three parties is entered under the one that comes first in alphabetical order, like the hard-to-recognize headings above for the FTA and NAFTA, but a treaty involving four or more parties is entered under title. A legal document not connected with any particular country may also be entered under title.

630	0	0	$a Treaty of Utrecht $d (1713)
130	0	0	$a Universal Declaration of Human Rights

13.10. COLLECTIVE ARTISTIC WORKS

Use "Laws, etc." also for parts of collections to which "Laws, etc." has been assigned, unless the part constitutes a subject compilation and has a citation title of its own. In the latter case, use the citation title of the part as the uniform title; generally, DO NOT make any further addition to the citation title when used as a uniform title.

Canada

[Criminal code]

not Canada

[Criminal code (Milligan)]

If it is necessary to provide a more precise subarrangement of works under the heading for one jurisdiction than can be achieved through the use of the *collective title* "Laws, etc.", use as an addition to the collective term a further designation such as title proper or a shortened version of the title, editor, translator, compiler, publisher, etc. The most appropriate designation is selected in each case and no specific order of selection is applied. Such additions should be made in all cases where a secondary added entry for the collection is used with the entry for a related work and the collective title "Laws, etc." has been used for more than one work under the heading for the same jurisdiction.

Ontario

[Laws, etc. (Statutes, 1974 - 1975)]

Statutes of the province of Ontario passed in the session...

13.11. COLLECTION OF REGULATIONS

Include within the scope of "legislative enactments" administrative regulations that fall under the provisions of rule 21.32B.For collections of regulations as covered under 21.32B deriving from more than one law enacted within the same jurisdiction, add to the uniform title the term "Regulations".

Northwest Territories

[Laws, etc. Regulations]

Revised regulations of the Northwest

Territories, 1980 : a consolidation ....

If it is necessary to provide a more precise subarrangement of collections of regulations under the heading for one jurisdiction, interpose between "Laws, etc." and "Regulations" a further designation based on the title, etc. If the scope of the collection of regulations coincides with the scope of a published collection of laws, choose as the designation for the regulations the same term as chosen for the laws.

Ontario

[Laws, etc. (Statutes, 1974-1975).

Regulations]

13.12. SINGLE LAWS ETC.

Include within the scope of "single legislative enactment" administrative regulations that fall under the provisions of 21.32B and derive from a single law.Use as the uniform title for administrative regulations as covered under 21.32B deriving from a single law the uniform title for the law followed by the term "Regulations".

British Columbia

[Health Act. Regulations]

13.13. COLLECTIVE ARTISTIC WORKS

Collective artistic works include motion pictures, television programs, etc. A uniform title is *not* created or used to avoid conflict with an identical 245 title already in the database (where the $h GMD and other information should make the situation clear). However, uniform titles *should* be created and used for these types of works whenever a 630 or 730 heading is called for, whether there is a conflict or not.

245	0	0	$a Hamlet, Prince of Denmark $h [videorecording]
630	0	0	$a Casablanca (Motion picture)

Uniform title qualifiers for works of this type should include a term identifying the type of work, followed if necessary by a date, personal name, etc. For artistic works with personal authors, such as paintings, uniform titles with qualifiers are unlikely to be needed unless there is a conflict, but any 600 $t or 700 $t heading will still be a uniform title.

13.14. MUSICAL WORKS

Uniform titles are established for virtually all music

scores. Generally, the same principles that apply to classic works are applicable to music.

Note regarding librettos: Retain the 240 tag in the bibliographical record.

* These are the texts/literary works which are set to music (operas). Although there is usually no music in these publications and they are classed in ML49 or ML50 (with books, not scores), they are catalogued with composer as main entry and therefore require Uniform Titles.

Due to rule changes and old cataloging practices, there is considerable cleanup of music headings to be done. The OPAC index displays are further confused by the fact that the records for many scores are in book format. Only those catalogued since 1988 are in the proper music format display.

13.15. MISCELLANEOUS RULES

Initial title elements consisting solely of the name of one type of composition.

Three categories of titles that are to be treated as "titles consisting solely of the name of one type of composition":

1) titles that consist of a name of a form;
2) titles that consist of a name of a genre;
3) titles that consist of a generic term frequently used by different composers.

The third category (and the third category only) should be evaluated with the final sentence of the footnote in mind also. This will be particularly true when the common term in question is accompanied by some modifier other than a medium or a numeral. One should consider that all modifiers other than a medium or a numeral make the phrase a distinctive title - no matter how common sounding it is. For example "Piece" is a generic term frequently used by different composers, but "Concert piece", "Little piece", etc., are considered distinctive titles.

13.16. STANDARD COMBINATION OF INSTRUMENTS

Giving a "full statement of medium" according to the last paragraph does not mean that one ignores the terms for groups of instruments in 25.30B5 and their prescribed use in 25.30B2(c).

[Quintets, piano, woodwinds, horn,
K. 452, E major]

not [Quintets, piano, oboe, clarinet,
horn, bassoon, K. 452, E. major]

13.17. CONTINUING RESOURCES

For continuing resources entered under title, construct a uniform title heading if the title proper for the work is identical to the title proper for another work in the catalogue, regardless of whether the other title proper is used as a main entry or only as an added entry.

Print version

130	#	#	$a Ottawa citizen (1986)
245	0	4	$a The Ottawa citizen.

Microfilm version

130	#	#	$a Ottawa citizen (1986)
245	0	4	$a he Ottawa citizen $h [microform]

Monographs (including sound recordings and audiovisual materials)

a) For monographs entered under title, construct a uniform title heading only if the title proper for the work is identical to the title proper for another work in the catalogue, and one or other of the works is cited by means of a formal note and/or added entry in a record for another work or part of the same work.

b) For monographs entered under person or corporate body, construct a uniform title (filing title) only if the title proper for the work is identical to the title proper for another work in the catalogue entered under the same heading, and one or other of the works is cited by means of a formal note and/or added entry in a record for another work or part of the same work.

13.18. STRUCTURE OF UNIFORM TITLE

To differentiate two works with identical titles proper, construct for each a uniform title using the title proper for the work, followed by a qualifying term and/or addition. Omit an initial article unless the uniform title is to file under that article.

Note that in certain cases involving items with identical titles proper, one (or perhaps both) of the items will belong to a group consisting of various manifestations (editions, translations, etc.) of a single work that requires a uniform title based on the title used in reference sources, the title of the original edition, a collective title, an official short title or citation title, etc. (see rules 25.3-25.4; 25.8-25.35). In such cases, construct a uniform title using the title called for in the applicable rule rather than the title proper on the item itself. Make additions to the uniform title for individual entries within the group, as necessary, to distinguish one language edition, etc., of the work from another.

If the work is entered under title, give the uniform title as the heading for the entry. If the work is entered under a heading for a person or corporate body, place the uniform title between the name heading and the title proper.

13.19. CHOICE OF QUALIFYING TERM

The term used to qualify the title proper will be selected according to the following order of preference:

1) Place
2) Corporate body
3) Date
4) Multiple qualifiers
5) Edition statement, other title information, etc.

The following criteria should be applied in determining which category of qualifying term is to be used:

1) Place of publication

Prefer place of publication as the qualifying term, unless one of the three conditions noted under 2) Corporate body below applies.

Arrow (Montréal, Quebec)

Arrow (Castlegar, B.C.)

Transactions of the Illuminating Engineering Society (London, England)

Transactions of the Illuminating Engineering Society (New York, N.Y.)

If the work is published in more than one place, choose as the qualifying term the place named first in the publication, distribution, etc., area.

2) Corporate body

Prefer as the qualifying term the name of the corporate body with which the work originated or by which it was issued or published if any of the following conditions apply:

a) main entry is under title and the title proper consists solely of a term or terms (other than articles, prepositions, and conjunctions) which indicate no more than the type of publication, or its periodicity;

Bulletin

Communiqué

Quarterly report

Technical report

or

b) main entry is under title and the title includes an initialism, acronym or other abbreviated form of the issuing body's name;

AIJ proceedings (American Institute of Journalists)

AIJ proceedings (Association of Iron Joiners)

or

c) main entry is under title and the addition of place as a qualifying term is inadequate to resolve the conflict because another work with the same title was published in the same place.

Contact (Toronto Nutrition Committee)

Contact (Real Estate Institute of Canada)

(Both works published in Toronto)

If in such a case the use of corporate body as a qualifying term is inappropriate or inadequate, the date of publication or the date of coverage of the first issue may be used as the qualifying term, notwithstanding the conditions enumerated in 3) Date below.

If more than one corporate body is associated with the work, choose as the qualifying term the name of the principal body according to the following order of preference:

(i) the first named in the statement of responsibility;

(ii) the first named in the publication, distribution, etc., area;

(iii) the first named in the issuing body note.

In case of doubt as to whether the criteria above are applicable, choose place of publication (see 1) Place of publication above) or other terms (see 3) Date, 4) Multiple qualifiers and 5) Edition statement, other title information, etc. below) as the qualifying element.

3) Date

Prefer the date of coverage of the first issue if all of the following conditions are met:

- the work has resumed publication under a title used previously and an intervening title change has occurred;
- the issuing body is the same and has not changed its name;
- no other conflict exists with an identical title proper (and a different issuing body).

British Columbia Ministry of Education.
[Annual report (1977)]
British Columbia. Ministry of Education.
[Annual report (1980)]
(Published in 1979 by:
British Columbia. Ministry of Education,
Science and Technology)

High River times (1905)

High River times (1982)

(Published 1976-1982 under title:

Times (High River, Alta.)

If the date of coverage of the first issue is unknown, use the date of the first issue or part of the publication that is available. If the first issue covers more than one year use the last named date. If necessary, add month or month and day to distinguish between two titles issued in the same year.

4) Multiple qualifiers

If the addition of place, corporate body, or date alone is inadequate as a qualifying term prefer as the qualifying term a combination of either place and date or corporate body and date following the general criteria for choosing these elements in 1) Place of publication, 2) Corporate body and 3) Date above.

Bulletin (Canadian Association of Medical Record Librarians : 1944)

Bulletin (Canadian Association of Medical Record Librarians : 1971)

(Published between 1968 and 1971 under title: CAMRL newsletter)

5) Edition statement, other title information, etc.

If none of the qualifiers listed above (in 1) Place of publication, 2) Corporate body, 3) Date, 4) Multiple qualifiers) is adequate, choose as the qualifying term any element or combination of elements extracted from the description of the work which will serve to distinguish it from other works entered under the same title or other works with the same title proper entered under the same heading.

Bakeries (Statistics Canada : Preliminary)
Bakeries (Statistics Canada : Final)
Canada (English edition)
Canada (Édition française)

13.20. MARC TAGS USED WITH UNIFORM TITLES

Uniform titles as a main entry in Marc tags 130 for translated, complex, or confusing works that do not have author main entries (including sacred scriptures, anonymous literary or historical works of various kinds, and serial titles).

If translated, complex, or confusing works *do* have author main entries, the uniform titles are entered in tags 240, (including works which have been translated or published in more than one form, and works which are grouped under general headings, including special headings for music and law).

A uniform title for any work with a title main entry, even if not translated or complicated in any way, may be used in a 630 field if it is a subject, or in a 730 field if it is considered to make a contribution to the book in hand. Likewise, a uniform title with an author main entry is used in a 600 $t or 610 $t if the work is a subject, or in a 700 $t or 710 $t if it makes a contribution, even if not translated or complicated.

In addition, a uniform title is the preferred form for use in linking tags (e.g. 776, 780, 785), since (at least in theory) it creates the best connection in the OPAC.

440, 830, and 800 $t series fields are also, strictly speaking, uniform titles.

Indicators

First		Nonfiling characters [0-9]
Second	#	Undefined

Subfield

$a	Uniform title (NR)
$n	Number of part/section of a work (R)
$p	Name of part/section of a work (R)
$l	Language (NR)
$h	Medium (GMD)
$k	Form subheading (R)
$s	Version (NR)
$m	Medium of performance for music (R)
$r	Key for music (NR)
$o	Arranged statement for music (NR)
$f	Date of a work (NR)

Punctuation

The field ends with a mark of punctuation (., !, ?, -) or a closing parenthesis.

Examples:

100	#	#	$a Montreson, Beni.
245	0	4	$a I saw a ship a-sailing /$c adapted by Beni Montreson.
730	0		$a Mother Goose.

100	#	#	$a Letters to Star trek / $c edited by Susan Sackett.
700	1	0	$a Sackett, Susan.
730	0		$a Star trek.

240 - Uniform Title (NR)

The uniform title for an item when the bibliographic description is entered under a main entry field that contains a personal (field 100), corporate (110), or meeting (111) name.

Indicators

First		Uniform title printed or displayed
	A	value that indicates whether the uniform title is printed or displayed.
	0	Not printed or displayed
	1	Printed or displayed
Second	Nonfiling characters [0-9]	
Subfield Codes	$a	Uniform title (NR)
	$d	Date of treaty signing (R)
	$f	Date of a work (NR)
	$g	Miscellaneous information (NR)
	$h	Medium (NR) A media qualifier.
	$k	Form subheading (R)
	$l	Language of a work (NR)
	$m	Medium of performance for music (R)
	$n	Number of part/section of a work (R)
	$o	Arranged statement for music (NR)
	$p	Name of part/section of a work (R)

$r Key for music (NR)

$s Version (NR)

Examples

240	1	4	$a The Pickwick papers. $lFrench
240	1	0	$a Laws, etc. (1969-1970)
240	1	0	$aTreaties, etc. $gPoland, $d1948 Mar. 2. $kProtocols, etc., $d1951 Mar. 6

CHAPTER 14
References

CONTENTS

14.0. GENERAL RULES

Forms of references

Reference entries direct a person while using the catalogue from one heading or from one entry to another heading or entry in the catalogue. The purpose of reference entries are: (i) To direct the user of the catalogue to refer to a particular name. (ii) It tells the user that there are no entries under which he is looking for but instead directs him to refer to another entry or entries and the requisite information can be found under those entries. (iii) It also tells the user that there are several more entries written by the author or on the subject he is looking for.

There are basically following types of references:

1. 'See' References
2. 'See also' References
3. 'Name-Title references

1. 'See' References: Make a see reference from a form of the name of a person or a corporate body or title of a work that might reasonably be sought to the form that has been chosen as a name or uniform title heading, or as a title entry.

2. 'See also' References: Make a see also reference from one name or title heading to another related name heading, uniform title, or title.

3. 'Name-Title references: Make a see or see also reference from a title (or uniform title) that has been entered under a personal or corporate heading in the form of a name-title reference beginning with the personal or corporate heading followed by the title concerned.

14.1. SEE REFERENCES

1) Name of persons: It is possible that some

authors may have more than one name. In such cases they may write under their different names.

a) **Dates.** Include dates in references if they have been included in the heading. If If the form of the reference conflicts with an established heading, resolve the conflict by using dates in the reference, although they are not used in the heading.

100	1	0	$a Zhang, Daqian, $d 1899-
400	1	#	$a Chang, Da-ch'ien, $d 1899-
400	1	#	$a Daqianjushi, $d 1899-

b) **Initials.** Do not combine different language forms or romanizations.

100	1	0	$a Chang, S. K. $q (Shi Kuo), $d 1944-
400	1	#	$a Chang, Hsi-kuo, $d 1944-, $d 1944-

Not:

400	1	#	$a Chang, S. K. $q (Hsi Kuo), $d 1944-

c) **Titles/epithets.** Include titles and epithets used in the heading in the reference unless, for titles, they are not appropriate to the form of the reference, or, for epithets, the purpose is to refer from a form containing a different epithet. For variant language forms for a person entered under surname, include titles of nobility and terms of honor and address in the form found in the source for the reference. If the source for the reference does not include the title, etc., use in the reference the term used in the heading, although it is in a different language.

100	0	#	$a Sejong, $c King of Korea, $d 1397-1450
400	0	#	$a Sedzhon, $c King of Korea, $d 1397-1450
400	0	#	$a Seijong, $c the Great, $d 1397-1450 , $c King of Korea, $d 1397-1450

d) Compatible headings. Normally, construct the reference to "match" the AACR2 compatible element in the heading. Exception: Do not use "pseud" in references.

100	0	#	$a Moren, $c pseud.
400	0	#	$wnne $a Mo-jen, $c pseud.
400	0	#	$a Mo, Ren.

e) Different names. Refer from a name used by a person, or found in reference sources, that is different from the name used in the heading for that person.

100	0	#	$a Premcand.
400	0	#	$a Dhanpat rai.
400	0	#	$a Munshi Premchand.

f) Chang name. If chang the name, choose the latest name or form of name unless there is reason to believe that the earlier name will persist as the name by which the person is better known.

In following case the Miss Anna Katherine Green changed her name after marriage and adopted her husband's surname. i.e. Rohlfs but continued to write some books in her maiden name i.e. Anna Katherine Green.

100	0	#	$a Rohlfs, Anna Katherine.
400	0	#	$a Green, Anna Katherine.

g) Different entry elements.

100	0	#	$a Polnay, Peter de.
400	0	#	$a De Polnay, Peter.

2) Corporate names: The name of a place found in reference sources that is significantly different from the form used as the entry element in a heading.

a) **Qualifiers.** Include qualifiers in the reference if appropriate to the form in the reference even if the qualifier has not been used in the heading because of earlier policies or because it is not appropriate here. Exception: Do not add a qualifier to a reference consisting solely of an initialism.

110	2	#	$a Taehan Min'guk Kungnip Chungang Tosogwan.
410	2	#	$a National Central Library (Seoul, Korea)(Seoul, Korea)
410	2	#	$a National Central Library (Seoul, Korea)(Seoul, Korea)

b) Terms of incorporation. Construct the reference to "match" the heading with regard to the presence, absence, or form of a term of incorporation.

110	2	#	$a Daian, Kabushiki Kaisha.
410	2	#	$a Daian Bunka Boeki Kabushiki Kaisha.

c) **Different forms of the name.** Refer from a form of name used by a body, or from a form of name of a place or body found in reference sources or resulting from a different romanization, if that form differs significantly from the form used in the heading for that body or place.

110	2	#	$a Nations Unies.
410	2	#	$a United Nations.

d) **Initials.** If a heading consists of an initialism or acronym and, in the catalogue, initials with full stops are filed differently from those without full stops, refer from one form to the other.

110	2	#	$a U.N.E.S.C.O.
410	2	#	$a Unesco.

110	2	#	$a E.E.E.
410	2	#	$a European Economic Community.

e) **Numbers.** If, in the catalogue, numbers expressed as words are filed differently from numbers expressed as numerals, follow the instructions sbelow if a heading begins with a number.

110	2	#	$a Twentieth Century Heating & Ventilating Co.
410	2	#	$a XXth Centu·y Heating & Ventilating Co.

14.2. SEE ALSO REFERENCES

1) Name of persons: If the works of one person are entered under two different headings, make a see also reference from each heading to the other. For personal names (including any pseudonym), when the entire form in the first line of a reference and the entire form in an established heading are the same, attempt to resolve the conflict by additions to the name in the reference. If there are no data available to resolve the conflict, make a see also reference. This applies whether the cross reference is already in the file or is the result of the item being cataloged.

100	1	#	$a Wen, Agnes Chung.
500	1	#	$a Zhong, Kun.

NOTE: The reference conflicts with the heading Zhong, Kun (..); no data available to resolve the conflict.

2) Corporate name: Refer from the name of a place found in reference sources that is significantly different from the form used as the entry element in a heading.

110	2	#	$a Aix-la-Chapelle (Germany)
510	1	#	$a Aachen (Germany)

Generally, trace a reference from variant forms of entry that apply to the name chosen for the heading. However, do not trace a reference that would normalize to the same form as the heading on the same record or to the same form as a heading on another record. For variant forms of a name, generally, trace only one reference from each variant, normally, constructing it in the form in which it would be constructed if chosen as the heading.

Normally, make references only to connect immediately adjacent headings, thus creating a chain of see also references leading from one heading to another. However, if the relationship is not clear, it is permissible to connect several headings.

Make see also references between independently entered corporate headings for bodies that are related:

110	2	#	$a Xing zheng yuan nong ye fa zhan wei yuan hui (China)
510	2	#	Joint Commission on Rural Reconstruction (China)

14.3. SEE REFERENCE UNIFROM TITLES

a) Treaties, etc.

(1) Different names or variants of the name

110	1	#	$a China. $t Treaties, etc. $g Portugal, $d 1887 Apr. 13. $l Polyglot.
430	#	0	$a Zhonghua Renmin Gongheguo zheng fu he Putaoya Gongheguo zheng fu guan yu Aomen wen ti de lian he sheng ming $d (1987)
430	#	0	$a Declaração conjunta Sino-Portuguesa sobre a questão de Macau $d (1987)

b) Treaties, etc. between two or three governments (21.35A1, 25.16B1). Refer from the name(s) of the government(s) not chosen as the main entry heading, followed by the uniform title Treaties, etc., and the date (year month day).

110	1	#	$a Japan. $t Treaties, etc. $g Russia, $d 1905 Sept. 5.
430	#	0	$a Korea (South). $t Treaties, etc. $g Ireland, $d 1990 July 18.

Different titles or variants of the title. Refer to the uniform title from the different titles and variants of the title under which the work has been published or cited in reference sources.

130	1	#	$a Feng shen yan yi.
430	#	0	$a Feng sheng zhuan.
430	#	0	$a Feng shen bang.

Collective titles.

When a collection of, or a selection from, a person's works is catalogued under a collective uniform title, refer from the name and title taken from the chief source of information or found in a reference source to the name and collective title, unless the title taken from the chief source of information or found in a reference source is the same as, or very similar to, the collective title.

100	1	#	$a Sima, Qian, $d ca. 145-ca. 86 B.C. $t Shi ji. $k Selections.
400	1	#	$a Sima, Qian, $d ca. 145-ca. 86 B.C. $t Xiao He, Han Xin.

14.4. REFERENCES TO ADDED ENTRIES FOR SERIES AND SERIALS

If an added entry is made under the heading for a series to which separately cataloged parts belong, refer to the heading for the series from different forms of the heading under which it might reasonably be sought.

In title references (subfield $a, subfield $n, and subfield $p) and title portions of name/title references, omit an initial article unless it is to be filed on. Add a qualifier to a reference if it conflicts with the heading of another publication.

Add the qualifier "(Series)" to a reference if it is identical to a personal or corporate (including geographic) name.

(1) Give a name/title proper reference for the situations listed below. If the heading includes a parenthetical qualifier, do not include that qualifier when recording the title proper in the reference.

When a body responsible for the series is a noncommercial one or is a commercial one whose responsibility extends beyond that of merely publishing the series; in this context, consider university presses as "commercial;"

130	#	0	$a Xianggang da xue Zhong wen xi wen shi cong shu.
410	2	#	$a University of Hong Kong. $b Dept. of Chinese. $t Xianggang da xue Zhong wen xi wen shi cong shu.

When the title of a numbered series consists solely of a form of a corporate body's name whether or not that form of name is identical with the name of the corporate body given as the heading on the body's name authority record.

130	#	0	$a Rodo Mondai Kenkyujo (Series)
410	2	#	$a Rodo Mondai Kenkyujo (Japan). $t Rodo Mondai Kenkyujo.
643	#	#	$a Osaka $b Rodo Mondai Kenkyujo (Series)

APPENDIX
A : Initial

Non filing character, users in tag number 130, 240, 242, 243, 245, 440, 630, 730, 740, 830

a	English, Galician, Hungarian, Portuguese, Romanian, Scots, Yiddish
a'	Scottish Gaelic
al	Romanian
al-	Arabic, Baluchi, Brahui, Panjabi (Perso-Arabic script), Persian, Turkish, Urdu (**Note:** *al-* is meant to cover all of the spellings in romanization (e.g., *"as" in "as-sijill"*))
am	Scottish Gaelic
an	English, Irish, Scots, Scottish Gaelic, Yiddish
an t-	Irish, Scottish Gaelic
ane	Scots
ang	Tagalog
ang mga	Tagalog
as	Galician, Portuguese
az	Hungarian
bat	Basque
bir	Turkish
d'	English

da	Shetland English
das	German
de	Danish, Dutch, English, Frisian, Norwegian, Swedish
dei	Norwegian
dem	German
den	Danish, German, Norwegian, Swedish
der	German, Yiddish
des	German, Walloon
det	Danish, Norwegian, Swedish
di	Yiddish
die	Afrikaans, German, Yiddish
dos	Yiddish
e	Norwegian
'e	Frisian
een	Dutch
eene	Dutch
egy	Hungarian
ei	Norwegian
ein	German, Norwegian, Walloon
eine	German
einem	German
einen	German
einer	German
eines	German
eit	Norwegian
el	Catalan, Spanish
el-	Arabic
els	Catalan

en	Catalan, Danish, Norwegian, Swedish
enne	Walloon
et	Danish, Norwegian
ett	Swedish
eyn	Yiddish
eyne	Yiddish
gl'	Italian
gli	Italian
ha-	Hebrew
hai	Classical Greek, Greek
he	Hawaiian
he	Classical Greek, Greek
he-	Hebrew
heis	Greek
hen	Greek
hena	Greek
henas	Greek
het	Dutch
hin	Icelandic
hina	Icelandic
hinar	Icelandic
hinir	Icelandic
hinn	Icelandic
hinna	Icelandic
hinnar	Icelandic
hinni	Icelandic
hins	Icelandic
hinu	Icelandic
hinum	Icelandic

hið	Icelandic
ho	Classical Greek, Greek
hoi	Classical Greek, Greek
i	Italian
ih'	Provençal
il	Italian, Provençal/Occitan
il-	Maltese
in	Frisian
it	Frisian
ka	Hawaiian
ke	Hawaiian
l'	Catalan, French, Italian, Provençal/ Occitan, Walloon
l-	Maltese
la	Catalan, Esperanto, French, Italian, Provençal/Occitan, Spanish
las	Provençal/Occitan, Spanish
le	French, Italian, Provençal/ Occitan
les	Catalan, French, Provençal/Occitan, Walloon
lh	Provençal/Occitan
lhi	Provençal/Occitan
li	Provençal/Occitan
lis	Provençal/Occitan
lo	Italian, Provençal/Occitan, Spanish
los	Provençal/Occitan, Spanish
lou	Provençal/Occitan
lu	Provençal/Occitan
mga	Tagalog

mga	Tagalog
mia	Greek
ʻn	Afrikaans, Dutch, Frisian
na	Hawaiian, Irish, Scottish Gaelic
na h-	Irish, Scottish Gaelic
nje	Albanian
ny	Malagasy
ʻo	Neapolitan Italian
o	Galician, Hawaiian, Portuguese, Romanian
os	Portuguese
ʻr	Icelandic
ʻs	German
’t	Dutch, Frisian
ta	Classical Greek, Greek
tais	Classical Greek
tas	Classical Greek
te	Classical Greek
ten	Classical Greek, Greek
tes	Classical Greek, Greek
the	English
to	Classical Greek, Greek
to	Classical Greek
tois	Classical Greek
ton	Classical Greek, Greek
ton	Classical Greek, Greek
tou	Classical Greek, Greek
um	Portuguese
uma	Portuguese

un	Catalan, French, Italian, Provençal/ Occitan, Romanian, Spanish
un'	Italian
una	Catalan, Italian, Provençal/Occitan, Spanish
une	French
unei	Romanian
unha	Galician
uno	Italian, Provençal/Occitan
uns	Provençal/Occitan
unui	Romanian
us	Provençal/Occitan
y	Welsh
ye	English
yr	Welsh

B: Glossary

This glossary contains definitions of most of the technical bibliographic and cataloging terms used in this rules.

Access point : A name, term, code, etc., under which a bibliographic record may be searched and identified.

Added entry : An alternate heading or title by which an item is represented in a catalog; a secondary heading. See also Main entry.

Analytic : A type of entry(record) for a work published as part of a monographic series is a bibliographic record, which is created using the unique title on the individual piece or pieces as the title proper.

Appendix : Notes, charts, tables, lists, or other detailed information that follow the main text of a book.

Area : A major section of the bibliographic description, comprising data of a particular category or set of categories. See also Element.

ASCII : An acronym for "American Standard Code for Information Interchange." A standard for defining codes for information exchange between equipment produced by different manufacturers. ASCII defines a specific set of alphanumeric characters, punctuation, and a few control characters (such as a carriage return).

Authority Control : Maintenance of established headings, both within an **Authority file** and within bibliographic files of library catalogs through the creation of one standard form of a name or word under which a person or concept can be indentified and searched within a catalog. Also involves the creation of cross-reference names or terms.

Authority File : A list of records for authorized headings used as access points in bibliographic records, also includes documentation justifying the form of the headings, and cross references to link common variant forms.

Authority Record : Includes the established form of a name or word that is used as an access point in a library catalog, as well as cross-references from other names or terms and documentation justifying the form of the heading.

Bibliographic Control : The process of managing library materials by creating surrogate records of descriptive information for each item and indexing them for retrieval.

Bibliographic record : The description of a discrete item, such as a book, a videorecording, or a serial. Machine-readable forms of bibliographic records are stored in and retrieved from automated online catalogs, either locally or nationally via the Internet, or magnetic tape provided by a vendor.

Bibliography : Lists sources used by the author in creating a work such as a book. Also may list additional sources on important subjects covered in the text.

Catalog : 1. A database of library material contained in a collection, a library, or a group of libraries, arranged according to specific rules. Access to the database may be provided in a print book of records, a traditional card file, on microform, or electronically via an OPAC.

2. In a wider sense, a database of materials prepared for a particular purpose (e.g., an exhibition catalog, a sales catalog).

Cataloging Source : Agency or institution responsible for the creation of the bibliographic record. Represented in USMARC record by field 008, position 39, and field 040, which gives NUC codes for the catalog agency, transcribing agency, and any agencies that modify the record.

Chief source of information : The location from which a bibliographic data may be taken in the construction of a bibliographic record (or portion thereof) is prepared. Example of the chief source are the title page of a book, the title screen of a video, or the title screen from a computer software product.

CIP : Cataloging in Publication, a program of the Library of Congress to make partial cataloging information available for items before they are published. This information generally appears on the t.p verses.

CJK : Chinese, Japanese, and Korean. The brief name for the RLG project to enable cataloging of these language items.

Classification : A system of assigning letters and/or numbers to books in order to collate items covering similar subject areas. Two prominent classification systems in the United States: LC - Library of Congress classification system developed at the largest library in the country, the Library of Congress in Washington, D.C. Composed of alphanumeric strings; DDC-Dewey Decimal System.

Collective title : The title proper for an item containing several individual works, such as essays or poems. The collected works... is a good example of a collective title.

Colophon : A statement at the back or end of an item giving information about one or more of the following: the title, author(s), publisher, printer, date of publication or printing.

Compiler : 1.One who creates or produces a collection by selecting and putting together matter from the works of various persons or bodies.

2. One who selects and puts together in one publication matter from the works of one person or body. Compilers are not listed as main entries.

Component Part or Accompanying material: An item that is physically part of a larger item (called the host item), and can be described by an analytic entry.

Claiming : The process of contacting a publisher or vendor to request supply of material missed or overdue on subscription, standing order, or backfile order.

Classed as Separate or Cataloged Separately or CAS : Volume(s) in a monographic series of a variety of subject areas; each volume receives its own call number and bibliographic record.

CONSER : Co-operative Online Serials Program, originally planned in 1973 as the Co-operative Conversion of Serials Program to convert manual serial cataloging into machine-readable records. The full CONSER data base resides on the OCLC online system. See now PCC.

CONSER record : A bibliographic record for a serial that has been authenticated by at least one participant in the CONSER program.

Continuing integrating resource : An integrating resource issued over time in a series of iterations with no predetermined conclusion. Most integrating resources are continuing.

Continuing resource : A bibliographic resource that is issued over time with no predetermined conclusion. Continuing resources include serials and ongoing integrating resources.

Content designator : A code (such as a tag, indicator, or subfield) that identifies the nature of a particular data element in a record.

Control number : A unique sequential number supplied by the system to each new bibliographic record when it is entered into the online catalog.

CORC : A cooperative framework for the sharing of metadata allowing integration of Marc and Dublin Core into a single system.

Corporate body : An organization or group of persons that is identified by a particular name and that acts, or may act, as an entity. Typical examples of corporate bodies are associations, institutions, business firms, nonprofit enterprises, governments, government agencies, religious bodies, local churches, and conferences. Corporate bodies may be main headings, added headings or subjects in a catalog record.

Copy Cataloging : Incorporating an existing bibliographic record that was created by another cataloging agency into the local catalog from a bibliographic utility's database and either accepting as is or editing the record.

Copy Holdings : In it is listed each copy owned, in process, or on order. Also in the copy holdings records is an item's location, call number, linkages to order and circulation records, date of cataloging, and type of cataloging.

Copyright : Legal document that the item's contents are the property of the author or publisher usually appears on the verso of the title page of a book

Copy-Specific Information : Details that apply only to a single copy of an item, as opposed to bibliographic data (normally applicable to all copies of an edition). This type of information should only be cited in a bibliographic record in a local field (e.g., 590)

Cover title : A title printed on the cover of an item as issued and not found on the title page of the item.

Current number : The last-issued number of a newspaper or serial publication and bearing the most recent issue number and/or date. Also called 'Current issue'.

Current serial : An individual serial (q.v.) publication to which the library has a continuous subscription, or has the expectation of receiving further issues.

DDC : Dewey Decimal Classification. A system for using numbers to put materials on similar topics together on the shelves, dividing materials into 10 broad main "classes" (main categories), then subdividing the classes into smaller and smaller groups. The top number in the call number on the label of a book is a classification number.

Delimiter : A special character used in conjunction with a subfield code to introduce each subfield in a variable field. Character may vary in design but typically is a or $.

Descriptive Analysis : The part of cataloging consisting of bibliographic description and the determination of access points.

Diacritic : Refers to a character or symbol, which

has no standard keyboard equivalent, such as + k {etc. Because they cannot be represented using a standard keyboard, diacritics are typically stripped from source data during the database building process. The pippin utility program is responsible for stripping/substituting city>place>diacritics.

Dublin Core : A set of standard descriptive metadata elements used with web resources to aid in resource discovery. The elements are intended as a starting point for resource description. All elements are optional, and are intended to be extensible to richer descriptive elements when needed. The 15 elements are: title, author/creator, subject/keywords, description, publisher, other contributor, date, resource type, format, resource identifier, source, language, relation, coverage and rights management.

Earliest entry cataloging : All changes to a serial title are kept on a single record with the description based on the earliest issue and title changes, etc. recorded in notes.

Edition : All copies produced from essentially the same type image (whether by direct contact or by photographic or other methods) and issued by the same entity. Intellectual content is unique and unchanged to the work. Significant variation of the content requires a new edition statement.

Editor : One who prepares for publication for an item not his or her own. The editorial work may be limited to the preparation of the item for the manufacturer, or it may include supervision of the manufacturing, revision, (restitution), or elucidation of the content of the item, and the addition of introduction, notes, and other critical matter. In some cases, it may involve the technical direction of a staff or person engaged in creation or compiling the content of the item.

Electronic serials : Serials in electronic format, which may be accessed at one or more sites, or from a remote server. They may be individual titles or part of electronic collections, some created by an individual publisher, and others aggregated collections covering a range of publishers.

Electronic Resource : A bibliographic format that includes data (information representing numbers, text, graphics, images, maps, moving images, music, sound, etc.), programs (instructions, etc., that process the data for use), or combinations of data and programs.

Element : A word, phrase, or group of characters representing a distinct unit of bibliographic information and forming part of an area of the description.

Entry : A bibliographic record of an item in a catalog. See also Heading.

Entry word : The word by which a bibliographic entry is arranged in the catalog, usually the first word (other than an article) of the main heading. See also Heading.

Enumeration : Numbering, as in serial volume and issue numbering.

Enumeration : The scheme used by a serial publication to identify distinct issues within a numerical sequence. Common enumeration elements are: volume/no. and month/year.

Extent of item : Description of the number and the specific material designation of the units of the item being described and, in some cases, other indications of the extent (e.g., duration). The first element of the physical description area.

Facsimile reproduction : A reproduction simulating the physical appearance of the original in addition to reproducing its content exactly. See also Reprint.

Field : One or more data elements that form a logical unit. In a bibliographic or metadata record, each tag corresponds to a single field.

Field number : Specification, typically 3 characters, beginning with 001 and ending 999. Synonym for tag.>

Field terminator : ending punctuation.

Finite integrating resource : An integrating resource issued over time with a predetermined conclusion; intended to be completed in a finite number of iterations.

Finite resource : A bibliographic resource that is issued once or over time with a predetermined conclusion; completed within a finite number of parts or iterations. Includes monographs and finite integrating resources.

Fixed field : A field in a machine-readable record in which each element, or unit of data, is limited to a prescribed size, content, and position in the record.

Format : In its widest sense, a particular physical presentation of an item, (e.g. monograph, serial, videorecording, map, Electronic resources, etc.).

Format Integration : A set of changes that aligns the individual bibliographic formats (such as books, serials, scores, etc.) and combines them into a single **USMARC** format for bibliographic data.

Frequency : Indicates the expected publication occurrence; any changes in the publishing frequency should be noted on the bibliographic record of a title.

Frontispiece : An illustration preceding the title page of a book and usually on the verso of the half title page.

General material designation : A term indicating the broad class of material to which an item belong. Indicated in field 245 subfield h (e.g., microfilm, sound recording, electronic resource). See AACR2 for authorized list of terms.

Half title : A title of a publication appearing on a leaf preceding the title page.

Heading : A name, word, or phrase placed at the head of a catalog entry to provide an access point. See also Access point.

Holdings : The volumes or parts of serial publications possessed by a library.

ILS : An integrated library system, such as SIRSI Unicorn, Endeavor Voyager, Library.Solution or CARL.Solution, integrate the system's modules acquisitions, cataloging, patron access catalog, and circulation - so they interact together. Therefore, when an item is cataloged, the system, in real-time, displays that item in the library's OPAC and circulation.

Imprint : The 260 field of a MARC record. Contains information on place of publication, publisher, and date of publication.

Index : Word-by-word or letter-by-letter lists, in alphabetical order, of important words, names, and places in the text of the book. Usually includes see and see-also references.

Indicator : A one-digit code that provides information to the computer about a variable field. The presence, meaning, and use of indicators will vary from field to field. Depending on the tag number of the field, either a numeric indicator value or a blank occupies each of the two reserved indicator positions in each field.

Integrating resource : A bibliographic resource that is added to or changed by means of updates that do not remain discrete and are integrated into the whole. An integrating resource may be finite or continuing. Examples of integrating resources include updating loose-leafs and updating Web sites.

ISBD : International Standard Bibliographic Description An internationally agreed upon framework for cataloging rules for description that states what essential items of information must appear in the bib record, the order in which those items will be given, and the standard punctuation that must be used.

ISBN : International Standard Book Number, carried in field 020 of the MARC record

ISSN : International Standard Serial Number. An internationally agreed upon standard number that identifies an item (serial) uniquely.

Issue : A particular publication, complete in itself, of a serial or periodical which is issued at intervals or in parts.

Issue date : The specified day, date, month or period by which the date of publication of a particular issue of a serial may be identified.

Issue number : The number given to a separately issued part of a serial to distinguish it from other issues. Numbers may run consecutively from the first issue onwards, but if the issues are divided into volumes, a new sequence of issue numbers commences with each volume.

Item : A document or set of documents in any physical form that is published, issued, or treated as a single entity, and as such forms the basis for a single bibliographic description.

Joint author : A person who collaborates with one or more other persons to produce a work in relation to which the collaborators perform the same function. See also Shared responsibility.

Journal : A newspaper or periodical. Particularly a periodical issued by a society or institution and containing news, proceedings, transactions and reports of work carried out in a particular field.

Latest entry cataloging : All changes to a serial title are kept on a single record with the description based on the latest (most recent) issue and earlier titles, etc. given in notes.

LC MARC : Another name for MARC II. All **LC MARC** records are **USMARC**, but most **USMARC** records are not **LC MARC**: that is other **USMARC** records outnumber MARC records generated by the Library of Congress.

LCCN : Library of Congress Control Number. Appears in field 010 of the MARC record. **LCSH** Library of Congress Subject Headings.

Leaf : One of the units into which the original sheet or half sheet of paper, parchment, etc. is folded to form part of a book, pamphlet, journal, etc.; each leaf consists of two pages, one on each side, either or both may be blank. The length of items consisting of pages of text on only one side is recorded in leaves.

Line number : The sequential numeric identification assigned by the system to each variable field in a record, appearing directly to the left of the field's tag. Also, the sequential numeric identification assigned to each entry in the display of a multiple record search result.

Loose-leaf publication : A serial publication which is revised, supplemented, cumulated, and indexed by means of new replacement pages inserted in a loose-leaf binder; such publications are used where the latest statements and revisions of information are important. See Updating loose-leaf.

Machine-readable cataloging : MARC bibliographic information, which is arranged in a prescribed format and on a medium, such as magnetic tape, that allows that information to be read by electronic data processing equipment, such as computers.

Main entry : The primary field of access. Usually the author or in the absence of a responsible person or body, the title of the work.

Main heading : The first part of a subject string that includes one or more subheading.

MARC : An acronym for MAchine-Readable Cataloging.

MARC format : A framework for communicating MAchine-Readable Cataloging (MARC) records, originally developed by the Library of Congress and used by many online systems, such as OCLC. The skeleton onto which the bibliographic information is built.

Mixed responsibility : A work in which different persons or bodies contribute to the intellectual or artistic content by performing different kinds of activities (e.g., adapting or illustrating a work written by another person). See also Joint author, Shared responsibility.

Magazine : A periodical publication as distinct from a newspaper, separate issues being independently paginated and identified by date rather than by serial number.

Metadata : Description of data. Generally used to refer to a descriptive schema to add in discovery of electronic resources.

Microfiche : A flat sheet of film, generally 4 x 6 inches, bearing in horizontal and vertical rows micro-images of the text of a publication. It may be positive or negative.

Microfilm : A strip of film, either 16 or 35 mm wide, bearing a number of micro-images in linear array. It may be positive or negative.

Microform : A generic term for any medium, transparent or opaque, bearing micro-images.

Micro-opaque : A copy of the whole, or part, of a book or other document made by means of microphotography, the print being on opaque paper or card. May be made solely by photographic means or by a printing method. See also Microcard.

Microcard : 1. a term, trade-mark of the Microcard Corporation which refers exclusively to a 5 x 3 inch card with images arranged in a specific manner and can be either transparent or opaque. 2. An opaque card of varying size on which microcopies have been reproduced photographically. It differs from other microforms in that the prints are positive as well as being opaque and cannot be directly reproduced. See also Micro-opaque.

Monograph : A type of publication which is nonserial - an item either complete in one part or complete, or intended to be complete, in a finite number of separate parts. Loosely used as an equivalent for book (examples: a novel, a set of encyclopedias).

Monographic Series : This is another term for "series".

Multipart item : A monograph complete, or

intended to be completed, in a finite number of separate parts. The separate parts may or may not be numbered.

Multivolume monograph : See Multipart item.

Monograph : A nonserial item (i.e., an item either complete in one part or complete, or intended to be completed, in a finite number of separate parts).

Multipart item : A monograph complete, or intended to be completed, in a finite number of separate parts.

Newspaper : A publication issued periodically, usually daily or weekly, containing the most recent news.

NACO : Name Authority Cooperative Project. A cooperative cataloging project established by the Library of Congress. Participants contribute name, series, geographic and uniform title authority records to the National Authority File.

NAF : National Authority File, a list of authoritative headings for persons and corporate bodies produced by the Library of Congress and **NACO** libraries.

Name-title added entry : An added entry consisting of the name of a person or corporate body and the title of an item. (Field 700 t)

NISO : National Information Standards Organization. The organization concerned with accreditation of voluntary technical standards for librarianship, publishing, and information science.

Non-filing characters : Typically, articles at the beginning of a title, such as 'a,' 'an,' or 'the' including the space that follows, that are not considered in the alphabetical organization of an item. 'The' would count as 4 non-filing characters (i.e. 3 letters, t h e plus the space).

NUC Code : Unique code that identifies a holding or contributing library in the National Union Catalog and, later, in MARC (or filing) records. This code appears in field 040.

OCLC Online : The largest shared cataloging service in the U.S.

OLUC Online : Union Catalog. OCLC'sdatabase of bibliographic records.

OPAC : Online Public Access Catalog. A term used to describe any type of computerized library catalog. A database of the libraries holdings made available via a computer for users.

Other title information : A title borne by an item that is not the title proper, a parallel title or a series title(s); also any phrase appearing in conjunction with the title proper, etc., indicative of the character, contents, etc., of the item or the motives for, or occasion of, its production or publication. The term includes subtitles, avant-titles, etc., but does not include variations on the title proper (e.g., spine titles, sleeve titles).

Pambinder : PAM BIND is an acid-free binder with a cloth spine reinforcement. Materials such as pamphlets, magazines, reports, manuals, scores, etc. are sewn in Title/author and call number labels are applied in-house to the pamphlet.

Parallel Title : The title proper in another language and/or script recorded in the title and **statement of responsibility** area (245 field).

Part 1 : One of the subordinate units into which an item has been divided by the author, publisher, or manufacturer. In the case of printed monographs, generally synonymous with volume; it is distinguished from a fascicle by being a component unit rather than a temporary division of a work. 2. As used in the physical description area, "part" designates bibliographic units intended to be bound several to a volume.

Periodical : A publication with a distinctive title which appears at stated or regular intervals, without prior decision as to when the last issue shall appear. It contains articles, stories or other writings, by several contributors.

PCC : Program for Co-operative Cataloging, formed in 1995 to expand access to collections by cataloging to a level that meets mutually-accepted standards. In 1997, PCC merged with CONSER, and the current situation is that PCC is the umbrella organization with four components - CONSER, BIBCO, NACO, and SACO.

PCC Partnership for Cooperative Cataloging : International cooperative effort aimed at expanding access to library collections by providing useful, timely, and cost-effective cataloging that meets mutually-accepted standards of libraries around the world.

Personal author : The person chiefly responsible for the creation of the intellectual or artistic content of a work.

Plate : A leaf containing illustrative matter, with or without explanatory text, that does not form part of either the preliminary or the main sequence of pages or leaves.

Portal : A site featuring a suite of information sharing tools, forums, chats, search engine, and news, serving as a starting point to the Web/internal service.

Preface : The author's discussion of the various aspects of the creation of the book that precedes the text of the work but follows the title page.

Preliminaries : The title page(s) of an item, the verso of the title page(s), any pages preceding the title page(s), and the cover.

Pseudonym : A name assumed by an author to conceal or obscure his or her identity.

Publisher : The agency that issued the book and assumed financial responsibility for its manufacture.

Recto : 1. The right-hand page of a book, usually bearing an odd page number.

2. The side of a printed sheet intended to be read first. Typically, the title page or leaf is a recto page or leaf.

Reference source : Any publication from which authoritative information may be obtained. Not limited to reference works.

Reprint : 1. A new printing of an item made from the original type image, commonly by photographic methods. The reprint may reproduce the original exactly (an impression or it may contain minor but well-defined variations (an issue).

2. A new publication of an edition with substantially unchanged text.

Retrospective Conversion : The process of converting bibliographic information from card or book records to computerized records for materials already held in collections before computer cataloging began. Also known as Retrocon, Recon, Retro, etc.

RLIN : The Research Libraries Information Network. The computer support for the database of the RL Group (RLG), and a large shared cataloging service.

Running title : A title, or abbreviated title, that

is repeated at the head or foot of each page or leaf. place>

SACO : The Subject Authority Cooperative Program (SACO) provides a means for libraries to submit subject headings and classification numbers to the Library of Congress.

Section : A separately published part of a bibliographic resource, usually representing a particular subject category within the larger resource and identified by a designation that maybe a topic, or an alphabetic or numeric designation , or a combination of these. See also Subseries.

Serial : A publication in any medium issued in successive parts bearing numeric or chronological designations and intended to be continued indefinitely. Serials include periodicals, newspapers; annuals (reports, yearbooks, etc.); journals, memoirs, proceedings, transactions, etc., of societies,; and numbered monographic series.

Series : 1. A group of separate items related to one another by the fact that each item bears, in addition to its own title proper, a collective title applying to the group as a whole. The individual items may or may not be numbered.

2. Each of two or more volumes of essays, lectures, articles, or other writings, similar in character and issued in sequence (e.g. Lowell's Among my books, second series).

3. A separately numbered sequence of volumes within a series or serial (e.g., Notes and queries, 1st series, 2nd series, etc.).

Sine loco (s.l.) : Without place (i.e., the name of the place of publication, distribution, etc., is unknown).

Sine nomine (s.n.) : Without name (i.e., the name of the publisher, distributor, etc., is unknown).

Statement of responsibility : A transcribed listing from the item being described, of the persons responsible for the overall intellectual or artistic content of the item, corporate bodies from which the content emanates, or persons or corporate bodies responsible for the performance of the content of the item.

Subfield : A subdivision of a variable field containing data logically identifiable as a discrete unit of that field. A typical publication field, for example, has three subfields: place, publisher, and date. Except for subfield "a" at the beginning of a field, each subfield is proceeded by a delimiter ( ) and a subfield code.

Subfield code : A character, usually lowercase alphabetic or numeric, that identifies the kind of data within a particular subfield.

Subheading : Part of a corporate or subject string other than the main heading.

Subject Analysis : Determining the focus/focii of the intellectual content of a work and translating it/them into subject headings and assigning aa appropriate classification number.

Subscription agent : A firm or organization which arranges, at the order of an individual or library, for the regular delivery of serials as published, and handles the financial records.

Subseries : A series or serial within a series (i.e., a series or serial that always appears in conjunction with another, usually more comprehensive, series of which it forms a section). Its title may or may not be dependent on the title of the main series. See also Section.

Successive entry cataloging : A new record is

made for each serial title or other major change (e.g., main entry); description is based on the latest issue (AACR1) or the earliest issue (AACR2).

Supplement. An item, usually issued separately, that complements one already published by bringing up-to-date or otherwise continuing the original or by containing a special feature not included in the original; the supplement has a formal relationship with the original as expressed by common authorship, a common title or subtitle, and/or a stated intention to continue or supplement the original.

Supplied title : A title provided by the cataloger for an item that has no title proper on the chief source of information or its substitutes. It may be taken from elsewhere in the item itself or from a reference source, or it may be composed by the cataloger.

Surrogate : A substitute for the issue of a serial on which a cataloging record is based. The surrogate consists of the title page or the title page substitute, and any other pages providing additional information on which cataloging is based. Surrogates are used when authenticating member cataloging, resolving problems, or performing authority work.

System Requirements : Minimum hardware/ software that a program/system needs to function.

Table of contents : Usually comes at the end of the preliminary material in a book and lists in order the book's main topics or the headings of the individual units and their page numbers.

Tag : A three-digit identifier, usually numeric, of a variable field, beginning with 001 and ending with 999.

Tag group : A collection of tags, beginning with the same first digit, that store similar kinds of information and share a similar function within a record. When referring to a tag group, the second and third digits are generally replaced with XX. For example, all tags in the 6XX tag group are subjects. <

Tattle Tape : A magnetic strip placed in each item for security purposes.

Technical services : A functional unit in thelibrary that generally includes cataloging, acquisitions, serials (processing of new materials) and preservations. (may also be called Bibliographic Services)

Text The main part of the book which contains the intellectual or creative content.

Thesaurus : Guide to use of terms, showing relationships between them, for the purpose of providing standardized, controlled vocabulary for information storage and retrieval.

Tip-In : A separately printed page not part of the print block that is fixed in position by being pasted to adjacent pages.

Title : A word, phrase, character, or group of characters, normally appearing in an item, that names the item or the work contained in it.

Title page : A page at the beginning of an item bearing the title proper and usually, though not necessarily, the statement of responsibility, and the data relating to publication. The leaf bearing the title page is commonly called the "title page" although properly called the "title leaf." Use t.p. to abbreviate the term.

Title Proper : The chief name of an item, including any alternative title, but excluding parallel titles and other title information.

Tracing : 1. A record of the headings under which an item is represented in the catalog.

2. A record of the references that have been made to a name or to the title of a item that is represented in the catalog. See also Access points.

Unicorn : Library computer system with access to library catalog, user services, database and archives.

Uniform Title : A collective title used to collocate publications of the same material produced under various titles or translated into other languages.

Updating database : An integrating resource that consists of a collection of logically interrelated data stored together in one or more computerized files, usually created and managed by a database management system.

Updating loose-leaf : An integrating resource that consists of one or more base volumes updated by separate pages that are inserted, removed, and/or substituted.

Updating web site : An integrating resource that consists of a web site that is updated

USMARC : The machine-readable cataloging format used in the country-region>place>U.S. Formerly known as **LC MARC**, MARC II, and MARC.

Validator : Software that provides access to NAF and authorized subject headings.

Variable field : A field in a machine-readable bibliographic record that is not limited to a prescribed size, content or position within the record.

Verso : 1. The left-hand page of a book, usually bearing an even page number.

2. The side of a printed sheet intended to be read

second. The verso of the title page shows the official date of publication and where the book was published.

Volume : 1. In the bibliographic sense, a major division of a work, regardless of its designation by the publisher, distinguished from other major divisions of the same work by having its own inclusive title page, half title, cover title, or portfolio title, and usually independent pagination, foliation, or signatures. This major bibliographic unit may include various title pages and/or pagination.

2. In the material sense, all that is contained in one binding, portfolio, etc., whether as originally issued or as bound after issue. The volume as a material unit may not coincide with the volume as a bibliographic unit.

Workflows : SIRSI library software featuring wizards that enables library staff to perform acquisitions, cataloging, and circulation tasks.

Z39.50 Protocol : Name of the national standard developed by the National Information Standards Organization (NISO) that defines an applications level protocol by which one computer can query another computer and transfer result records, using a canonical format. This protocol provides the framework for OPAC users to search remote catalogs on the Internet using the commands of their own local systems. Projects are now in development to provide Z39.50 support for catalogs on the Internet. SR (Search and Retrieval), ISO Draft International Standard 10162/10163 is the international version of Z39.50.